BALD

BALD

FROM HAIRLESS HEROES TO COMIC COMBOVERS

KEVIN BALDWIN

BLOOMSBURY

Published by Bloomsbury Publishing, New York and London
Distributed to the trade by Holtzbrinck Publishers

All papers used by Bloomsbury Publishing are natural, recyclable products made from
wood grown in well-managed forests. The manufacturing processes conform to the
environmental regulations of the country of origin.

Library of Congress Cataloging-in-Publication Data has been applied for.

ISBN 1-58234-394-2
ISBN-13 978-1-58234-394-5

First U.S. Edition 2005

1 3 5 7 9 10 8 6 4 2

Typeset by Palimpsest Book Production Limited
Printed in the United States of America by Quebecor World Fairfield

To Alison and Emily,
and in memory of
my Mum

CONTENTS

Introduction   1

Chapter One   The Causes of Calvities   5

Chapter Two   Cures for Coots   31

Interlude I   'I'm not bald . . .'   53

Chapter Three   Drugs, Plugs . . .   54

Chapter Four   . . . and Rugs   65

Interlude II   Proverbs for Pilgarlics   80

Chapter Five   Combovers and Other Covers   82

Chapter Six   Getting Scalped   93

Interlude III   'Oi, Spamhead!'   101

Chapter Seven   The Significance of Slapheadedness   104

Chapter Eight   10 Disadvantages of Depilation   119

Interlude IV   Slapping Back   131

Chapter Nine   40 Advantages of Alopecia   134

Interlude V   'As bald as . . .'   151

Chapter Ten   A Hairless History of the World   153

Chapter Eleven   Shining Examples   166

Interlude VI   Bald Eagles and Hairless Mexicans   191

Chapter Twelve   Bald? Join the Club   195

Interlude VII   Places to Baldly Go . . .   202

Chapter Thirteen The Last Strands   205

Acknowledgements   213

I lost my hair when I was sixteen.
What a card game that was.

Mick Miller,
stand-up comedian

INTRODUCTION

Looking back, I can see now that I've been preparing to write this book since I was at school. Throughout my formative years, I was known as Baldy. ('Sir, can't Baldy be on the other team?' 'You'd better own up, Baldy, we're not all staying in detention.' You get the picture.) Yet this was the one period of my life when I wasn't a baldy. It later crossed my mind that my classmates had detected some sign of my hairline's future migration north, but no; school photographs confirm that I looked like Chewbacca's long-lost twin.

The principal type of baldness examined in this book is male pattern baldness, sometimes referred to as androgenetic alopecia. This may be identified by the four basic patterns of hair loss: the 'Widow's Peak', where the hair recedes from the temples, leaving a narrow strip of hair down the centre of the head; the 'Naked Crown', where the hair recedes more quickly in the centre and more slowly at the sides; the 'Domed Forehead', where the whole of the hairline recedes; and the 'Monk's Patch', where a bald patch grows at the top and back of the head.

Of course, these patterns are not mutually exclusive – if a Widow's Peak and a Monk's Patch occur on the same head, the eventual result is a small 'Fantasy Island' of hair just above the forehead, surrounded by an expanse of bare scalp. (The fantasy being that the wearer imagines that he still has something resembling a head of hair.)

1

Of course, my nickname came from my surname – a name which turns out to have no historical connection with baldness. 'Baldwin' simply means 'bold one' and does not derive, as I had hoped it might, from the glorious victories of some great hairless warrior. All the same, being called 'Baldy' for years gave me an early insight into the lot of those who don't have a lot on top. And when my hair eventually disappeared, I was prepared for all the comments and jokes at my expense. They were like water off a coot's back.

I felt that I had the perfect background, if not the perfect location – Barnet, of all places – to study baldness. Few disputed my qualification to write a book on the subject. (As one friend has pointed out, the longer I spent working on it, the more qualified I became.) Some, however, have queried whether it is really a topic worthy of such consideration.

At one level, they have a point. Is it ultimately of importance whether or not a person has strands of dead cells hanging from his or her head? Besides, baldness is hardly an unusual phenomenon; millions have lost their hair. The proportion of men experiencing a significant degree of baldness roughly matches their age: around 30 per cent of 30-year-olds are bald or balding, around 40 per cent of 40-year-olds, and so on. It comes to most men who live long enough – or it leaves them, depending on how you look at it.

Baldness, however, is big business. According to the November 2002 issue of *Harvard*

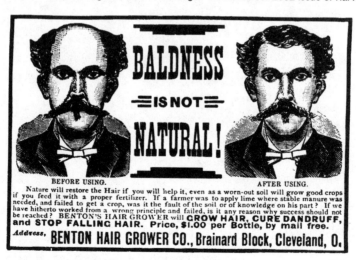

Oh yes it is

Men's Health Watch, Americans alone spend around $1.5 billion a year on attempts to combat hair loss. For an estimate of worldwide expenditure today, this would need to be multiplied several times.

More attention and concern has been devoted to the subject over the centuries than even these figures would suggest. Throughout history, the bald and balding have been mocked, have suffered anxiety and have tried their utmost to cure or conceal the condition. Many of the world's great thinkers – in both scientific and literary fields – have applied their minds to the various aspects of baldness: its possible causes, its possible cures, its symbolism and its social consequences.

A study of baldness is a study of human nature. Shallowness and vanity – and the foolishness they induce – are in evidence everywhere. The self-delusion of those who believe that their wig or combover is undetectable is simultaneously hilarious and depressing. To these traits we may add desperation; people will put up with any amount of pain, embarrassment and expense in an effort to deal with baldness. Where there is desperation, deceit is usually close at hand. There have long been people offering so-called cures for hair loss with the sole aim of relieving the gullible of their money. Intolerance and prejudice also raise their ugly heads – not just in the way that the bald are treated, but in the various theories put forward to explain why some people go bald and others do not.

However, more admirable human characteristics do shine through, not least the ability to turn an apparent disadvantage into a source of strength, and an all-conquering sense of humour. A lack of hair may even become a symbol of comradeship and solidarity, of pride and self-definition.

Whether this book handles the subject with insight and intelligence is not for the author to judge. Yet it is hoped that the sentiments of the sixteenth-century scholar Abraham Fleming may apply here. In the introduction to his translation of a pro-baldness treatise written in the fifth century by Bishop Synesius of Cyrene (or 'The Bald Bishop', as we shall come to know him), he declared:

> For, such is the nature of wisdom, that where she dealeth,
> she leaveth beautie: yea, even in so base a thing as Baldnes
> is, though it seme but a fable at the first blush.

In other words, wonderful things may be revealed by disappearing hair.

CHAPTER ONE

The Causes of Calvities

The ridiculous statement has been made that radiation from ceiling panels may be a cause of baldness; there is no justification for this.
— *Warming for Health and Comfort* (1938)

It is only in the last fifty years that the true cause of male pattern baldness has been identified and generally accepted. If you don't already know what this is, you will have to remain in suspense for a little longer while we look at an A–Z of the different and It often downright bizarre theories which have been put forward over the years.

A is for . . . Arsenic (as it says in *Baby's First Book of Lethal Toxins*). At the 80th convention of the American Chemical Society in 1930, a paper was presented by a group of doctors from the New York Skin and Cancer Hospital, including the euphoniously named Binford Throne and Herman Felt. They claimed that many cases of baldness were caused by the absorption of lead, and of arsenic – which, at the time, was used in the spraying of fruit and vegetables and was present in various foods, beverages and drugs (including many baldness 'remedies'). However, they were at pains to point out that this was not the primary cause of baldness: eliminating arsenic was not to be regarded as a universal cure.

B is for . . . Beards Many bald men cultivate a big, bushy display of facial fungus. This proof that they are capable of growing hair somewhere presumably compensates for their appearing to have their heads on upside down. Some people, however, have ended up blaming the beard for the loss of hair. In 1913, during the *New York Times'* Great Baldness Debate (more of which later), the correspondent J. W. E. commented: 'Take a man whose whiskers grow early and luxuriantly, and what does time discover? A thinning of the hair of the hair of the head and a coarsening of the whiskers!' Moustaches and beards, claimed J. W. E., use up all the hair-growing energy of the head, drawing away all the nutrition that would otherwise go to the scalp. He went on to suggest that this is why women rarely go bald; since they do not grow a profusion of facial hair (outside the circus, at any rate), they do not lose it on the top of the head.

In May 1994, China's *Disaster Reduction Press* claimed that beards cause baldness because they trap chemical pollution. The beard's capacity for trapping substances in the environment is indisputable (egg, soup and cornflakes, in particular); its relation to hair loss, however, is rather more dubious.

. . . Brain (activity of) It was widely believed in the nineteenth century that baldness resulted from 'brain expansion' brought on by the overuse of that organ. (One can imagine Victorian parents deterring their sons from reading: 'Pack that in or you'll go bald.') One British investigator into the condition asserted that 'butcher-boys, valets and the lower classes of the Irish' rarely went bald, whereas lawyers generally did. American medical students of the time were taught that slaves, Indians, women and donkeys never go bald because of their small and undeveloped brains. G. R. Brandle subscribed to this view – at least as far as the fair sex is concerned – in his 1897 'Treatise on Premature Baldness':

> The most liable of all seem to be those who indulge in excessive brain-work and are continually wearing heavy head-gear. The fact that men come under the influence of these conditions more than women is an adequate reason why baldness is so much more prevalent amongst them than women.

As recently as 1978, Dr M. Wharton Young from the University of Maryland claimed that although the skull and scalp stop growing after about 20 years, the brain continues to do so

The Feeble Follicles of the Philosophical

Lao Tzu (c. 570–490 BC), Chinese philosopher reputed to be the founder of Taoism.

Socrates (c. 469–399 BC), Greek philosopher.

Plato (c. 428–348 BC), Greek philosopher and founder of the Academy of Athens.

Aristotle (384–322 BC), Greek philosopher.

Seneca (c. 4 BC–AD 65), Roman philosopher and writer.

Thomas Hobbes (1588–1679), British philosopher and political theorist.

Jeremy Bentham (1748–1832), British philosopher.

John Stuart Mill (1806–1873), British political philosopher. ('His eyes go twinkling and jerking with wild lights and twitches; his head is bald, his face brown and dry.' Thomas Carlyle)

Herbert Spencer (1820–1903), British social theorist, regarded as one of the first sociologists.

Henry Adams (1838–1918), American historian and philosopher of history.

Henri Bergson (1859–1941), French philosopher and winner of the Nobel Prize for Literature.

Michel Foucault (1926–1984), French philosopher.

for several more decades, especially if one's job involves a great deal of mental stimulation. As the brain expands, the scalp area is supposedly stretched thin, hindering the blood vessels within in their supply of nourishment to the hair. Regrettably, there are more than enough stupid bald men around for this theory to seem even thinner.

. . . **Brain (wasting of)** A view put forward by Hippocrates, the father of medicine: 'The wasting of the brain which leads to baldness.' Rather revealing when you consider that Hippocrates was bald himself.

. . . **Brush bristles** In November 1901, the correspondent C. F. S. stated his conviction in the *New York Times* that the stiff bristles of a brush were the primary reason for the loss of hair. When the sharp point of a bristle punctures the cell at the base of a hair, he argued, the cell is destroyed and the hair dies. And this must be true, because a barber told him it was. He went on to elaborate that bald people are almost always bald on top, while retaining hair on the temples and the back of the head, because the brush strikes the scalp perpendicularly on top, so that the bristles penetrate deep down, but merely glances over the other parts of the head without touching the hair roots. Men with thick, curly hair are less likely to go bald, as the dense mass of hair protects the scalp from the bristles. And women, who are generally thought to spend more time tending to their locks, do not become bald because they hold the hair off the head when they brush it – though C. F. S. noted that women do suffer loss where they part the hair, since the sharp points of the comb eventually injure the scalp.

C is for . . . Calcification of the skull In 1942, Dr Frederick Hoelzel of Chicago claimed in the *Journal of the American Medical Association* that baldness occurs when such hardening of the skull bones 'apparently has not only firmly knitted the cranial sutures but

Clever Cleric Cordially Commends Coot-Condition

The Flemish monk Hucbald of St Amand, born around AD 840,
produced an astonishing composition in praise of baldness,
dedicated to Hatto, the bald Archbishop of Mainz. His 'Ecloga
de Calvis' consists of 146 lines – and every single word begins with
the letter 'c'. For example:

> Carmina, clarisonae, calvis cantate, Camenae.
> comperies calvos columen conferre cerebro;
> comperies calvos capitis curare catarrhos;
> comperies calvos caecas curare catervas.

Hucbald sees a bald head as a natural tonsure or crown,
and considers that all the greatest men have been hairless.
He mentions the prophet Elisha, St Paul, clerics, kings, religious
hermits, men of learning, poets, soldiers – and, in the following
extract, he praises the skill of bald doctors:

> Sing loudly, O Muses, songs in praise of the bald. You
> shall learn that the bald bring together brains of the
> highest order; that they can cure the common cold,
> heal crowds of blind people, and that even chronic
> consumption and cancer yield to them. They can bring
> an end to colic, which so weakens one's stomach.
> Wielding the scalpel, they make judicious incisions in
> the nape of the neck to keep bad blood from the head.
> Why do I sing their praises so much? They prevent all
> mysterious and debilitating diseases and mend broken
> bodies. Sing loudly, O Muses, songs in praise of
> the bald.

also closed or narrowed various small openings through which blood vessels pass'. This phenomenon was said to be more common in men than women, which at least provides the latter with a useful riposte: if men claim that they go bald because they have more active brains, women can appropriate Dr Hoelzel's assertion that men are more bone-headed.

. . . **Cold water** In the early part of the twentieth century, this was considered by many to be the worst thing one could apply to the hair. Theodor Koller in *Cosmetics* (1902): 'It is impossible to warn too strongly against a too frequent use of cold water – such as washing the hair daily with cold water, since this practice will inevitably result in baldness.' *Harper's Weekly* in September 1910 strongly agreed: 'Cold water is unnatural and has a tendency to do serious harm not only to the hair and head, but to the whole system.'

'Unnatural'? One can't help wondering what they thought that wet stuff frequently falling from the sky might be.

> Down come de scaldin' water . . . Ole Brer Rabbit, he lean fum out de steeple en 'pollygize de bes' he kin, but no 'pollygy aint gwine ter make ha'r come back whar de b'iling water hit.
>
> —Joel Chandler Harris, *Nights with Uncle Remus* (1883)

. . . **Cycling** was put forward by the aptly named Professor G. H. Wheeler in his snappily titled *An Abridged Lecture . . . on the Prevalent Disorders of the Hair, Causing Greyness and Baldness* (1899). 'Immoderate cycle riding has now become recognised as one of the many common causes of hair falling,' he states. Those who indulge in this pernicious practice will render any hair-loss remedies ineffective: 'So long as the patient continues cycling with unfavourable conditions there will always be the liability of a relapse.' Realising that he sounds like a killjoy, Professor Wheeler interjects, 'I want it to be clearly understood that I in no way disapprove of cycling'.

Trying to explain exactly how a boneshaker is a hair-shaker, he claims that overtiredness and overheating brought on by vigorous cycling can 'induce a disturbance' in the normal functions of the body, while the sebaceous glands can get overexcited and produce an excess of grease on the scalp. Furthermore, one could become exposed to the cold and damp while waiting for a slower friend to catch up. Even if a cyclist should manage to avoid baldness, there is a high risk of turning prematurely grey:

> Gentlemen, in addition to these, there is another, and I am convinced, a frequent cause of white hairs in cycle riders, a cause which I believe is not sufficiently recognized . . . and that is the undue retention of urine. Young cyclists should pay proper attention to this matter and to the proper adjustment and hygienic make of the saddle so as to do away with any injurious effects of pressure

On your bike, Professor Wheeler.

D is for . . . Deficient secretions from the basement membrane (obviously). H. P. Truefitt, who declares in the preface to his 1863 book *New Views on Baldness* that he will use only 'simple and untechnical language', explains the theory thus: 'This follicle itself we have seen to be produced by an involution of the basement membrane whose vitality, and consequently the function of which, are maintained by the vessels ramifying in the derma below.' Er – quite.

. . . Diet was often suggested as a primary cause of male pattern baldness during the nineteenth century. In *Baldness: Its Causes and Cures* (1875), Michel Carlin ascribed the condition to 'stomachic disturbance' brought on by eating 'fleshmeat' too often. Twenty years later, that old enemy of excitement, Professor Wheeler, took the view that 'various over-seasoned foods and condiments taken by persons of a highly strung nervous temperament directly and indirectly excite the nerves with which the hair and scalp is so liberally provided'. So if you and your mates insist on going for a bike ride, perhaps you shouldn't go for a curry afterwards.

E is for . . . Evolution This theory is a simple one; since man descended from hairy apes and eventually lost the thick covering of body hair, men who go bald must be even further along the evolutionary chain. It's an attractive idea, and one which the bald frequently promote.

. . . **Eye fatigue** was put forward as a cause of baldness by Dr George Carlson of Lincoln, Nebraska, in November 1934. In his address to local optometrists, he declared that nine out of ten people with thin hair or bald patches suffered some kind of eye strain: 'Nerves and muscles of the head are deprived by eye strain of energy that should go to the roots of the hair.' Dr Carlson does not, however, mention any correlation between eye fatigue and the microscopic print on bottles of hair restorer.

F is for . . . Fish mentioned as a possible cause by Tom Robinson in *The Etiology, Pathology and Treatment of Baldness and Greyness* (1882). Hairless pates were said to be 'common in localities where the inhabitants have chiefly a fish diet. According to R. Monteith (*Description of the Orkneys*), baldness was for this reason quite common in the Shetlands. It has also been stated that baldness is more common at Brighton and its vicinity than at other places.'

G is for . . . Germs In January 1926, the *New York Times* reported that in Kittanning, Pennsylvania, a 'strange germ' which defied diagnosis was rapidly denuding the heads of young men. In just two weeks, more than 300 men between the ages of 19 and 30 had sought medical treatment for the condition.

This was not the first time germs had been blamed. Reacting to the 'ridiculous' theories of other contributors to the Great Baldness Debate of 1913, a Mr H. B. Sheffield stated with absolute conviction that hair loss was caused by 'a specific microbe that permeates the hair roots and destroys them, unless killed before much damage had been done'. The germ, he said, was usually carried by combs and brushes. The tendency of baldness to affect several members of the same family was explained by their sharing the same comb and brush. Men were more likely to be bald than women, since women rarely went to barbers' shops, where the same comb could be used on hundreds of men, and were 'as a rule . . . more particular about using their own comb and brush'. Mr Sheffield suggested that men should

> Robert Holton removed several dark hairs from his comb and wondered if his hairline was receding. He squinted for a moment at himself in the mirror and decided that he was not losing his hair, not yet anyway.
>
> —Gore Vidal,
> *In a Yellow Wood*

take their own comb and brush to the barber's and declared that in most instances baldness may be cured in its early stages by suitable germ-destroying antiseptics.

H is for . . . Hair treatments Even today, these can cause the hair to fall out if used to excess; repeated bleaching, for example, causes the hair shafts to become brittle, dry and liable to break.

However, modern hair preparations are nothing like as harmful as their predecessors. In *Daring Do's: A History of Extraordinary Hair* (1994), historian Mary Trasko describes the measures taken by men in ancient Greece to turn their hair blond. As well as applying industrial-strength bleaches, they would use lead combs to get rid of unwanted grey hairs. The result was widespread baldness and death by toxic poisoning.

Women in Ancient Rome also suffered after using noxious treatments on their hair. Ovid takes one unfortunate to task in Book I of his *Amores*:

> I told you to stop using those treatments on your hair, and now you have no hair left to dye. Why couldn't you leave it as it was, when it was so luxuriant, and reached all the way down to your sides? . . . Your hair was delicate and soft as down, but oh! what torture it had to bear. How long it had to suffer heated irons, so that it could be twisted into tight ringlets! 'It's criminal,' I told you, 'absolutely criminal to singe your hair like that. It's fine as it is. Spare your head, you obstinate woman. Stop using such violence on it. Your hair is not for scorching' . . . The loss you are experiencing was caused entirely by what you did. You put that harmful mixture on your head yourself.

Just the kind of thing a girl likes to hear after suddenly losing all her hair.

. . . Hats were for years seen by many as the chief cause of baldness. The belief was that a tight hat would reduce the flow of blood and air to the top of the head, with a resultant loss of hair above the zone of the hatband. (This, it was thought, was why the hair at the back and sides of the head did not fall out.) Dr J. O. Cobb of the US Public Health and Marine Hospital Service outlined this theory in the *New York Medical Journal* in 1909:

HAIRDON'TS

Specific hairstyles have frequently been held responsible for hair loss. In March 1927, Dr Leonard Williams warned that the fashion for shingled hair (a style in which the hair is cropped short at the back) would have dire consequences: 'The present generation of young women certainly will go bald. Most women with shingled hair wear tight hats like men, with the result that when they get to the age of about 30 or 40 they will find their hair falling out'. A female doctor wrote to the *New York Times* shortly afterwards to dispute this, though she did believe that shingling would cause women to grow moustaches and beards.

Dr Williams' prediction proved inaccurate, but other hairstyles can cause baldness, particularly if they involve pulling the hair tight. Drawing the hair back into a ponytail or bun may cause balding at the front hairline – though this does not explain the alarming number of balding middle-aged men who sport ponytails. Sikh boys twisting their uncut hair tightly on the top of the head may experience some loss, and Afro-Caribbean styles featuring tight braiding, especially corn-rows, can also cause traction alopecia.

The Afro itself may damage the hair. Using a hot comb, claimed Dr Algie C. Brown of Emory University in a lecture to the American Medical Association in 1972, could injure the hair shafts, while the lack of washing necessary in maintaining the style increased the chances of infection and subsequent hair loss.

If a man's head is very wide, or if he is very prominent fore and aft, that man will become bald in time, because such a person, to make his hat fit snugly, invariably pulls it down tight. The man with low brow and thick, heavy hair rarely is bald. If one wears the hair long and thick it acts as a cushion and prevents in a large measure the constriction caused by the hatband.

Dr Cobb suggested that 'in this age of contrivances in shoes, suspenders and braces, somebody ought to be ingenious enough to make a hat that will stay on in a breeze without impeding the circulation in the scalp'. Failing that, there was always the simple alternative put forward by M. D. in the *New York Times* in 1913: 'A few generations of hatless men would probably make baldness as infrequent in men as in women.'

Poor circulation is not the only damaging effect attributed to hats. H. P. Truefitt advises in *New Views on Baldness* that wearing '*bonnets de nuit*' in bed would prevent perspiration from evaporating and would thus cause the decay of hair roots with the eventual loss of hair. And a century later, Anthony J. Parrotto mentions in *Baldness, Grayness, Dandruff* (1963) the old belief that wearing a hat indoors causes baldness because it offends God.

I is for . . . Inadequate blood supply to the scalp Erasmus Wilson suggested in 1852 that baldness occurs on the top of the head because 'the integument is bound down somewhat tightly on the bones of the cranium' and therefore restricts circulation. *Harper's Weekly* in September 1910 made the same assertion: 'As a result the hair dies and the head becomes bald, first in spots, then all over, wherever the roots of the hair do not receive nourishment, just as grass dies on a prairie whose irrigating canals run dry.'

The theory was still being espoused in 1994 by Andy Bryant in his book *The Baldness Cure*. In his view, blood has difficulty getting through to the hair follicle because tension causes the blood vessels to narrow. The blood which does get through supposedly carries insufficient nutrients for hair growth, and it is difficult for the waste products of cellular activity to drain away from the scalp.

However, poor blood supply can hardly be the principal factor behind baldness, as proved by the success of hair transplants. If poor blood supply on the top of the head caused hair to fall out, the hairs transplanted from elsewhere on the head would not last in their new location – but they do.

Overall verdict on theory: not bloody likely.

. . . Improper breathing If by now you are thinking that simply breathing may make you go bald, you are not the first. At a meeting of the American Dermatological Association in Washington, D.C., in December 1910, Dr Andrew P. Biddle of Detroit stated that for many years one of his colleagues had proved to his own satisfaction that hair loss was caused by a poison produced by 'improper breathing'. He was less forthcoming as to which sort of breathing might be considered 'improper'. Short pants, perhaps?

J is for . . . Jealous husband In April 1996, the *Independent* reported the story of a man who discovered that his wife was having an affair and decided to inflict on her lover the most humiliating punishment he could think of. He seized his rival, held him down and rubbed hair remover into his head. All of his hair duly fell out.

. . . Jobs In *Baldness and the Care of the Hair* (1966), Ian Martin-Scott states his conviction that demanding occupations have much to answer for:

> In my own experience, psychological trauma is one of the
> commonest precipitating factors; and of these in men the
> main causative stimulus is increasing responsibility at work,
> and secondly financial worry due to overwork in keeping up
> hire-purchase payments in the buying of domestic
> appliances beyond one's means.

Ordinary workers, by contrast, are less prone to hair loss: 'It is seldom one sees a labourer on roadwork or building sites who has become bald at an early age, and I have never seen premature baldness in a ghillie or gamekeeper.'

Of course, men are not the only breadwinners in the modern world, so we should not be too surprised that they are not the only hair-losers. In November 1997, the *Sunday Times* reported that thousands of women were shedding their hair as a result of taking roles which had traditionally been male preserves. The need to adopt a more aggressive and competitive attitude to get ahead was said to lead to a general thinning of the hair and a widening of centre partings. One quoted study, by the University of Portsmouth, indicated that 30 per cent of women in their twenties and thirties were experiencing some degree of loss. It's a harsh way to learn how bigwigs got their name.

Sometimes it may not be the job itself which leads to baldness, but the overbearing nature of one's superiors at work. This was recognised as long ago as the eighteenth century by the English poet John Collins in *Ben Black*:

'Why, my Lord,' replied Ben – 'it with truth may be said,
While a bald pate I long have stood under;
There are so many Captains walk'd over my head,
That to see me quite scalped were no wonder!'

Male Stripper

. . . Joseph Smietana was a one-man baldness plague in the US in the late 1970s and early '80s. In 1978, the 33-year-old former longshoreman was charged in Indiana with phoning women and persuading them to cut off all their hair or to treat their heads with caustic solutions. In one case he even persuaded a woman to bend over a flaming stove jet. He claimed to be a doctor treating their husbands for a mysterious scalp disease and told them that they needed to lose their hair so that it would not spread to them.

On that occasion he was found not guilty by reason of insanity. But three years later, he began a new campaign in Montana using a more 'hands-on' approach. This time he turned up on doorsteps calling himself 'Smitty' and trying to pull the hair out of housewives' heads. Fifty complaints were made against him, and he was eventually given a year's probation and ordered to seek psychiatric help.

K is for . . . Keeping the face clean-shaven This theory was put forward by J. Gardner of Newark, New Jersey, during the *New York Times*' Great Baldness Debate:

> Without doubt, nature provided hair on man's face for some purpose. What this was I do not profess to know, but it is her law, and nature always provides punishment for violation of her laws. Shaving is the violation, and baldness the punishment.

L is for . . . Laughter During the 1950s, the US physicians Szasz and Robertson insisted that baldness resulted from the muscular contractions caused by having a chuckle. The apes from which man descended, they argued, had static, hairy faces; as man developed, he learned how to express different emotions by facial contortions. Eventually he lost most of his facial hair, retaining only the hair on the top of the head. This remaining hair, claimed Szasz and Robertson, was now being attacked by ever more violent emotions and facial movements – in particular, by laughter. They concluded that only a return to the brutishness of prehistoric ages could save mankind from the completely hairless fate awaiting it. Titter ye not.

. . . Leprosy one of a number of diseases which can cause the hair to fall out, though this is not male pattern baldness. Robert Browning refers to the effect in 'Childe Roland to the Dark Tower Came': 'As for the grass, it grew as scant as hair / In leprosy.'

M is for . . . Musical instruments The *Scientific American* in August 1896 reported on an investigation by an unnamed English statistician into the hirsuteness or otherwise of musicians. It led to some surprising conclusions:

> Thus, while stringed instruments prevent and check the falling out of the hair, brass instruments have the most injurious effects upon it. The piano and the violin, especially the piano, have an undoubted preserving influence. The violoncello, the harp, and the double bass participate in the hair-preserving qualities of the piano. But the hautboy, the clarinet, and the flute have only a very feeble effect. Their

Unfinished Symphonists

1 Antonio Vivaldi (1678–1741)

2 Charles Gounod (1818–1893)

3 Johann Strauss the Younger (1825–1899)

4 Antonin Dvorak (1841–1904)

5 Jean Sibelius (1865–1957)

6 Erik Satie (1866–1925)

7 Arnold Schoenberg (1874–1951)

8 Igor Stravinsky (1882–1971)

9 Sergei Prokofiev (1891–1953)

10 Aaron Copland (1900–1990)

action is not more than a fiftieth part as strong. On the contrary, the brass instruments have results that are deplorable. The cornet-a-piston and the French horn act with surprising surety and rapidity; but the trombone is the depilatory instrument par excellence. It will clear the hair from one's head in five years. This is what the author calls 'baldness of the fanfares', which rages with special violence among regimental bands.

Some conflicting evidence has appeared in the years since: Elton John, for instance, could hardly testify to the 'undoubted preserving influence' of the piano.

The totally hairless head of Jean Sibelius is celebrated in 'Baldness and the Swan', a poem by Winfield Townley Scott first published in his 1945 collection To Marry Strangers. The swan is an allusion to Sibelius' composition The Swan of Tuonela:

This matter of baldness: we do it badly.
We tend to be incomplete about it: obscene:
Not the semi-nude, merely the semi-clothed.
The scalp half undone, the scalp fringed
With remnants of tired hair, the scalp scalped –
All this is a weariness and a near-beer.
If baldness, then let it be full-grown,
Wonderful as first pubic hair, an attainment:
Sibelius' head, bare, virile, a completion, an
Aged and naked dome for the accomplished body.
This will be a courage against decoration, wonderful as
Where upon shadowed waters with rhymeless music a dark
    swan moves forth.

In addition to these great bald composers, there have been several great bald conductors, including Arturo Toscanini, Pablo Casals, William Steinberg, Sir Georg Solti and Bernard Haitink. Solti was once labelled 'the screaming skull' by an orchestra member.

N is for . . . Not reading novels by Julio Cortázar It was the poet Pablo Neruda who suggested that this may be detrimental to one's hairline: 'Anyone who hasn't read Cortázar is doomed . . . something similar to a man who has never tasted peaches. He would quietly become sadder, noticeably paler, and probably, little by little, he would lose his hair.'

Hard to believe, I know. But then, have you read anything by Cortázar? And are you losing your hair?

. . . **Nest** as in Bird's Nest Droop. In *Folk Medicine: A Chapter in the History of Culture* (1883), W. G. Black records an old belief from the west of Scotland that, if a bird used human hair in the building of its nest, the person whose hair had been used would become bald.

O is for . . . Overindulgence blamed for causing baldness by the Roman philosopher and playwright Seneca:

> The great founder of the study and profession of medicine [Hippocrates] said that women never lost their hair or suffered with their feet; and yet now their hair is going and they suffer from gout . . . In matching the licentious behaviour of men, they have suffered the same physical afflictions which beset men. They stay up just as late, and drink just as much; they challenge men to wrestling bouts and wine-drinking contests . . . In fact, they are even as lustful as the men; although they were born to be the objects of passion (may the gods and goddesses destroy them!), they invent and initiate perverse types of lewd behaviour with men. How much of a surprise is it, then, that the greatest and most skilled physician might be judged to have uttered a falsehood, when so many women are bald . . .

If only hard-drinking, promiscuous women really did go bald in this manner. It would make it much easier to find them.

P is for . . . Pessimism In November 1992, the *Montreal Gazette* reported on a survey carried out by a Japanese cosmetics company which concluded that men with certain psychological characteristics are more likely to lose their hair. Men who are pessimistic, methodical and irritable are apparently most at risk. The survey did not consider the possibility that their subjects were pessimistic and irritable because their methodical search for a baldness remedy had proven fruitless.

. . . **Plant** A certain plant (or rather, an uncertain plant, since it is not named) is said to cause baldness by Aristotle in *On Marvellous Things Heard*: 'It is said that a lethal drug grows in Italy near the mountain Circe and has this property: when it is sprinkled on someone, it makes that person fall immediately and causes his hair to fall out.'

. . . Pollution The baldness epidemic which affected hundreds of children in the Ukrainian city of Chernovtsy in 1988 was believed to be caused by the chemical element thallium, though its source was unclear. Ten factories in the city were closed and checked, but they were cleared of blame. A chemical plant 42 miles away in Romania was also suspected. However, the likeliest source of the pollution was a mixture containing thallium being put into cars because of an acute petrol shortage. Cars were banned from the city centre and most children were evacuated to the countryside. The children who remained became very nervous; one five-year-old was constantly putting her hands on her head 'so that my hair doesn't fall out'.

Q is for . . . Quick weight loss A team of doctors from the Letterman Army Medical Centre reported in the *Journal of the American Medical Association* in 1976 that a severe restriction on calorie intake can precipitate hair loss. Some of the subjects studied were on starvation diets of 500 calories a day, and one 50-year-old man was still suffering loss four months after the end of his course. In such cases, the hair usually grows back again. But it is as well to be wary of crash diets which promise you a new thin look; they may be referring to more than your waistline.

R is for . . . Rubbing In October 1974, the *National Observer* featured this novel reason for baldness, given by Roy Palmer from North Carolina: 'Too many car doors when a teenager and too many headboards since.'

S is for . . . Salamander There was a belief in Ancient Rome that touching a salamander would make a man lose his hair. In Petronius' satirical romance *Satyricon*, Lichas confronts some shorn men and asks, 'Who was the salamander that singed off your eyebrows?' Jonathan Swift also refers to the belief:

> This Serpent is extreamly cold,
> So cold, that put it in the fire,
> 'Twill make the very Flames expire,
> Beside, it Spues a fith Froth,

(Whether thro' Rage or Love, or both)
Of matter purulent and white
Which happening on the skin to light,
And there corrupting to a Wound
Spreads Leprosy and Baldness round.

. . . **Severe shock** may trigger hair loss all over the body as well as on the top of the head. Professor Wheeler, that bold berater of bicycles, gave in his *Abridged Lecture* of 1899 the example of a young boy whose hair fell out within a week: 'It appeared on enquiry that his loss of hair was the direct result of shock to his system, occasioned by a thrashing with a rope which his father gave him for breaking a window'. Wheeler concluded: 'The cause of this peculiar patchy baldness is undoubtedly of neurotic origin inasmuch as it can generally be proved to occur after bicycle accidents, railway accidents, news of the sudden death of one of the family or a dear friend and other similar nervous shocks'.

Other examples of hair loss being caused by shock include:

• In 1980, a woman from Trenton, New Jersey, filed a suit for damages when the shock of an explosion at a nearby chemical plant apparently led to the loss of all her hair. She claimed to have spent over $1,500 on wigs, and was afraid to go horse-riding, swimming, 'fast dancing' or riding on fairground amusements for fear of losing her hairpiece.

• Olympic champion swimmer Duncan

> **Trouble has done it, Bilgewater, trouble has done it; trouble has brung these grey hairs and this premature balditude.**
> **—Mark Twain, *Adventures of Huckleberry Finn***
>
> **. . .why do I yield to that suggestion**
> **Whose horrid image doth unfix my hair**
> **And make my seated heart knock at my ribs,**
> **Against the use of nature?**
> **—William Shakespeare, *Macbeth* I.i.134–7**

Goodhew lost all his hair at the age of ten after he fell out of a tree.

• In July 1965, *The Times* reported on a prisoner in the US who underwent a series of trials for murder over a period of three years. Ten weeks after he was finally found guilty, he began to shed hairs at the rate of more than a thousand a day.

• A combination of shock and fear was evident in the case of a Shropshire man who in 1994 lost every hair on his body following a 200-foot bungee jump. He woke up one morning to find the last of his hair lying on his pillow. He looked in a mirror in a panic and to his horror saw a completely hairless man staring back. His wife was equally uneasy about his new bald state, remarking that when she woke up in bed beside him in the dark she couldn't tell which end she was touching.

Note: Hair loss caused by shock or stress is not male pattern baldness; this usually patchy form of baldness is known as alopecia areata. It seems to be a type of auto-immune disease, in which the immune system suddenly sees the hair as foreign and rejects it. It is often temporary, and steroid injections into the scalp are commonly used to reverse the condition. That said, the more extreme form called alopecia universalis involves the loss of all body hair and can be permanent.

. . . **Sex** You probably guessed this was, ahem, coming. The philosopher Socrates declared that baldness was the result of too much sex (yes, he was bald). Bald men have always promoted the fallacy ('phallusy'?) of heightened virility, so it is hardly surprising that having it off should so often be seen as the cause of the hair falling off. In *The Generation of Animals*, Aristotle offers an explanation as to how sex might have this effect:

> The cause of this condition [baldness] is a lack of hot fluid, the principal hot fluid being greasy fluid . . . sexual intercourse has a cooling effect, since it involves the emission of some of the pure, natural heat, and as the brain is by its nature the coldest part of the body, we should therefore expect that it is the first part to feel the effect . . . So if you take account that the brain

itself has very little heat, that the skin surrounding it necessarily
has even less, and that the hair, being the most remote of the
three, must have even less heat than this, it is to be expected
that those with an abundant amount of semen will go bald at
about this stage of life . . . Women do not go bald because their
constitution is like that of children: both are incapable of
emitting semen. Eunuchs do not go bald either, because they
have converted to the female condition.

The Hippocratic collection of writings offers a different view of the process, in *The Nature of the Child*:

Those who are bald become this way because they have a
phlegmatic constitution; during sex, the phlegm in their heads is
agitated and heats up, and when it comes into contact with the
epidermis it burns the roots of their hair, which then falls out.
This is why eunuchs do not become bald; they do not
experience the vigorous movements of sex which would heat
the phlegm and cause it to burn the roots of the hair.

Having sex with the wrong people can certainly cause baldness – see **Venereal diseases**.

. . . Sun (overexposure to) In December 1910, Dr George F. Harding of Boston, Massachusetts, told a meeting of the American Dermatological Association that prolonged exposure to the sun's rays was a prominent factor in hair loss among the young. He claimed that many of the people he studied went out into the summer sun bare-headed every year.

According to current thinking, some 'moulting' in warmer weather can occur, and is quite normal – but any marked change during the summer is more likely to be the result of excessive hair-washing. Using a shampoo which is too strong, or a hairdryer which is too hot (and using it too often) is commonly to blame.

T is for . . . Tallness On 1 April 1973 (make of the date what you will) the *New Orleans Times-Picayune* carried a story with the headline 'Betty Has Hairy Theory'. The paper featured the view of a Mrs Betty Roney, who ran a hair clinic in London. She claimed that tall men tend to lose their hair sooner than short ones, since blood has further to travel to the top of the head and thus finds it harder to deliver nourishment to the roots of the hair. Betty was also of the opinion that chubby men were likely to go bald; the *Times-Picayune* did not say whether she believed that this was because the blood had so far to travel around them.

. . . Tobacco takes its toll on the hair as well as on the heart and lungs, or so said Graham Lee Hemminger in his eulogy to the evil weed, 'Tobacco': 'It takes the hair right off your bean/It's the worst darn stuff I've ever seen, I like it.'

Although smoking can have a constricting effect on blood flow, it is unlikely to be a cause of baldness. All the same, one can't help wondering whether warnings such as 'Smoking makes you bald' on the front of cigarette packets would deter more people than 'Smoking kills'.

. . . Trichotillomania a genuine cause of baldness, though not of the male pattern variety. For one thing, it chiefly affects women. And for another, it is the name given to the compulsive pulling-out of the hair (often including the eyebrows and eyelashes). This condition is much more common than one might imagine. Estimates of the number of female sufferers in the United States have been as high as eight million. Some comb the remaining strands of hair across the head, some wear wigs, while others claim to be having chemotherapy. Yet social embarrassment is not the only problem caused by trichotillomania; in many cases, the women eat the hair they have pulled out and require surgery to remove huge knotted balls from the stomach.

U is for . . . Ungodliness considered to be a cause of distress up above by C. S. L. in the *New York Times* in May 1913. He claimed that believing oneself to be in the hands of a Supreme Being would insure against baldness. 'I would hazard the statement that 99 per cent of the sincere religious leaders have full heads of hair,' he declared. With a non-believer, on the other hand, worry and depression about the pointlessness of life would cause the formation of uric acid around the brain, which would then act upon the roots of the hair.

The following day, the newspaper editorial took issue with C. S. L., citing the example of certain bald old deacons and asking whether their piety should now be considered 'to have been only a cloak or semblance. They seemed to be good, and passed for such in their respectful communities'. However, the leader writer had to admit that 'the theory falls in beautifully with the universally recognized superiority in morals of women to men and the greater tenacity with which they cling to – and practice – the tenets of ancestral faiths'.

A day later, there was a further attack from a J. W. B. who wondered whether C. S. L. had ever seen 'a bald pagan or heathen or agnostic. My experience is that they are as rare as dead elephants.' (A slightly odd simile, given that all elephants eventually die, but you get his meaning.)

Undeterred, C. S. L. hit back, claiming that some unbelievers do not lose their hair because 'they do not know enough to worry or are too busy to find time to worry, while there are many religious men whose hair began to fall before they realised that worry would eventually kill them, and that the basis of worry was the fear of the future'.

Shortly afterwards, C. S. L. actually received some support. A correspondent wrote of a religious community he knew in his youth, which comprised around twenty men aged 55 to 93 – none of whom even had a bald spot. 'They were, I believe, distinctly men of the type your correspondent had reference to. They were men of a strong dominant religious faith, of great piety and purity of life.'

(See also **Zeal**.)

Sure, Mum?

Though they are not the principal cause of baldness, it seems that underarm anti-perspirants can have a detrimental effect on the scalp. This is because they seal up the pores under the arms, causing an increase in perspiration on the head. Sweat contains lactic acid, and this may cause damage to the hair follicles. This is not to say, of course, that one should avoid anti-perspirants at all costs. Any benefit to one's hair would be overcome by the stench of fetid armpits – as would anyone standing downwind.

V is for . . . Venereal diseases 'Some of your French crowns have no hair at all' in Act I of *A Midsummer Night's Dream* is a veiled reference to 'the French disease', or syphilis, which can cause baldness. Some of Shakespeare's contemporaries were rather more explicit, such as John Davies of Hereford in his epigram 'On Kate's Baldness':

> By's beard the Goat, by his bush-tail the Fox,
> By's paws the Lion, by his horns the Ox,

By these all these are known; and by her locks
That now are fallen, Kate's known to have the pox.

Ellis Pratt, an eighteenth-century London hairdresser, describes in a poem titled 'The Art of Dressing the Hair' how the disease may be contracted from ladies of the night and how it then courses through the body:

Oh, if some Nymph of Drury's artful Race
Should tempt You thoughtless to her lewd Embrace,
While in her Blood the dire Infection reigns,
And more than Lust inflames her throbbing Veins;
Should the foul Poison upward force its Way,
Taint your young Bones, and on your Marrow prey,
Unbated its corrosive Influence spread,
And shake the Tresses from your drooping Head . . .

He does offer a remedy – albeit one which involves tearing the intestines out of a freshly slaughtered creature and applying the fat to the head:

On your bare Temples shed the copious Store,
Till the rich Unction gluts each thirsty Pore:
And soon th'Effusion of that magic Dew
Shall the lost Honours of your Head renew.

W is for . . . War In March 1943, the *New York Times* reported that a man had failed to report when drafted into the US Army, since he believed that his thinning hair would not be saved if he had to go to war. He was picked up in due course – as, presumably, was all of his hair.

The same year, Herbert Agar, special assistant to the US ambassador to Britain, told the same paper that many men and women in London were losing their hair through anxiety about the war. 'London doctors tell people the only thing to do is to go away for two or three weeks of rest and peace. Since

The Falklands thing was a fight between two bald men over a comb.

Jorge Luis Borges

no one can do that, they might as well tell them to go six miles straight up to Heaven.' The government refused permission to clerical workers to take a holiday as a hair restorer, since it was feared that this would open the way for many other requests of a similar nature.

More surprisingly, the end of hostilities has also been blamed for baldness:

> In the services [during the Second World War], in spite of worries about personal safety, most ranks had an easy and sheltered way of life . . . On return to civilian life they had a cool awakening to the vital necessities of life without any assured income. Hair loss was also commoner after the war in the occupied countries than during the war when all things were under military control. When the individual was left to himself to deliberate on the continued survival of himself and his family, baldness often ensued.
> —Ian Martin-Scott, *Baldness and the Care of the Hair* (1966)

War. Huh. What is it good for? Companies that make wigs or hair restorer, apparently.

X is for . . . X.X.'s theory. X.X. was another (presumably pseudonymous) correspondent to the *New York Times* in May 1913. This was his suggestion as to why men go bald:

> As men cut the hair so often it must be kept in a constant state of growth, making a great strain on the roots and whatever nourishes them. Many hairs give up the struggle and fall out; and the remainder illustrate the survival of the fittest. We shall never know what the normal length of men's hair is except in the case of Indians.

The best that can be said for this theory is that it offers an argument, albeit a feeble one, to use against a mother who keeps nagging you to get your hair cut.

Y is for . . . Youthful over-exuberance In the *Sunday Times Magazine* in May 1998, actor David Swift (best known for playing bewigged newsreader Henry Davenport in the sitcom *Drop the Dead Donkey*) pointed the finger at his brother Clive (famous as Richard

Bucket in *Keeping up Appearances*). He recalled the fierce fights they had as boys, during one of which Clive swung the belt of his mackintosh around like a medieval mace and caught him a nasty blow on the head. David's hair had to be cut away so that the wound could be tended – and he claimed that this episode was to blame for his subsequent baldness.

Z is for . . . Zeal (religious) In 1913, M. F. of Cape Cod contributed to the Great Baldness Debate in the *New York Times* in response to the theory of C. S. L. (see **Ungodliness** above.) He told the story of his friend Captain Zach Truebody, a sailor with luxuriant hair who upon retiring 'experienced religion' and lost all his hair 'under the strain of holy fervour'. M. F. was backed up shortly afterwards by W. Juell, who was adamant that 'one of the best-known causes of baldness, very generally promulgated and accepted, is praying in damp cellars'.

The True Cause

So, what is the true cause of male pattern baldness? The almost universally accepted answer is a combination of testosterone and heredity.

The role of testosterone was proved conclusively by an experiment carried out at the Winfield State Mental Hospital in Kansas during the 1940s. Patients were castrated as a matter of routine, and all had thick, luxurious hair. One patient was visited by an identical twin brother who had started to lose his hair at 20, and at the age of 40 was almost completely bald. A doctor noticed the contrast and decided to see what would happen if the hairy twin were given an injection of testosterone. The result was that the patient's hair fell out almost immediately and never grew back.

Of course, testosterone actively triggers the growth of hair in certain places on the male body. In some men, however, the action of an enzyme called 5-alpha-reductase converts the testosterone to dihydrotestosterone. This 'switches off' the hair follicles on the crown so that they produce thinner and thinner hairs until nothing sprouts at all. Whether or not this process occurs in a man depends on whether he has that particular genetic trait. If your body is programmed to react to testosterone in this way, you will go bald; if it isn't, you won't. The genetic trait can be passed on to you by either parent; the belief that it comes only from the mother's side is a myth.

CHAPTER TWO

Cures
for Coots

It is thought that the ashes of an
ass pizzle will make the hair to grow thick.
    — Pliny the Elder, *Natural History*

— Is there anything which will stop my hair falling?

— Yes, the floor.

This joke is as old as time – but that is the point. Man has been searching for a baldness cure ever since he evolved into *Homo slapiens*.

Ancient Cures

The earliest known anti-baldness preparations are those described in ancient Egyptian papyri – and judging by their number, the subject was of enormous importance. The Ebers papyrus, dating from around 1500 BC, contains a number of treatments, such as 'a poultice of equal parts of the fats from the ibex, lion, crocodile, serpent, goose and hippopotamus . . . together with the burned prickles of a hedgehog immersed in oil, fingernail scrapings and a mixture of honey, alabaster and red ochre.'

This was to be administered with invocations to 'the eternal, steadfast Aton [literally, a disc; the sun] to fight the malign divinity that ruled the summit of the bald head'. Another preparation consisted of equal parts of date blossom, the heel of an Abyssinian greyhound and asses' hooves boiled in oil.

Queen Cleopatra had her own special tonic for the hair, which she reputedly recommended to Julius Caesar. In December 1997, the *Sunday Times* tried to recreate the tonic, although it was necessarily a rough approximation with ingredients such as 'toasted horse's teeth', 'deer's marrow' and 'vine rag' difficult to find at Tesco. The result was a substance with the consistency of stuffing and a very strong smell. The remedy has long been overlooked as a contributing factor in Caesar's downfall: perhaps Brutus and his mates simply couldn't stand the stench any longer.

Pliny the Elder described a number of baldness treatments in his *Natural History*. The nettle, for example, in Book 22 (we are using here the entertaining translation provided by Philemon Holland in 1601): 'Applied in a liniment to the bare and naked places of the head, it causeth the hair to grow again, and bringeth all to the former beauty.'

Don't fancy rubbing nettles on your head? Try Book 24: 'As for the little round balls or apples found upon the oak . . . if they be incorporate with bear's grease, they cause the hair to come thick again, where it is shed, in case the bare or bald place be anointed therewith.'

We find all sorts of excrement in Book 29: 'The naked places in head or beard are replenished again with hair by a liniment of the ashes of sheep's dung incorporat in cyprin oil and honey'. And by the time we reach Book 32, Pliny appears determined to make every creature an endangered species:

> The ashes of the fish called the sea-horse, mingled with sal-nitre and swine's grease, or applied simply with vinegar, replenish the bare places with new hair, and cause it to come up thick again: and for to apply such medicines for this purpose, the powder of a cuttle-bone prepareth the skin well beforehand. Also the ashes of the sea-tortoise incorporat with oil; of a sea urchin likewise burnt and calcined flesh and all together: as also the gall of a scorpion, be appropriate medicines to recover hair that was lost. In like manner, take the ashes of three frogs burnt together alive in an earthen pot, meddle them with honey, it is a good medicine to cause the hair to grow: but the operation will be the better, in case the same be tempered with liquid pitch or tar.

Plant Cures

Virtually every plant and tree you can think of (except, perhaps, for the bald cypress) has been tried in the search for an effective treatment. Romans rubbed **berries of myrrh** into the scalp. Tribes in the Bahia region of Brazil used **cactus sap**. And **boxwood** was a traditional English country remedy – which may have given rise to another ancient joke: 'What would help me to keep my hair?' 'A box would'.

The seventeenth-century French physician Jean Adrien Helvetius listed the parts of the human body and suggested which **herbs and plants** should be used to treat them; for the hair, he recommended asparagus, fennel, vine roots, flax and goat's-beard. To these we may add mint leaves, capsicum, yarrow, quince seeds, fleurs-de-lis and leaves from St John's wort. Oh, and fern roots, burdock soaked in rum, garlic, parsley, basil, tomato juice, sage tea, castor oil and grapevine sap. Not forgetting coconut oil, mustard oil, artichoke juice, dates, rosewater, pine bark, sorrel, wormwood, linseed oil, wheat bran and bruised almonds.

And then there are all the combinations of plants to consider. In April 1975, the *Sunday Times* reported that 'a famous London goalkeeper' who wished to remain anonymous was trying a remedy containing a mixture of 'pure herbs'. Apparently this did nothing for his hair

I have discovered an essential oil that will make the hair grow, a Comagene oil! Livingston has set up a hydraulic press for me to make it from hazelnuts which, under great pressure, will yield all their oil. I reckon to earn at least a hundred thousand francs within a year. I'm thinking about doing a poster with the headline: 'Down with wigs!' It will cause a sensation. You don't know how many sleepless nights I've had. I've been losing sleep for three months now over the success of Macassar Oil. I want to ruin Macassar!
— Honoré de Balzac, *César Birotteau*

but did give him very long, strong fingernails.

Mrs Beeton offered a **rosemary** recipe in her *Book of Household Management* (1861):

> To promote the growth of hair:
> Ingredients: Equal quantities of olive oil and spirit of rosemary; a few drops of oil of nutmeg.
> Mix the ingredients together, rub the roots of the hair every night with a little of this liniment, and the growth of it will very soon sensibly increase.

The virtues of **southernwood** were extolled in a book of medical recipes dating from 1610:

To remedye baldnes of the heade – Take a quantitye of
Suthernwoode, and put it upon kindled coales to burne; and
being made into powder, mix it with the oyle of radishes and
anoynte the balde place, and you shall see great experiences.

Willow twigs were often used during the Middle Ages in accordance with the Doctrine of Signatures prevalent at the time. This was a theory that plants exhibited some outward sign of their useful attributes – and willow twigs can grow hair-like roots if they are damp. The hirsute gooseberry, for some reason, did not catch on in the same way.

Grapefruit juice and alum were suggested by John Capps III (founder of the Bald-Headed Men of America): 'It won't make your hair grow, but it'll shrink your head to fit what hair you have left.'

Animal Cures

Some of the animal-based remedies mentioned by Pliny the Elder went on to be used for centuries. **Bear's grease** was recommended by William Bulleyn in the 'Book of Simples' (1562):

The bear is a beaste whose flesh is good
for mankynd; his fat is good, with laudanum,
to make an ointment to heale balde-headed
Men to receive the hayre agayne.

It was still common in the late nineteenth century, though by that time the name seems to have become a synonym for hair tonic, and the ointment contained no direct ursine contribution. **Frogs** have also been used since Pliny. In November 1990, the *Spectator* reported that Terence Kealey, a scientist who had succeeded in growing hair in a test tube, had been contacted by a man with a patent method based on frog extracts. But even Pliny could not have anticipated the variety of animal-based remedies tried in subsequent centuries. It seems that substances from every animal, indeed each end of every animal, have at some point been smeared on to bald heads.

To wash with dog's piss causeth hair to grow on bald heads.
—*The Poor Man's Physician* (1731)

Bat milk – or as Robin might say, 'Holy bat milk!' It was reported in 1989 that a Swiss farmer called Gerhardt Flit had been in a barn with bats in the rafters when something splashed on his head. It wasn't what he first thought; it proved to be milk from a female bat. The farmer wiped it off – and the next morning he found hair sprouting on his head and hand where the milk had touched them.

Intrigued, Herr Flit returned to the barn, caught a female bat and somehow managed to milk it. He applied the milk to his head, and soon hair was 'growing like wild weeds'. Seized by enthusiasm – rather than by the men in white coats – Flit took to grabbing female bats and rubbing them on his scalp. Eventually, he realised the money-making potential of his discovery. He attracted hundreds of bats to his barn, fed them with as many moths as he could get, obtained the milk from the females and started to sell it for around £2,000 an ounce. So, perhaps not quite as daft as he seemed.

Cow licks were touted as a cure for baldness in 1984 when John Coombs, a farmer from near Salisbury, claimed that hair had been restored to his balding pate by one of his cows slobbering over it. The news made headlines around the world, and one American company made plans to launch a product called 'Likkit'. The cow in question, called Primrose, became known as the 'Friesian 2000' cow and was saved from the abattoir by her grateful owner.

It has also been claimed that horses and dogs can lick baldness. In 1997, Dr William B. Yancey wrote to the *Chicago Tribune* to plead the canine case: when his dog was recovering from an operation for which it had had to be partially shaved, the hair appeared to grow fastest in those areas where the dog licked most.

Then again, consider the bits all dogs lick most often; they are not the hairiest parts of a dog's body.

Beef marrow was often melted and applied to the scalp in the Victorian era in an attempt to combat baldness. The same treatment was still being proposed by Karen Thesen in her 1979 book, *Country Remedies from Pantry, Field and Garden.*

Donkey's teeth, ground down and boiled in oil, have been suggested as a remedy – as have boar's teeth. The Rawlinson manuscript in the Bodleian Library in Oxford offers the following advice: 'Take the toothe of a boores mouth and anoynte wher thou wilt, and it xal [shall] make the heer to grow thou ther [where] growthe neuere [never] non beforn [before].'

A combination of **hoof and horn** from animals was developed in the 1920s by the physiologist Professor Nathan Zuntz and marketed under the name 'Humagsolan'. In his 1926 book *The Loss of Hair and its Treatment by Light*, however, Franz Nagelschmidt remarked: 'I have prescribed Humagsolan in a good many cases of loss of hair, and have seldom observed any marked results.'

Drs von Hovorka and Kronfeld, writing in Stuttgart in 1908, reported that in the region of Swabia, the **boiled flesh of a mole** was commonly rubbed on the scalp. In the mountains of North Carolina, on the other hand, **mole's blood** was seen as a cure. It is unlikely that either treatment had any effect – apart from producing bumps all over the head, perhaps.

A fourteenth-century Gaelic manuscript contains the following potent recipes, translated from the *Lilium Medicinae* (c. 1305), written by Bernard of Gordoun in Montpellier:

> For baldness: let calcine a **raven**. His ashes boil in sheep's suet. Rub to the head and it cures. With **mice**, fill an earthen pipkin, stop the mouth with a lump of clay and bury beside a fire, but so as the fire's too great heat reach it not. So it be left for a year and at a year's end, take out whatsoever may be found therein. But it is urgent that he that shall lift it have a glove upon his hand, lest at his fingers' ends the hair come sprouting out.

Patrick Logan describes a peculiar process in *Irish Country Cures* (1981): 'The person making it up must fill a jar with **worms** and bury the jar in the manure heap; at the end of a month the jar may be dug up and the contents rubbed on the scalp.'

Exactly why a sealed jar needs to be buried in manure is not clear. Perhaps smearing dead worms on one's head was not unpleasant enough, and needed this extra twist to bring the cure up to code.

Pigeon poo was used by the Egyptians and by Hippocrates, who mixed in opium, beetroot and horseradish before smearing it on his scalp. A fourteenth-century English barber recommended a pomade of **goose droppings**, and a suggested treatment three centuries later was 'a strong paste made from cow dung and old soles of shoes burnt to powder, with a little rosemary'. In addition, the efficacy of poultices made of **chicken manure** has long been an old wives' tale (presumably to have a laugh at the expense of their old husbands).

Snakes have frequently been used to make lotions and potions. **Python fat** has been applied to the head, but snake oil has historically been far more common and was still being hawked around the US during the nineteenth century by travelling salesmen. (By contrast, the third-century physician Quinto Samonico mentions in his *Liber Medicinalis* the Roman superstition that snake poison, expelled occasionally into the air, was detrimental to the hair.)

Lanolin, a fat derived from sheep's wool, was once marketed as a remedy with the slogan: 'Have you ever seen a bald sheep?' Which may sound convincing, until you discover that some do suffer from falling fleece. In 1931, Dr B. Norman Bengtson of Chicago claimed to have grown new hair on completely bald men by injecting them with an extract from a sheep's pituitary gland. The treatment did not catch on, though it is not known whether this was because the side-effects were baaad.

Spider's webs have been tried, possibly because they can look like wisps of hair. And Friedrich-Christian Lesser suggested in his *Théologie des Insectes* of 1742 that the **housefly** might cure baldness if crushed and applied to the bald spot – though this sounds dangerously like another excuse for slapping a baldy on the bonce.

Magnified one thousand
times, the insect
Looks farcically human; laugh if you
will!
Bald head, stage-fairy wings, blear
eyes,
A caved-in chest, hairy black
mandibles,
Long spindly thighs.

—Robert Graves, 'The Blue-Fly'

Painful Cures

Ow! In 1995, Mr Pil Chun of Tewksbury, Massachusetts, patented a method of acupuncture to remedy baldness. The patent covers three types of treatment: i) inserting needles; ii) inserting needles and applying pressure; iii) inserting needles and passing an electrical current

Corporal Replenishment

Various parts of the human body have been used to create baldness remedies:

- **Hair** In *Magic and Healing* (1946), C. J. S. Thompson refers to 'a liquor distilled from human hair, mixed with honey' which could be used as 'a stimulating application for a bald head'.
- **Blood** The principal active ingredient of 'Capsuloids', a treatment common in the early 1900s, was haemoglobin, the red oxygen-carrying pigment found in red blood cells.
- **Earwax** Any effect this had on one's appearance would probably have been down to the ear hair that came with it.
- **Placenta extracts** formed part of a preparation made by a French company during the 1980s.
- **Urine** was commonly used in Co. Kerry and Co. Clare, according to Patrick Logan in *Irish Country Cures*: 'Human urine is poured into the bladder of a goat which is then hung up in the chimney above the fire and it must remain there until all the liquid has evaporated. When this has happened, the bladder is taken down, ground up and rubbed on the scalp.'

through them. Mr Chun admitted in his patent application that 'the exact mechanism by which the present acupuncture treatment technique works to treat baldness is not fully understood'.

Oww! 'I'm bald. So bite me.' In the US, this would be a simple statement of defiance. But as Sir James George Frazer described in his classic anthropological work *The Golden Bough*, this could once have been a request for help in central Australia:

> To promote the growth of a boy's hair, a man with flowing locks bites the youth's scalp as hard as he can, being urged thereto by his friends, who sit round watching him at his task, while the sufferer howls aloud with pain. Clearly, on the principle of capillary attraction, if I may say so, he thus imparts of his own mature abundance to the scarcity of his youthful friend.

Owww! A technique called 'popping' was practised by German-born Rita Hartinger in New York during the late 1960s. This involved tugging so hard at tufts of hair on the client's head that a noise like an exploding kernel of popcorn was made as the scalp was pulled away from the skull. 'When you lift up the scalp from the bone structure by popping,' Frau Hartinger explained, 'it stimulates circulation and nourishes the tissue. Then the hair is strengthened, and it is less likely to fall out.' Nightly washings 'in water as hot as possible' were also recommended.

It sounds excruciating – and of course it was. Patients were given a rod crackling with electricity to hold to keep their minds off the pain. Even Rita's husband refused the treatment, she admitted: 'He won't let me near him because it hurts so much.' Yet some people were prepared to endure the agony – including, reportedly, Leonard Bernstein and Anthony Perkins.

Aarrgghh! In 1980 lightning was said to have restored the hair of a 62-year-old man in Falmouth, Maine. Edwin Robinson, who had become blind and deaf after a road accident in 1971, was searching for his pet chicken in his backyard when he was struck. He miraculously regained his sight and hearing (and his chicken, one assumes) – and shortly afterwards began to sprout hair on his bald pate, as the family doctor confirmed. All the same, it probably wouldn't be a good idea for bald men to run around waving golf clubs in the air during thunderstorms in an attempt to emulate this.

Baldness treatments involving high charges? Nothing unusual there then

Lower doses of electricity have frequently been tried over the years, however. Our old friend and traducer of two-wheeled transport Professor Wheeler was in favour: 'The mild electrical treatment that we use is pleasant, very soothing, quite harmless, and easily applied . . . at the time it benefits the hair, it also has relieved depression and melancholy by its exhilarating and restorative powers or influence'. Doesn't that sound suspiciously like EST?

Aaarrrgggghhh!! C-c-castration. Since testosterone plays a key role in hair loss, cutting off the supply will prevent baldness. This was observed as early as Hippocrates' *Aphorisms*: 'Eunuchs neither get gout nor go bald.' There are stories of desperate young men, from families in which baldness is common, asking doctors to castrate them before they lose any hair; though I have yet to uncover any, er, firm examples. If the stories are not apocryphal, one can only hope that the men were motivated by something more than their desire to stay sexually attractive. Undergoing castration to that end would be like blowing all your petrol money on a top-of-the-range sports car.

Harmful Cures

The very thought of some baldness treatments would make your hair curl. That is, if you have any left to curl.

Lead-based remedies were common in the late nineteenth and early twentieth

Eyebrow-Raising

If some of these suggestions make you raise your eyebrows, they are helping you to keep your hair – at least, according to 'Hirsute', a contributor to the *New York Times* in March 1914. He argued that men needed to develop their scalp muscles to provide the hair with more nourishment, and that eyebrow-raising was the best way to do this:

Man can soon learn to raise his forehead for several inches above his eyebrows, and it will then be only a short time before he can move his scalp in any direction he pleases. As soon as this has been learned all fear of baldness is gone. I cured myself, and I know, and I now go to the barber's so often that I had to cut down on my smoking. This method tried consistently for six months will give a good head of hair ... Don't scoff: try.

centuries. Allen's Hair Restorer, the New London Hair Restorer and the Royal Windsor Hair Restorer were all preparations containing lead – some even proudly announcing their 'plumbiferous' nature on the packaging.

During the 1930s, German doctors claimed that **mustard gas** promoted hair growth. This, of course, was not the purpose for which it was originally developed.

Ammonia was an important constituent in Erasmus Wilson's Hair Promoter, a preparation widely used in the nineteenth century.

Turpentine formed part of a remedy devised by the Hôpital Saint Louis in Paris in the late nineteenth century. And **paraffin** has sometimes been applied to the scalp to act as an irritant. Strike a light. No, on second thoughts. . .

Radioactive paint was mentioned as a treatment by Ian Martin-Scott in *Baldness and the Care of the Hair* – though having a head which glows in the dark would not seem to be the best way to conceal one's bald spot.

Tying arteries in the temples and at the back of the head was a method developed in the early 1960s by the Belgian doctor Raymond Maréchal. The idea was that by cutting off the blood supply, testosterone might be prevented from reaching susceptible areas of the scalp. By 1987 the practice had been condemned as highly dangerous and banned outright in both France and the United States.

Not Entirely Unpleasant Cures

Massaging the scalp was stated by that vituperator of velocipedes Professor Wheeler to be 'a remedy of great regenerative power', and indeed it does seem to be of some use. In fact, the very action of rubbing in potions and lotions is probably more effective than most of the preparations themselves. In some cases, however, it can be harmful. When the hair is in the 'resting' stage of its cycle, or when the hair shafts are fragile, a massage could pull out huge handfuls.

Countless **shampoos** have been promoted with inflated claims for their restorative properties, and have often come with an inflated price. Hair Today, for example, was a herbal shampoo launched in the US in the early 1980s which cost $2,000 for six months' supply. While shampoos and mousses designed to thicken the hair shaft may bring about a marginal improvement in the early stages of balding, it seems fair to say that any shampoo claiming to cure the condition will prove to be both sham and poo.

Professor Wheeler, incidentally, believed that washing the hair regularly could be beneficial, but was keen to recommend products which 'have quite taken the place of the old-fashioned shampoo'. These products, including the Medicated Scalp Atomiser, the Wheeburshoe Hair Douche and Kentilt Head Fomentations, just happened to be available at his hair-treatment establishments. They were said to be 'most serviceable in prolonged hair falling from a variety of causes and impairments of functional vitality, which are brought about by illness, chills, bad nerves, headaches, internal troubles, operations, confinements, over-exertion from pleasure . . . late hours, and sedentary habits or occupation' and, of course, 'excessive bicycle riding'.

Whether **aromatherapy** is any more effective in treating hair loss than in treating a broken leg is debatable. Still, if you set any store by it, mix five drops of essential oil of sage with five of cedarwood in 30ml of surgical spirit. Or add three drops of both rosemary and ylang-ylang oils to a teaspoon of vodka before making this up to a tablespoonful with orange-flower water.

Love, according to Penny Perrick in *The Times* in March 1985, not only makes the heart leap, but causes hair to sprout too. She reported that Olympic swimming champion Duncan Goodhew had begun to grow hair after getting married. A heart-warming tale . . . but unfortunately untrue.

Comical Cures

In the early 1900s, helmets equipped with powerful **vacuums** were devised and marketed, the idea apparently being to draw blood to the scalp and suck hair out of it.

An advertisement for the Evans Vacuum Cap Co. of London demonstrates how ludicrous the user would look; the device looks like an oversized German soldier's helmet hanging from a birdcage stand. The medical endorsement could probably have been secured from a more convincingly named physician than Dr I. N. Love – if only with second opinions from his colleagues, Dr I. N. Thehouse, Dr A. T. Large and Dr A. T. Sea.

Magnetic insoles have also been proposed, the idea being to create 'a

How many ladies did read this, only to be worried that they would end up looking like the picture on the right?

favourable negative field in the feet to encourage a hair-raising positive polarity in the head'. It's a wonder the makers didn't suggest sprinkling iron filings on the scalp to complete the effect.

In 1924, the Frenchman Emile Coué visited New York to promote his 'method of **conscious auto-suggestion**'. One of his employees told the *New York Times* of a case where this technique had had spectacular results: 'A young man who came to the New York institution was suffering from pains in the head. We told him what to do to cure himself. He had not been using the method long when all over his head, which had been completely bald, hair began to grow.'

So what does 'conscious auto-suggestion' involve? Coué was happy to explain: 'By repetition of the formula "Day by day in every way, I am getting better and better", the unconscious self begins to right the things that are wrong in the body . . . When auto-suggestion begins to work, the follicles begin to close up and to secrete normally, and soon the hair grows.' He even offered advice on how to make the technique less tiresome: 'If you are too lazy to say the words, have them put on a phonograph record and hear them regularly that way.'

Inversion – or to put it another way, putting your body the other way up – was promoted by Andy Bryant in his 1994 book *The Baldness Cure*. It formed only part of his 'SIDES' therapy (stress management, inversion, diet, exercise, shampoo), but it was unsurprisingly the aspect which attracted the most media interest. Readers were advised to buy one of his inversion machines (for just a few hundred pounds), which would grip their ankles and allow them to tip themselves upside down. By dangling for a minute or two twice a day, they would supposedly stimulate the flow of blood and nutrients to the head.

Bryant claimed a high success rate (more than 90 per cent) for his topsy-turvy method, and received endorsements from Labour MPs Bryan Gould and Keith Vaz. As further evidence of its effectiveness, he launched a hair-growing competition in 1995; the winner succeeded in reducing the width of his bald crown from 8.5cm to 6cm. Faced with suggestions that this was a small improvement to show for dangling upside down every day, Bryant remained defiant: 'Think of them [the finalists] as like the Wright brothers. They only flew for 59 seconds. But they showed that it could be done.'

Nevertheless, most trichologists remain sceptical; one remarked on television that dangling clients upside down is the quickest way to empty their pockets.

Cures to Make You Go 'Mmm!'

Many remedies based on edible or drinkable substances have been tried:

Applying **alcohol** to the scalp has been tried many times, and not just by those too drunk to remember where their mouth is. Vodka-based treatments – generally including cayenne pepper – have often been used. And in *Cosmetics* (1902), Theodor Koller remarks that 'after a long period of neglect, the beneficial effect of bay rum on the scalp is beginning to be more and more widely recognised on the Continent'. He also mentions the Capillarine Hair Restorer, a preparation composed of pure alcohol, onion juice, French brandy, Peruvian balsam, burdock root oil and juniper berry oil, with a soupçon of fat or tallow. It may not have been an effective restorer, but what a punch to serve at a party.

If you prefer to apply alcohol to the back of the throat rather than the top of the head, you'll be pleased to know that this too has been suggested as an antidote to hair loss. In 1977, George De Leon, a researcher in New York, noticed that the winos on the streets were rarely bald. He compared the frequency of baldness among them with that found in other groups of men, such as academics, businessmen and shopkeepers. Academics were most likely to go bald, with 71 per cent being affected; but only 36 per cent of the winos experienced any loss.

The reason seems to be that alcohol can act as a suppressant of testosterone. But beware. Even if alcohol does encourage growth on top, too much can cause shrinkage further down.

The American physiologist Professor Nathan Zuntz asserted in 1920 that certain **food elements** would encourage hair growth. Albuminous substances were particularly recommended, as were 'horny substances' (oysters, perhaps?) containing amino acids.

In 1995, there was a sudden and unexpected trend in the north of England for smearing **Marmite** on the head instead of on bread, in the hope that the vitamins in it would promote new hair growth. One Lancashire woman (surname: Burke) wrote to *Take a Break* to tell of her husband who had tried this before going to bed; the Marmite set solid and stuck his head to the pillow.

In 1996, the *Independent* reported that a West Midlands man had experienced some regrowth on his bald spot after rubbing **curry** into his scalp twice a day.

The School of Salerno, perhaps the leading medieval medical school, offered this advice in the *Regimen Sanitatis Salernitanum* (translated by Sir John Harington in 1607):

> For Oyntment iuyce of Onyons is assign'd,
> To heads whose haire fals faster then it growes:
> If Onyons cannot helpe in such mishap,
> A man must get him a Gregorian cap.

The French doctor Ambroise Paré was still suggesting in the seventeenth century that the balding should 'rub the scalp with a clean cloth, raw onions or fig leaves until it grows flushed'. And E. F. T., writing in the *New York Times* in November 1901, claimed that it 'produces remarkable results. If one can stand the dreadful odor long enough, the result will be efficacious'. Perhaps the real benefit of onions lies in keeping others at such a distance that they do not spot your bald spot.

During the nineteenth century, cold Indian **tea** and fresh **lemon juice** were applied to many a thinning scalp throughout England. Eventually, though, it was conceded that hair loss is the one thing in the country which does not stop for tea.

Dearth of a Nation

On occasions, baldness remedies have caused mass hysteria.

In Hungary, former factory supervisor Andras Banfi announced in 1979 that he had invented a miracle hair restorer, inspired by studying Egyptian manuscripts. When Mr Banfi's Lotion went on sale in Budapest, moulting Magyars packed the shops, and the queues frequently became so long and unruly that the police were sent in to keep order. Customers able to get hold of the lotion were offered as much as ten times its price for it, and many bottles found their way to Austria, Poland and Czechoslovakia, where they were sold for a fortune on the black market. As many as 1.2 million bottles were sold in the first eight months, though demand slowed considerably after that – probably because of its terrible smell, though its nasty brown colour and stickiness couldn't have helped.

Around ten years later, Beijing was going mad for 101 Hair Regeneration Liniment, so named because its inventor Zhao Zhangguang had developed it after 100 unsuccessful attempts. Despite the course of treatment costing around a third of the average annual income in China, demand greatly exceeded supply. Bald visitors flocked to Beijing from Japan, while '101 fever' was triggered in Taiwan. Chinese students bought it and sold it on in the United States and Canada for several times the original cost.

Cures to Make You Go 'Huh?!'

It has been jokingly suggested that the only sure-fire ways to keep your hair are to arrange to be born into a family in which all the males keep their hair, or to knot your hair from the inside so that it doesn't fall out. These are scarcely more ridiculous than the following methods:

Get yourself treated by a **doctor wearing black**. Sir James George Frazer in *The Golden Bough*:

> An ancient Indian cure for a scanty crop of hair was to pour a solution of certain plants over the head of the patient; this had to be done by a doctor who was dressed in black and had eaten black food, and the ceremony must be performed in the early morning, while the stars were fading in the sky, and before the black crows had risen cawing from their nests . . . the black clothes of the doctor, his black food, and the swarthy hue of the crows unquestionably combined to produce a crop of black hair on the patient's head.

In January 1926, a physician advocated in the *New York Times* that having the hair cut during **the moon's last quarter** encourages it to grow more thickly. 'Sceptics will smile at this. However, "fools deride, philosophers investigate",' he declared. All the same, it is difficult to ignore the shared etymology of 'lunar' and 'lunatic'.

Dr William H. FitzGerald of Hartford, Connecticut, claimed in *American Medicine* in January 1922 that **rubbing the fingernails** of one hand against those of the other (including the thumbnails) very briskly for two to three

'I've got a plan for keeping your hair from falling off,' said the White Knight. 'First you take an upright stick. Then you make your hair creep up, like a fruit tree. Now the reason hair falls off is because it hangs *down* – things never fall upwards, you know.'

— Lewis Carroll, *Through the Looking Glass and What Alice Found There* minutes a day would cause the scalp to tighten and thus reduce or stop altogether the loss of hair.

Singeing the hair was often advised by barbers after a haircut in order to prevent 'the vital fluid' from escaping out of the newly trimmed ends. This theory was already being debunked at the end of the nineteenth century, in G. R. Brandle's *Treatise on Premature Baldness*:

> Misinformed hairdressers . . . when questioned by their customers to account for the increasing thinness of their hair, reply by stating that it is either constitutional or that it is in consequence of the escape and waste of nutrition from the ends of the hair, and recommend as a preventative to have them singed. This is of course a gross error, as the hair grows and is pushed out from the root and does not increase in length in the same manner for instance as an icicle.

The word 'error' seems rather generous: after all, what better remedy than a service which may be performed on the spot?

Strangely Familiar Cures

A number of substances and activities mentioned earlier as supposed causes of baldness have also been suggested as remedies.

A combination of arsenic and prayer was declared to be effective by a Hungarian priest towards the end of the eleventh century. A tartrate of arsenic was mixed with salts and various mysterious ingredients and dissolved in Tokay before being applied to the scalp. (The priest's prayers were presumably that he wouldn't be blamed if the patient died.) In Franz Nagelschmidt's *The Loss of Hair and Its Treatment by Light* (1926), arsenic is still being mentioned as a commonly prescribed measure.

Frequent shaving – of the whole head as well as the face – was recommended frequently between the two world wars. This was based on the false belief that hair grows back more strongly after being cut. It doesn't work, but persisting with the method may help balding men to grow accustomed to the look which awaits them.

Specific **headgear** for bald heads has been designed, notably 'Lichtmann's Improved Cap for Promoting the Growth of Hair', patented in 1904. This looked like an ordinary nightcap, but contained an inner layer impregnated with an alcohol-based mixture intended to increase blood circulation.

Eel fat was tried during the eighteenth century, while in 'The Magic Art' Sir James George Frazer mentions a fish-oil treatment favoured by the Lkuñgen tribe of Vancouver Island.

Brushing the hair has been proposed as a cure as often as it has been blamed for hair loss. As Dr William P. Cunningham of Harlem Hospital stated in *The Medical Record* in 1915: 'The practice of brushing the scalp briskly with a good stiff implement will stimulate the blood and nerve supply and prevent the development of the condition.'

Various brushes have been devised specifically for this task. One marketed in Japan came with the instruction that the buyer should strike himself upon the head with it 200 times, twice a day. (The brush had a built-in counter In case the user lost track.) Still more surprising than this was the slogan used to sell the brush: 'Japanese men are beaten at work, they are beaten at home, and beating makes strong men!'

Exposure to **sunshine** was proposed as the best remedy by Joseph McAfee in the *New York Times* in September 1925:

> These young fellows . . . who keep their scalps open to the
> free air and the vivifying rays of the sun, will preserve
> enough human hair to enable the next generation of bald
> offspring of bald men and balder women to catch a
> remaining glimmer of a glory which will then have departed.

A year later, Franz Nagelschmidt was extolling the virtues of ultra-violet light in *Loss of Hair and Its Treatment by Light*. He claimed that after treating 200 patients – suffering from hair loss caused by illness or alopecia areata rather than male pattern baldness – 82.2 per cent were cured completely, 10.8 per cent were improved and 7 per cent remained unaffected. This means that 21.6 people improved and 164.4 people were cured completely. Unfortunately Herr Nagelschmidt did not explain what constitutes 0.6 or 0.4 of a person.

In *Baldness and Hair Care* (1980), D. J. Drabble refers to UV-focusing antennae designed to be attached to the bedhead. It's surprising that no one thought of converting the 'deely-bobbers' popular at the time for this purpose.

Today, the most common light-based treatments for male pattern baldness involve lasers. In December 1994, the *Sunday Mirror* reported that snooker star Jimmy White had spent around £12,000 on this method. Four years later, footballer John Hartson was said to have signed up for a course of 'advanced laser therapy' – though he has since opted for a completely shaven look.

Since testosterone is a crucial factor in causing male pattern baldness, one would think this is the last thing one would apply to the scalp – yet it has been tried. In February 1965, the *Journal of the American Medical Association* reported that a cream containing testosterone had succeeded in stimulating hair growth on some bald heads, though the lack of subsequent positive reports points to the method's long-term inefficacy.

It is perhaps less surprising that the female hormone oestrogen has been employed to counteract the depilatory effects of testosterone. It has been applied to the scalp as well as taken internally, and it does help to preserve the hair. But there are drawbacks. Large, pendulous drawbacks.

Men taking large doses of oestrogen will find that their bodies become feminised. Losing the beard may not seem so bad; after all, no one enjoys shaving. But the loss of one's sex drive – perhaps even permanently – is a rather more serious matter. (One treatment, Androcur, was originally developed for the treatment of sex offenders in Sweden.) The breasts may also be enlarged. This, perhaps, is the way oestrogen really acts as a baldness treatment: while people are gawping at your knockers, they do not notice your receding hairline.

INTERLUDE I
I'm not bald . . .

'I'm not bald, I'm alive!'
—Squidward in *Spongebob Squarepants*

I'm not bald. . .

I'm follicularly challenged.
I'm differently hirsute.
I'm trichologically understated.
I have a minimalist coiffure.
I have slight hairing difficulties.
I'm being economical
  with the roots.
I have a hairdo of
  restricted growth.
I have a wider than
  average parting.
This is a no-hican.
This is a short back
  and sides and top.
I have a tall face.
I'm slightly too tall for my hair.
I'm letting my head go barefoot.

My hair is preservative-free.
I'm lying fallow.
I'm conducting a limited
  experiment in streaking.
I'm going topless.
I have a hole in my haircut.
I've had a sunroof fitted.
I'm a hair donor.
I have edited highlights.
I'm reducing my overheads.
I'm aerodynamic.
This is a solar panel for a
  sex machine.

CHAPTER THREE

Drugs, Plugs . . .

It will be apparent that I have provided a novel means of securing a fiber to a follicle . . . I have used hairs from animals which have been previously treated with a disinfectant and preservative such as a 40% aqueous solution of formaldehyde. I have also used fibers or hairs made from synthetic materials such as nylon, Dacron or other materials and have used vegetable fibers, as for example, hemp.

— Extract from US Patent No. 3,062,214 (1962) for a method of transplanting hair

As the twentieth century started to run out, large numbers of men whose hair was doing likewise turned to drugs and hair transplants in an effort to combat it. Both methods had been tried earlier in the century, but with little or no lasting success.

In response to the huge number of ineffective drugs on the market, the Food and Drug Administration in the US felt obliged to introduce strong measures in 1989. The FDA issued a rule regarding all 'over-the-counter hair-grower and hair-loss prevention drug products as not generally recognized as safe and effective and as being misbranded'. The following year, all non-prescription creams and lotions claimed by their makers to grow hair or prevent baldness were banned.

However, two medical treatments have been approved and confirmed as effective by the FDA: **minoxidil** and **finasteride**.

Minoxidil

Minoxidil, marketed as 'Regaine' in the UK and 'Rogaine' in the US (where the FDA thought that the former name promised too much), was discovered in Kalamazoo, Michigan, in 1964. Developed from a chemical extracted from rat's urine, its original application in the early 1970s was as an oral medication intended to lower high blood pressure. Some users soon noticed an unusual side-effect, however: they grew thick hair between the eyebrows, on the temples, and on the shoulders, arms and legs. So thick was the new hair that this became known as the 'werewolf effect'.

Upjohn, the drug company involved, spotted the potential and set about developing a lotion which could be applied directly to the scalp. Regaine was eventually launched in 1987, and approved for use in the UK by the Committee on the Safety of Medicines in 1988. Regaine Extra Strength followed around ten years later to encourage further growth of both hair and profits.

So how does it work? Upjohn spokesperson Jan R. AufderHeide offered the following explanation in March 1987: 'No one knows.' However, the two strongest possibilities are: a) that minoxidil expands blood vessels to increase the supply of blood to the scalp (though other drugs which do this have no effect on the hair); and b) that it partially enlarges follicles which have begun to shrink and extends their lives so that they can go on producing hair.

A more important question, you might think, is: 'How well does it work?' Frankly, it depends – not just on the individual using it, but on which set of figures you believe and what you understand by such terms as 'good results'. Upjohn claimed that one-third of

Homer's Hair-Doh!

In an episode of *The Simpsons* titled 'Simpson and Delilah', Homer sees an ad for a hair-growth product called Dimoxinil and is desperate to give it a try. (His bathroom cabinet is already full of products such as Hair Chow, Bald Buster, Hair Master, Gorilla Man Scalp Blaster and U Wanna B Hair E.) He pays for the expensive treatment by claiming on his company insurance, on the grounds that it will keep his brain from freezing. When his hair grows back, he is ecstatic, as is his wife Marge who is delighted at his new-found friskiness.

At work, he is perceived as being young and dynamic and is soon promoted and given the key to the executive washroom. He is invited to address a large gathering of executives – but before he can do so, his son Bart spills the remaining Dimoxinil and Homer's hair falls out again. The assembled executives no longer take him seriously.

regular-strength Regaine users experience reasonably luxuriant regrowth, while another third show some improvement and the remaining third are unaffected. After four months, 8 per cent of patients show good results, and this figure rises to 39 per cent after a year. By the makers' own admission though, the product stands a chance of working only if the user is just starting to lose his hair; a spokesman commented that applying it to a shiny bald head was likely to be as successful as a farmer pouring fertiliser on to a concrete yard.

In January 1989, the *Journal of Clinical and Experimental Dermatology* published a paper which took a critical look at the way Upjohn evaluated hair growth. The company's preferred method was to count the hairs in a circle one inch in diameter, visually. The paper suggested that the operator could, on a later count, spot hairs which had always been there but had previously been overlooked, either because minoxidil darkens fluffy hairs and makes them more visible – or simply because they had become more skilled at counting hairs. The author of the paper preferred the method of plucking out the hairs as they were counted, even though this rather defeats the object of using hair restorer. Upjohn subsequently scrapped their counting method.

The paper concluded that Regaine might prove to be useful to only one person in 200. Hair loss might be halted for two or three years, but it would probably resume after that. It was considered unlikely that the product would be effective in the long term.

There had already been criticism of Regaine's test results in the *Lancet* the previous year. A report by three clinical pharmacologists concluded that the drug worked for fewer than 1 in 10. Terms such as 'dense' and 'moderate' used to describe regrowth were considered vague and unhelpful. It was pointed out that in a trial conducted for Upjohn with

**Early enthusiasm for minoxidil spread like wildfire.
Unfortunately the hair didn't**

56 men, 25 experienced no change, while the eight individuals who enjoyed an 'excellent' improvement had shown an average increase of only 6 per cent, which is scarcely noticeable.

The Minuses of Minoxidil

Before you run down to the pharmacist's to give minoxidil a try, here is a rundown of the disadvantages:

1) The treatment involves considerable expense – and you have to pay the price for ever. Should you ever stop using minoxidil, you will quickly lose your hair to the extent that you would have done if you had never used it at all.

2) As well as being a constant drain on your finances, it is a constant inconvenience since it must be applied twice a day.

3) It has to be used for four months (or two in the case of the extra-strong variety) before you can tell whether you are going to be one of the lucky few to experience 'substantial' regrowth.

4) The chances of growing a lot of new hair are very slim. Minoxidil seems to be effective in helping users to retain the hair they have. If you have only just begun to recede, it may be just what you need. But if you need your roof substantially rethatched, you are unlikely to be satisfied. Reports of one incident claim that a client of a hair clinic in New York was so furious that his minoxidil treatment had produced no new hair that he barged into the building brandishing a gun and a knife. After trying to shoot and stab two men, he was eventually subdued – and in the struggle, his hairpiece fell off. 'The rug was on the rug,' a police detective commented to the *New York Post*, who ran the story under the headline: 'COPS: BALDIE FLIPS WIG, TRIES TO KILL HAIR-CLINIC BOSS'.

5) When minoxidil does make new hair grow, it tends to do so on the crown, rather than at the front of the head where most people want to see the benefit.

6) As with any drug, there is a possibility of side-effects. Minoxidil brings a risk of water retention (with resultant weight gain), increased heart rate and shortness of breath.

Finasteride

Like minoxidil, the hair-restoring properties of finasteride were discovered by accident. Marketed as 'Proscar' by the pharmaceutical company Merck Sharp and Dohme, it was taken for the treatment of enlarged prostate glands. When users reported new hair growth on their heads, the company considered how to make use of this side-effect.

Trials using pills with a reduced dosage of finasteride (1 mg as opposed to the 5 mg contained in Proscar tablets) were carried out in the mid-1990s, and the results were encouraging: 83 per cent experienced no further loss of hair or grew more, and around two-thirds showed a visible improvement. This form of the drug, named 'Propecia', was approved by the FDA in December 1997 and became available on prescription in the US soon afterwards.

Finasteride works by suppressing the enzyme 5-alpha-reductase which converts testosterone to dihydrotestosterone (DHT) – the hormone which 'switches off' some hair follicles. It has a number of advantages. Since it comes in pill form, it is not as time-consuming or as inconvenient to use as minoxidil. It promotes growth towards the front of the scalp, rather than on the crown. And of course, it will prevent your prostate from growing.

The Downside of Finasteride

1) Like minoxidil, it does not come cheap. And as with minoxidil, you have to keep taking it for life.

2) It takes around three months to see any results. You need to shell out a tidy sum before you know whether it will be of any benefit to you.

3) Finasteride must not be used by women, since it can cause birth defects.

4) It can lead to reduced libido, impotence and – when a user can manage it – less ejaculatory fluid. The makers claim that only 1.8 per cent of men experience any diminution of their sex drive, but would you be prepared to take the risk? Some would, of course – and there's always the (very) odd one who sees this as a bonus. One man who had been using the drug for six months complained, 'I was hoping to be cured of lustful thoughts, but it didn't work.' It didn't have much effect on his hair loss either.

Transplants

One of the first methods of implanting hair in the scalp was practised in Hungary in the early twentieth century. It was patented by Dr Aurel Popovics in 1909, but in the July 1914 edition of *Scientific American* published a detailed description written by a Dr Szekely, who claimed to have perfected the technique. Those who underwent the procedure may have been nervous at first, but they were soon hooked:

The end of a gold wire $\frac{1}{500}$" in diameter is bent to form a
loop, barely visible to the naked eye, which is threaded with a
woman's hair of the desired colour, soft, fine, and from 8–12"
long. The wire is introduced into a short, fine Pravaz
hypodermic needle and drawn forward until the threaded
loop is just inside the point of the needle. The wire is then
bent back and cut to a length of $\frac{1}{12}$" to $\frac{1}{8}$", forming a tiny
hook. Several hundred needles are prepared in this way and
are thoroughly sterilised before they are used.

The part of the scalp to be treated was sterilised and 'made insensitive'. About 625 pairs of
hairs were planted per square inch, with 400–500 planted in a single session of 30–40
minutes. The total number of hairs implanted could range from 10 to 50,000; 20,000 would
cover a bald crown, but 50,000 would be needed for a completely bald head.

The discomfort of the operation – and of walking around afterwards with thousands of
tiny metal hooks anchored inside one's scalp – can only be guessed at. Brushing or
combing the hair must have been agony, yet Dr Szekely made light of this. He
acknowledged that a slight inflammation developed on the reforested area, but declared
that this 'quickly subsides' and is succeeded by a scar 'which attaches the hair still more
firmly to the scalp'. Besides, 'the soreness caused by the inflammation is trifling, and is
scarcely appreciable after 10 to 12 days'.

Dr Szekely was not exactly modest in describing the finished result:

> The implanted hair presents so natural an appearance that it
> deceives the ordinary observer . . . It can be brushed,
> combed and washed . . . In short, this method of planting hair
> is hygienic, cosmetic and practical. The permanence of the
> result is indicated by the fact that in one case, where the
> whole crown of the head was thus covered, the implanted
> hair has remained in perfect condition for seven years.

The fact is that such a method involved a huge risk of infection; the 'ordinary observer'
would be less likely to be 'deceived' than to wonder who that poor chap in the corner with
a septic head might be.

Disturbingly, a similar procedure was still being used more than fifty years later. In January 1971, the Federal Trade Commission in the US took action against a California company called Medi-hair. The company had been inserting plastic-coated steel wire anchors into the scalp, which reportedly caused bleeding, infections and headaches. Four doctors signed affidavits claiming that the technique could even cause tumours. Not the sort of growth which clients would have wanted to show off.

The man generally credited with refining and popularising the transplant method favoured today is the New York dermatologist Dr Norman Orentreich. In the 1960s, he showed how complete hairs, including the whole hair bulb, may be taken from the back and sides of the head where there is generally a plentiful supply, and implanted in bare areas on top.

Hundreds of thousands of bald men, possibly millions, have had hair transplants since Dr Orentreich demonstrated the technique's possibilities. American research indicates that policemen, construction workers and salesmen are keenest on the procedure, but a number of celebrities have also opted for the root-moving route. Elton John's transplants were carried out in Paris in the late 1970s. 'I had the operation because I did not like being bald,' he said at the time. 'I admit it is 100 per cent vanity – and I am thrilled with the result.' He

A side-splitting *New York Times* cartoon on early hair transplants

was evidently less thrilled by the early 1990s, when he invested in his hairpiece. Francis Rossi of Status Quo is another singer believed to have undergone the procedure, as is Gary Numan. According to rock legend, a particularly ardent fan of the latter had hair implants in his honour, even though he didn't need them.

The advantages of transplants are clear. The results are permanent. You are using your own hair to cover your losses, rather than someone else's in the form of a wig. And the outcome can be impressive. In 1971, Bobby Hull – a star player in the Chicago Black Hawks ice-hockey team – spent $900 on transplants to cover his bald spot, and was chosen soon afterwards to star in a TV commercial for shampoo.

The Trouble with Transplants

1) Transplants can be spectacularly expensive.

2) The result can look unnatural. If large hair grafts are used, it makes for a particularly 'pluggy' appearance – variously described as 'Barbie-doll head', the 'colander', 'toothbrush' or 'corn row' effect, and the 'planted forest' look. Even if the doctor is able to carry out micro-grafts (a painstaking and very expensive technique whereby individual hairs are transplanted in a random pattern for a more natural appearance), the coverage is still likely to look thin. Anyone who expects to end up with a full, dense-looking crop on top is heading for disappointment.

   It also has to be remembered that the transplanted hair is coming from other places on the head; there is not an infinite supply. However, this did not deter one man in France. Having run out of spare hair at the back of his head, he insisted that his pubic hair be used to cover his remaining bald spots.

3) It is not just the finished result which can look peculiar. Since the procedure has to be carried out in stages, one's interim appearance may attract a lot of attention.

   Even wearing a hat isn't always an option; there are, after all, many situations when hats are inappropriate. In May 1972, Senator William Proxmire of Wisconsin tried to cover up his new hair transplant with a bulky white turban in the senate and at committee meetings. He insisted that bald men on TV looked 'grotesque' and that their appearance was a distraction from what they were saying. Few, however, would have followed this argument, diverted as they were by his heavily bandaged head.

4) A hair transplant is a surgical procedure, and comes with all the attendant discomfort and disfigurement: bruising, scarring, swelling and pain – and that's just when the surgery goes well.

5) In the worst cases, the procedure may cause infection, excessive bleeding and permanent scars. The trauma of the operation could cause hair loss to accelerate. And there is always the possibility, however slight, that the surgeon will make a mess of things. In one case in the US, a doctor fashioned a hairline in the shape of an inverted triangle which came to a sharp point low in the centre of the patient's forehead. There have been other cases when grafts have been planted the wrong way so that the hairs require buckets of industrial-strength gel to flatten them in the right direction.

6) If you have transplants while still in the early stages of hair loss, you cannot know how much you will eventually lose. You can cover bald or thinning areas in the short term, but these areas will continue to expand over the following years – and it may transpire that the final extent of your baldness is too large to be covered satisfactorily. By that time, the first reseeded areas may look odd and isolated. Moreover, you could have hair moved to the top of your head, only for this to disappear because it would have done so in its original location.

Perhaps the safest and cheapest course of action would be to follow the advice of bald comic Lee Hurst. He suggested having transplants on the palm of the hand, so that when you stroke your pate, it feels like you've got a full head of hair. On the other hand, those who get some sort of thrill from extreme surgical procedures have a few more gruesome alternatives available to them:

The 'flap operation', sometimes known as the 'Juri flap' after the Argentinian doctor who developed the technique in the 1960s. This involves slicing a strip of scalp up to two inches wide and eight inches long on the side of the head, then rotating it through 90 degrees so that it lies across the bare pate. The gaping hole at the side is closed by stretching the skin and stitching it together. Not surprisingly, bleeding and scarring are inevitable, and there is a risk of permanent disfigurement.

The Lamont method, which involves removing the sideburns and planting them across the hairline.

The scalp reduction. This is the surgical removal of the bald spot; an oval-shaped piece of bare scalp is cut out and the edges pulled together and sutured. The result is frequently a thin line down the centre of the head, as well as pain and a lingering feeling of tightness.

This procedure may be repeated over a number of months to reduce the bald area gradually, though there is a way to eliminate the whole bald spot in one go. A balloon may be inserted under the scalp and gradually inflated by weekly injections of saline water. After two or three months, the scalp should have stretched to such an extent that the hair-bearing areas may be pulled together to completely cover the bare region. You will have spotted the huge drawback to this method, though; one's head looks so swollen and deformed during the process that it is best to stay indoors to avoid scaring children in the street.

The singer Tom Jones reportedly admitted in 2003 that he had undergone a scalp reduction, unable as he must have been to bear the thinning of his green, green grass of home. Come on, Tom: it's not unusual.

CHAPTER FOUR

. . . and Rugs

ORTON: This is on me.
HALLIWELL: And this is on me.

— Joe Orton treats his lover and murderer Kenneth Halliwell to a
wig in the Alan Bennett-scripted film *Prick Up Your Ears*.

Wearing a wig may sound a better option than rubbing animal dung on your head, paying a small fortune for drugs which may make you limp or having your scalp sliced to pieces.

In ancient Egypt, wigs were status symbols. The Pharaohs and their families shaved their heads and wore highly stylised ceremonial wigs, usually made of human hair but occasionally of vegetable fibre or even grass. This arrangement presumably allowed the ruling class to cool their bare heads in private when the weather was especially hot. By contrast, slaves were forced by law to retain their own hair.

Wigs were also worn by Assyrians, Persians, Phoenicians, Greeks and Romans. The poet Martial refers to the furry covering worn by his acquaintance Phoebus: 'Since you cover your temples and the crown of your bald head with kidskin, Phoebus, that man said a funny thing when he told you your head was well shod.' The Roman emperor Caligula is said to have worn a wig to disguise himself when out at night in search of pleasure.

It was during the seventeenth and eighteenth centuries that wearing wigs became extremely fashionable in Europe. The trend was probably started by Louis XIV of France, who started to go bald at the age of 32 and concealed it with unfeasibly large black creations. The change in attitudes in England was particularly dramatic. At the start of the seventeenth century, bald Englishmen had preferred wearing hats indoors and out – sometimes sewing bunches of hair to the brim of their hats – to wearing a wig. Yet by the second half, even those with a full head of hair were shaving it off so that they could sport someone else's on their head. A wig became a sign of status and wisdom. Oliver Goldsmith in *The Citizen of the World*: 'To appear wise, nothing more is requisite than for a man to borrow hair from the heads of all his neighbours and clap it, like a bush, on his own'.

But by 1765, the fashion for wigs was starting to decline – to such a degree that in February of that year, a group of wigmakers marched through the centre of London with the intention of petitioning King George III to give their business a new boost. It wasn't a particularly successful exercise; on their way there, the watching crowd noticed that most of the wigmakers did not have wigs on. Those not wearing their wares were seized and forcibly shorn.

The eighteenth-century playwright and poet Oliver Goldsmith was laughed at in the street when he covered his bare head with a curled wig and carried a sword; a passer-by said he looked like a large fly stuck on a pin.

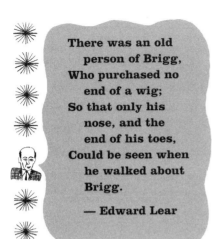

There was an old
person of Brigg,
Who purchased no
end of a wig;
So that only his
nose, and the
end of his toes,
Could be seen when
he walked about
Brigg.

— Edward Lear

During the nineteenth century, wigs remained out of favour. As the *Evening News* in London commented in 1886: 'Wig-wearing outside the theatrical profession is rare, though a few foolish old men, ashamed of being bald . . . give some employment in the manufacture of wigs, patches and fronts.' They did not become popular again until the late 1950s and early 1960s. This rug renaissance may have been prompted by the realisation that many celebrities were wearing them – a 1954 article revealing the secret of then-young singer Tony Bennett is thought to have had a significant impact – but probably had more to do with hairpiece companies making strenuous efforts to broaden their market. They employed hard-sell techniques and gimmicks (those selling 'Crown Toppers' in the 1960s would often wear one during a consultation and then surprise the potential customer by whipping it off) and they made wigs more affordable. Prices were squeezed even more by other businesses coming into the market; in 1967, Woolworth's started selling wigs from just £2 each. Sales continued to rise during the 1970s, with a huge leap of 30 per cent in the US in 1973 alone. Wig shops became so profitable that they became the targets of crime; in March 1974, two armed robbers held up a wig shop in Manhattan and stole thousands of dollars from the till and customers.

Improvements in styles and techniques contributed to the boom. Hair weaves in particular became increasingly popular. This involves attaching a small hairpiece, carefully matched for colour and texture, to the customer's remaining hair. The wearer's own hair may even be drawn through the mesh of the hairpiece to blend in more convincingly. A weave is certainly preferable to a full wig, since the wearer is still using much of his own hair and there is no need for glue or tape.

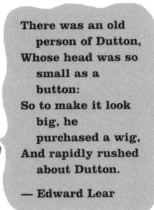

There was an old
person of Dutton,
Whose head was so
small as a
button:
So to make it look
big, he
purchased a wig,
And rapidly rushed
about Dutton.

— Edward Lear

The large number of famous wig-wearers might be taken as further endorsement of the practice. However, most are reluctant to admit it in public. And since it is such a source of embarrassment, others naturally take delight in exposing them whenever they can. In August 1992, the *Sun* had a 'Syrup Week' (syrup of fig = wig) and named a host of stars suspected of a cover-up. Among those listed were:

Adam Ant, who presumably didn't want people familiar with his hit 'Stand and Deliver' telling him that the way he looked, he'd qualify for next year's old-age pension.

Terry Wogan, who has always refused to admit to wearing a hairpiece, but has nevertheless often been dubbed 'Terry Wigon'.

Burt Reynolds, who was reported in 1996 to owe more than $100,000 to a Los Angeles wigmaker. He was also reported to be so desperate for a part in the film *Striptease* that he threw his toupee against the wall in the audition.

Bruce Forsyth ('Shall I wear it higher, higher or lower, lower?').

Ted Danson, whose character Sam Malone in *Cheers* was fiercely proud of his hair.

The list of other stars believed to have carpeted their crowns is impressive, including: Fred Astaire, Gene Kelly, John Wayne, Burt Lancaster, Rex Harrison, Bing Crosby, Henry Fonda, Charlton Heston, Tony Curtis (alleged by his hairdresser to have superglued his wig to his head to prevent it from being dislodged), and Humphrey Bogart. Frank Sinatra was once said to have employed a man who did nothing but look after his hairpieces – more than a hundred of them. Lorne Greene, star of the TV series *Bonanza*, apparently took five or six silvery pieces wherever he travelled; they were made of yak hair and angora, and constantly had to be replaced because they turned yellow so quickly.

> **'Can't act. Slightly bald. Can dance a little.'**
>
> **—Early screen-test verdict on Fred Astaire**

One of the few celebrities to have spoken openly and frankly about wearing a hairpiece is the actor John Nettles, best known for his TV roles in *Bergerac* and *Midsomer Murders*. He came clean in his 1991 autobiography *Nudity in a Public Place*:

Now, I wear a wig, but I introduced it gradually, so that my legion of fans, who will have no truck with the ageing process, would not be suddenly shocked by the appearance of a luxurious growth of hair of doubtful colour in all kinds of new places. Following the advice of my friend and mentor Terence Alexander, I diplomatically and surreptitiously applied small quantities of burnt cork to those areas of scalp showing beneath the thinning hair. As these areas increased in size, I gently, secretively, unobtrusively introduced small and then longer hair pieces, and I shall continue to do so.

Marlon Brando on Frank Sinatra: 'He's the kind of guy that, when he dies, he goes up to Heaven and gives God a bad time for making him bald'.

Thunderbald

Sean Connery differs from most wig-wearing actors in that he wears them only for film roles. When he landed the role of James Bond (for which the rugged Burt Reynolds was also a contender, incidentally), the producers decided that he would have to don a toupee to look more dashing and virile. Connery accepted this, but would not wear it elsewhere. On set, an observer had the job of making sure the wig was always on properly; in an early scene of *Thunderball*, she pointed out that the join was clearly visible, which the director had failed to spot.

When Connery returned to the role of Bond in *Never Say Never Again*, the wig question caused him some concern. A toupee matching his now-silvery hair had to be made, as the black style he had worn in the 1960s looked very odd. 'When I put it on,' Connery remarked, 'it looked like a balaclava.'

Wigs clearly have their plus points. They can make the wearer look younger. There is some evidence that a hairpiece can improve one's performance at work. And for those who are very confident, a wig can provide a great source of amusement. The jazz drummer Lenny Hastings used to wear one, and at the end of every show he would throw it in the air and shout, 'The grouse season has started!' As it started to fall, he would pretend to shoot it by giving a double-roll on the drums.

But, as you may have expected by now, there is also a plethora of drawbacks:

A hairpiece can be very noticeable, especially if it is a cheap one or if the wearer has been completely bald for years.

It can be extremely distracting to others. In September 1992, *The Times* columnist Matthew Parris devoted a whole column to recounting how his attention at a recent performance by the London Philharmonic Orchestra had been taken up by a wig sported by one of the violinists.

Once a wig has been twigged, the social embarrassment for the wearer can be enormous. It is not so much that the secret of one's baldness has been discovered; it is the vanity or insecurity which prompted the purchase that is revealed to the world.

You can never be sure that those entrusted with the secret of your hairpiece will not reveal it to a sniggering world. In 1993, the true appearance of later-disgraced pop singer Gary Glitter was laid bare by a woman in the know. She revealed that he was completely bald apart from one or two wisps of grey hair above his ears. His touchiness on the subject allegedly caused him to fly into a rage if his wig was not on properly - though he sought to prevent this by spending two hours putting it on, using enough glue to withstand a hurricane. It would then stay there for weeks to avoid the risk of being spotted changing it.

You cannot even be sure that your wigmaker will not reveal your secret. In 1998, the Hollywood rugmonger Charles Alfieri spoke publicly about famous wearers. He stated that William Shatner's wig 'has too much hair' and that Charlton Heston's 'should be recut to recede a little'. The one belonging to Burt Reynolds, on the other hand, 'looks natural', while Elton John's has a 'nicely layered cut and soft colour'. If your wigmaker can't keep it under his hat, who can?

The *Hairdressers' Weekly Journal* commented in 1886 that 'One great misfortune connected with wig-wearing is the opportunity it affords for small boys to call out, "Hullo Wiggy! Keep your hair on, old boy."'

It is not just small boys who poke fun. William Shatner, who as Captain Kirk in *Star Trek* refused to baldly go anywhere, was once asked at a convention in front of 3,000 fans whether he was wearing a wig. He was not pleased. 'Bad question, boy,' he yelled back. 'Do you have a brain?'

Charlton Heston was furious when a fellow guest on a TV show told him to keep his hairpiece on. And the American comedian George Burns was highly displeased when a newspaper columnist mentioned that he wore a wig, and later reproached the writer. 'But George,' the columnist replied, 'I didn't think you'd mind.' 'If I didn't mind,' snapped Burns, 'why would I wear a toupee?'

Even when the jokers claim to be laughing with, rather than at, their target, you can never be sure. Members of a Bruce Forsyth appreciation society formed in Plymouth in 1987 wore six square inches of shag-pile carpet on their heads in honour of their hero, as well as a couple more inches under the nose. But some of the society's other activities suggested that wigs, rather than Brucie, might have been the chief interest. Stickers proclaiming 'Toupees are for life – not just for Christmas' were produced, a spoof of a Sex Pistols hit was written ('Anarchy in the Toupee'), and members also starred in *Reservoir Wigs*, a TV send-up of Quentin Tarantino's first film.

Wigs involve a lot of expense. They need replacing every twelve to eighteen months – and in the case of hair weaves, reattaching to the wearer's hair every four to six weeks. Consequently, you need at least two, so that one can be worn while the other is being cleaned and refurbished. The initial cost of each hairpiece can run to thousands of pounds. Even in Samuel Pepys' day, wigs were relatively expensive:

> By and by comes Chapman the periwig-maker, and [upon]
> my liking it, without more ado I went up and there he cut off
> my haire; which went a little to my heart at present to part
> with it, but it being over and my periwig on, I paid him three
> pounds for it; and away went he with my own hair to make
> up another of.

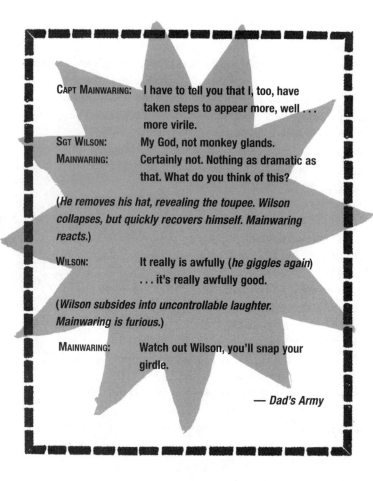

CAPT MAINWARING: I have to tell you that I, too, have taken steps to appear more, well . . . more virile.

SGT WILSON: My God, not monkey glands.

MAINWARING: Certainly not. Nothing as dramatic as that. What do you think of this?

(*He removes his hat, revealing the toupee. Wilson collapses, but quickly recovers himself. Mainwaring reacts.*)

WILSON: It really is awfully (*he giggles again*) . . . it's really awfully good.

(*Wilson subsides into uncontrollable laughter. Mainwaring is furious.*)

MAINWARING: Watch out Wilson, you'll snap your girdle.

— *Dad's Army*

When his second wig was delivered, Pepys was surprised to see how much it cost considering the source of the materials: 'After dinner came my Perriwigg-maker and brings me a second perriwigg, made of my own hair; which comes to 21s and 6d more than the worth of my own hair.'

A hairpiece works out to be even less value for money if it quickly falls to pieces. In March 1994, a man from Elgin, Morayshire, hit the headlines when his £2,000 'hair replacement system' disintegrated within two weeks leaving him looking like 'one of those troll dolls'. When he phoned the firm in Aberdeen which had sold him the hairpiece, he found that they had left the building.

Owning several hairpieces may lead to confusion and considerable hilarity at the wearer's expense. A leading figure in the London advertising world owned wigs of different hair lengths which he would wear in turn to make it appear that his hair was growing. When he had worn the longest for a while, he would announce that he was going for a haircut and return with his shortest on again. One evening, he returned home somewhat the worse for wear after an awards dinner, and was still so groggy the following morning that he put the wrong hairpiece on. His staff at the office were amazed, and not a little amused, to see that his hair had apparently grown by three or four inches overnight.

The most embarrassing thing that can happen if you are wearing a wig is that it becomes loose in public. For instance, a New York realtor on holiday in Florida got chatting to two stunning women on the beach and hit it off with both of them. They decided to take a swim in the sea together – but when they slipped into the water, his hairpiece did the same. Horrified, he swam underwater as far as the next hotel, leaving his shoes, clothes and two puzzled women behind. He flew straight back to New York, where his lawyer brother filed a suit against the wig company, who ended up settling out of court.

It must have been bad enough for the Brooklyn supermarket owner whose wig was speared from his head by a low branch as he walked past one day. But even greater humiliation was endured by a judge attending an assizes service in Oxford towards the end of the nineteenth century. As he entered the church, his wig caught on a projection above the doorway and hung there, revealing him to be quite hairless. The sermon – on the subject of

The expression 'Keep your wig on!' derives from the eighteenth-century practice of removing the hairpiece before a fight. We can only guess at how many of those altercations began because someone laughed at the wig in the first place.

The expression 'to go for someone baldheaded' (i.e. boldly, without holding back) originates from a cavalry charge at Warburg in 1760 led by the Marquis of Granby, whose wig fell off in the battle.

diminishing respect for authority – was illustrated by the story of Elisha in the Second Book of Kings, who was taunted for being bald.

Some public occasions are even more embarrassing. Frederick the Great's wig fell off as he raised his hat to the crowd while riding through Berlin in the 1770s, though he apparently carried on unconcerned. A syrup-sporting non-league footballer in the north of England once went for a header during a match and his wig fell off near the penalty spot. As play moved to the other end of the pitch, a boy ran from behind the goal and picked it up. It was then passed around the crowd for the rest of the game – not the best advertisement for the player's hairpiece-selling business.

The audience is greater still when the story makes the national papers. In October 1997, the *Sun* reported the sorry tale of a man from County Durham, whose £880 hairpiece blew off in front of a bus full of people the first time he wore it. His baseball cap went one way and the wig went the other way into the gutter, from where he had to rescue it. Everyone roared with laugher at him, with the result that he declared himself to be too ashamed ever to get on a bus again.

A former editor of the *Sun* has suffered a similar experience, according to the *Guardian*. When David Yelland was appointed to the post in June1998, the broadsheet told the 'possibly apocryphal' story of how a tube train had once snatched a luxuriant blond wig from his head. The wig, worn to conceal a scalp made totally bald by alopecia, was supposedly never seen again by Mr Yelland who duly resolved to do without hairpieces in future.

If true, Yelland's experience with a train was not unique. In 1997, the railway authorities in Kent put up posters in stations passed by Eurostar trains, warning:

> Trains can create strong gusts as they pass through stations.
> They can be strong enough to lift objects such as pushchairs
> (and wigs) into the air. So please stay as far back from the
> yellow line as possible.

Three years earlier, the management at Blackpool Pleasure Beach had issued a similar warning when more than a dozen men lost their wigs in the first week after the opening of 'The Big One' – Britain's tallest roller-coaster, which reaches speeds of around 85 mph. The first incident occurred within hours, and soon the lost-property office had become one of the funfair's biggest attractions.

Frankie's Flyaway Hair

By this time in his career Frankie Howerd's hair had receded so much that he resorted to a toupee. Perhaps Stanley Dale had got it for him cheap but, costly or not, it came to be known by those of us who wrote for him as the 'dead ferret'. It did look as if some poor mangy animal had crawled onto his head and died there. For outdoor wear he sported a pork pie hat, and the story is told of his emerging from the stage door to greet his fans at the variety theatre at New Brighton, when, through no fault of his own in a very high wind, both hat and toupee flew off his head, and he disappeared rapidly to the seclusion of his dressing-room until the embarrassment wore off.

— Barry Took, *Star Turns: The Life and Times of Benny Hill and Frankie Howerd*

One radical method of keeping the hairpiece in place was pioneered in 1992 by cosmetic surgeon Anthony Pignataro of Buffalo, New York. The first step is to embed titanium sockets in the top of the skull. Writing in the *American Journal of Cosmetic Surgery*, Pignataro offered the reassurance that 'all drill bits and taps employ a depth guard to insure against overdrilling and possible intracranial injury'. After the sockets have fused with the bone, which takes around twelve weeks, gold snaps are screwed into them. A plastic mould is taken of the head and human hair is sewn on to it. This hairpiece can be snapped on and off – and Pignataro claimed that the whole process is reversible, since the gold snaps can always be unscrewed.

Dr Pignataro persuaded his father – also a surgeon, you will be relieved to learn – to carry out the operation on him. And despite the bone-chilling, or bone-drilling, nature of the operation, not to mention the expense involved (an implantation plus a snap-on hairpiece cost around $4,000 at the time), Pignataro found a hundred customers in the next four years.

When periwigs came first in wear,
Their use was to supply
And cover the bald pate with hair,
To keep it warm and dry.

For this good end, our Cavalier
Determined one to buy,
Which did so natural appear
That it deceived the eye.

But riding out one windy day,
Behold! A sudden squall
Soon blew his feathered hat away,
And periwig and all.

He joined the laugh with noddle bare,
And sang in concert tone,
'How should I save another's hair,
Who could not keep my own?'

<u>Moral</u>
To take upon oneself a joke,
Good humour shows and wit,
Which may a second laugh provoke,
And leave the biter bit.

— 'The Bald Cavalier' (1757)

Then there is the problem of thatchsnatchers: once others are aware that you wear a wig, it is liable to be stolen as a trophy. In August 1992, two of Sean Connery's wigs – each costing around £800 – went missing on the set of *The Rising Sun*. Nor do you need to be as famous as Sir Sean: the chairman of a leading football club was also the victim of an alleged wig-snatch during a match. A guest of a sponsor had apparently been enjoying the corporate hospitality rather too much before the game, and in the directors' box he decided to lurch over and make a grab for the obvious hairpiece. A struggle ensued, but he was prevented from hurling the wig on to the pitch and ejected from the ground.

In 1990 a 'rug war' broke out between DJs at rival radio stations in Chicago. Robert Murphy of WKQX was constantly being accused by the WBBM morning show of wearing a toupee, even though he didn't. So when he spotted WBBM's Joe Bohannon sporting an obvious wig at the cinema, he saw his chance for revenge. He offered a $500 bounty on air to the first 'rug ranger' to bring him Bohannon's piece. WBBM responded by giving away 20 toupees, supposedly from Bohannon's collection, and urging all the recipients to take them to WKQX to claim the reward. WKQX refused to pay up, but renewed its call for the original specimen to be seized and brought in. WBBM then offered to hand $1,000 to a charity if Murphy came over to get the wig in person.

It's not just humans that need watching. Birds have been known to prey on wigs, presumably because of their similarity to furry rodents. In 1992, a hawk at a falconry display in Devon swooped on a man in the crowd and knocked his hairpiece to the ground. It then dived and seized the wig, took it back to its perch and ripped it to bits. Staff gave the man a baseball cap to hide his pate, if not his shame. In 1994, a barn owl at the Gentleshaw Wildlife Sanctuary near Lichfield removed the wigs from two spectators at displays – and in 2003, it was reported that a snowy owl had performed the same trick at the same sanctuary.

The victim of the most famous wig theft was the artist Andy Warhol. It occurred at a book-signing session in New York in October 1985, and it left Warhol so angry and upset that it was days before he brought himself to mention it in his diary. A young woman snatched the silver wig from his head and threw it over the balcony to a male accomplice, who ran out of the bookshop with it. The woman was grabbed and held while the police were called, but Warhol declined to press charges. Since there was still a long queue of people waiting to have their books signed, he pulled the hood of his Calvin Klein coat over his head and carried on. By coincidence, a friend called a few days later to say he had just seen a shop in L.A. called 'Andy Warhol's Wigs' and wondered whether he owned it.

A wig which has lost its head isn't always what it appears to be. The legendary newsreader Reginald Bosanquet once lost his rug when filming in Africa. He had to stoop to enter a mud hut, and the cameraman following him in suddenly noticed a large hairy creature on the ground. He quickly stamped on it as hard as he could – only for Bosanquet to shout angrily at him that he had ruined his hairpiece and that he would not now be able to wear it on camera.

The loss of a wig can even be incriminating. A burglar in Basingstoke lost his hairpiece in a struggle at the scene of his crime, and was traced using the serial number stamped on the inside by the wigmaker. When the case came to court, he wept in the dock as he stood with his bald head bowed.

In the case of a Chicago salesman, it caused the misdemeanour in the first place. As he left a company party one Christmas Eve, one of the Windy City's stronger gusts whipped off his wig and carried it down a dark side-street. The salesman fetched his car and looked for his rug by driving slowly up and down the road – until a policeman spotted him, arrested him for drink-driving and took him to the cells where he spent Christmas night.

A wig may prove lethal. In 1991, a man from Abbeville in France bought a new wig and could not wait to get home to try it on. He sat in his car, liberally applied the special glue he had been given and carefully positioned his new purchase. He was so satisfied with his new look that he sat back and lit a cigarette – only for this to ignite the glue fumes which had built up inside the car, turning it into a fireball.

It could even be injurious to the soul. At least, that was the view of the early Christian Church. Clement of Alexandria declared in the first century AD that a wearer could not receive a blessing through the laying-on of a priest's hands, since the blessing would not pass through the hair of a stranger. The following century, the writer Tertullian was vehement in his condemnation:

> All wigs are such disguises and inventions of the devil . . . if
> you will not throw away your false hair as hateful to Heaven,
> let me make it hateful to you by reminding you that it may
> well have come from the head of a damned person or an
> unclean person.

In 692, the Council of Constantinople excommunicated a number of Christians who persisted in wearing wigs. And in the seventeenth century, when wig-wearing was at its height in Western Europe, the Bishop of Toul in France was warning that the fashion was unchristian and worse than not praying at all. Priests even came to blows on the subject. Dr Jean-Baptiste Thiers revealed in his book *Histoire des Perruques* (1690) that there had been a number of scuffles in vestries, with some priests trying to knock off the wigs of others.

A final word of warning. Once you have decided to proceed down Syrup Street, it is very difficult to turn back. If others think it is your natural hair, you cannot suddenly

HENRY DAVENPORT:
Look, once I've done
the midday bulletin I
need a longish lunch
to relax. To let my hair
down.
SALLY SMEDLEY: You
don't let your hair
down, Henry. You take
it off and put it in a
box.
—Drop the Dead
Donkey

be seen without it; and if people suspect that you are bald, you will be loath to come clean and take it off.

Only a few celebrities have been brave enough to take this step. Ray Milland came out as a proud pilgarlic in *Love Story* in 1970, having worn a toupee in every film he had made for the previous fifteen years. He declared that he had always hated wearing it and was quite unperturbed by the public's shock at suddenly seeing him without it. When anyone asked what had happened to his hair, he told them it was in a box in the South of France.

The magician Paul Daniels used to sport a rather obvious wig; in fact, in his advertisements for Wimpey Homes (fitted carpets included) it was difficult to tell it apart from the cat which was the company symbol. But eventually, and to his credit, he decided to make the hairpiece vanish.

INTERLUDE II
Proverbs for Pilgarlics

A hair on the head is worth two in the brush
— Oliver Herford

A good man grows grey, a rascal grows bald. (Czech Republic)

Of ten bald men, nine are deceitful and the tenth is stupid. (China)

Hair is not to be mentioned in a bald man's house. (Latvia)

The bald pate talks most of hair. (Latvia again)

He is bald-headed and keeps a pair of combs. (Punjab)

Change of women makes bald knaves. (From John Ray's 1670 *Compleat Collection of English Proverbs*)

It is time, not the comb, that makes men bald. (Czech Republic)

If you swear at your hair when combing it, it will all fall off. (Suffolk)

Hair an' hair makes the carle's head bare. (Scotland) [carle = old man]

A man with greying hair had two mistresses – one young, one old. The older woman was ashamed of having a younger man as her lover, and when he was with her she kept plucking the black hairs from his head. The young woman, who was not keen on the idea of being with an old man, would pluck out his grey hairs. Between them, the two women eventually made him completely bald.

— Aesop, *Fables*

A bald-headed man cannot grow hair by getting excited about it. (Congo)

The man who has lost his head does not cry for his hair. (Nikita Khrushchev)

We shall all be bald a hundred years hence. (Spain)

Regarding one's own comfort, a bald head; regarding others, luxuriant hair is preferable. (Tamil)

The blind man is laughing at the bald-head. (Iran)

Long hair, short wit. (France)

A bald head is soon shaven. (Britain)

Grey hair is to be honoured; a bald head deserves a bow. (Estonia)

Bald-headed men are ready-made Buddhist priests. (China)

God grant no nails to the bald. (Hindustan)

A person waiting for hair is not bald. (Wales)

CHAPTER FIVE

Combovers and Other Covers

... Hair thin and thoughtfully distributed over the head like fiddle strings, as if to make the most of it (pah!).

— J. M. Barrie *The Little White Bird*

If using someone else's hair to mask your bare pate doesn't appeal, there is a way of using your own which doesn't involve transplants. All you need is plenty of hair on one side of your head. Yes, we are talking about the dreaded combover.

The combover is known by other names, notably the 'Bobby Charlton' (despite the footballing legend having dispensed with the style several years ago – even admitting in 2001 that it looked ridiculous), the 'sidewinder' and (if the hair being swept across has become matted together to form a single unit) the 'Shredded Wheat'.

Creating a combover might seem to be a simple matter of sweeping the hair over the head, with no need for special skills or training. This was not the view of Eric Oakley, however. His snappily titled book, *A Method of Disguising Your Male Baldness Using Your Own Hair from the Sides* (1975), offers detailed instructions on the technique. Oakley seems to believe that he is doing mankind a great service by explaining his Method (he gives this word a capital letter throughout, like God; as we shall see, this is about as standard as his English gets):

> I am firstly confident that I am being of practical service to all
> bald men like myself with their own hair at the sides but,
> secondly . . . we can face the future together with confidence
> knowing now that our top hair has gone, we now have a
> great alternative that can be adapted as we get older.

From both sides you gather up your scanty hair, Marinus, and try to cover up the vast expanse of your gleaming bald head with the hair which still grows on your temples. But when it is blown about, your hair comes back at the bidding of the wind and forms big curls on either side of your bare head . . . Why don't you, to make things simpler, admit that you are an old man? . . .There is nothing that looks worse than a bald man pretending to have hair.
— Martial, *Epigrams*

There is, it seems, madness in his Method. He concedes that he is not its inventor; rather, he is the man who has perfected it:

> It is vitally important to appreciate that the system of
> disguise outlined here is not new, it has been used for
> several years now in various inferior forms but what you
> are about to have described to you is not what to do but
> how to do it described in great detail and featuring, step by
> step, photographs of the author and the secret of this
> Method's success with you, is that you will be shown
> graphically and have it detailed in writing for your
> continued reference.

These details, he avows, took him 'years of practise [*sic*] research and study' to refine. Before sharing these with us, however, he outlines the advantages of the Method over other means of masking a bare pate. He objects to wigs because: they are more expensive 'in terms of money'; they do not allow the hair to be stroked (as if a combover does); and they deceive no one (see previous parentheses). Hair transplants are quickly dismissed on the grounds of cost, and the radical idea of being bald and proud of it is not considered appropriate for the ordinary man. While Oakley is 'in no way denying the popular appeal of Yul Brynner and Telly Savalas', he is sure that 'you and I wouldn't want to go to work looking like them'.

The Method, by contrast, maintains an appearance of youth while being entirely natural:

> You can conceal your baldness and carry with you the
> confidence of your family and friends and as you have simply
> improved your appearance BUT and it is a big BUT it is all
> your own hair that people are noticing simply trained in a
> better way to improve your appearance.

Oakley points out that the 'principal' of the Method is already used by many famous personalities, such as Frank Bough, David Hamilton, and Arthur Mullard. One should not expect to look quite as good as these celebrities, though; it is important to 'bear in mind that the above have great makeup and coiffure facilities available that you and I do not enjoy'.

Eventually, Oakley divulges his sidewinder secrets. It is not just a matter of plastering hair across the pate; the aim is to 'add height to your overall hair profile'. First, you need to decide which side of your head is going to provide the hair to be combed over. The hair needs to be long – 'long enough in fact to go right across your head, reach the other side with some length to spare' – and could take some time to grow to the required length. While you are busy doing this, you also need to decide where your parting will be:

> This may mean going farther down the side of your head
> than normal but this doesn't matter, as it is the end result of
> improvement that is important, nothing else . . . it doesn't
> matter how far down the side of your head you go, within say
> 1" of your ear.

Once the strands of hair at the side are long enough, you can continue with the key steps of the Method. You wet the hair and brush it over the bald area, bringing it towards the front of the head. More water is applied until it lies completely flat, and then the hair is left for several minutes. This done, a hairdryer is used to make the hair look fluffy and thick. (By lifting it like a mat, the damp scalp underneath may also be dried.) The hair is then rubbed vigorously with a towel to disarrange it even more, and 'give it a more natural appearance'. A brush may be used to give the hair shape, so long as care is taken not to flatten it. 'Your hair now is trained to rest on top and is light and fluffy and away from your scalp but it is now deliberately exaggerated [*sic*] to effect volume in appearance.'

The side hair is guided over the scalp towards the front of the head. 'Do not worry about the back,' Oakley advises. (After all, who is going to think you look ridiculous with a gaping hole at the rear? Hands down, everyone.) When it meets the hair at the other side, it is imperative that you . . .

> FREEZE. YOU MUST HOLD THIS APPEARANCE. YOU MUST NOT
> DISTURB ONE HAIR ONE [*sic*] YOUR HEAD.

At this point Oakley remembers that he should have told you to put on any garments which have to be put on over the head (if you have already reached this stage, it's too late to do anything about it now). The mat of hair is secured to the hair on the other side with a liberal application of lacquer. This will help you to 'resist in the main [i.e. not all the time] wind, knocks, accidents and occasional wearing and removal of a hat'. The lacquer is hardened by further use of the hairdryer.

And that's it. The hallowed Method consists of fluffing up the hair so it is even more noticeable, and welding it to the other side of the head.

Even Oakley is vaguely aware that his readers may have misgivings about employing this technique, so he endeavours to reassure them by answering the questions he thinks they would ask:

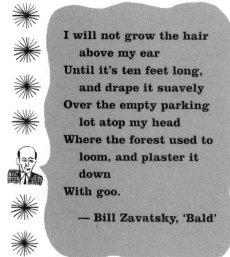

I will not grow the hair
above my ear
Until it's ten feet long,
and drape it suavely
Over the empty parking
lot atop my head
Where the forest used to
loom, and plaster it
down
With goo.

— Bill Zavatsky, 'Bald'

Q What happens as the hair at the sides continues to recede?
A Simply lower your parting and you will never run out of hair.

Q Surely with a side parting in my hair so low and near my ear I will look ridiculous, won't I?
A No. It is a much more accepted practise [*sic*] with men these days and you will look a lot younger with top hair as a result of using this Method to make your low side parting of no importance.

Q Won't my new top hair attract the same sort of ridicule [as a wig]?
A No . . . I can honestly say that in my case and all others using this Method that it doesn't attract the attention or the ridicule of a wig.

Unfortunately, Oakley then starts to come up with questions to which he cannot supply encouraging answers:

Q What happens if it rains?
A You will need to use a hat or umbrella, as the water will make your hair look streaky.

Q What happens when I go swimming?

A This is one activity where you simply cannot maintain your top hair disguise.

Q Can I play football without spoiling my top hair appearance?

A No. With both rubgy [*sic*] and soccer I can only observe that it is not possible to play and keep your baldness disguised.

Sensing that he is undermining his own Method, Oakley makes a final valiant attempt to defend it:

> There is absolutely no point in me avoiding the negative aspects nor indeed do I ever make any attempt to gloss over the snags of this Method because you will still share my view, that despite the snags, it is the only practical and masculine way to disguise male baldness.

So, do we share his view? Do we forelocks.

Two years after the publication of Oakley's magnum opus, however, a very similar method was successfully patented in the United States by Frank Smith and his son Donald, both from Orlando, Florida. With this combover technique, 'the hair styling requires dividing a person's hair into three sections and carefully folding one section over another'.

It took some time for this patent to receive wide recognition, but in September 2004 Donald Smith received the Ig Nobel prize for engineering on behalf of himself and his late father at a ceremony at Harvard University. (These annual awards, handed out by Nobel Prize winners, recognise scientific research that 'makes you laugh, then makes you think'.)

Furthermore, a number of otherwise highly intelligent men have had common cause with Oakley and the Smiths. The noted anthropologist Desmond Morris, for instance, tried to hide his bald pate by sweeping his hair over it. It is remarkable that such an authority on human behaviour should have failed to identify the societal subtext of this action; that is, it sends a clear message to other members of the species that the perpetrator is very sad.

Robert Robinson, the revered host of such cerebral TV shows as *Ask the Family*, also persisted with his combover for years, but fooled no one. It once thoroughly distracted actor John Nettles when the latter appeared as a guest on *Call My Bluff*:

From where I was sitting, I could observe in detail the Byzantine complexity of the coiffure . . . the hair which appears lying serenely athwart the upper dome of that distinguished skull has its origins in the nape of the neck, whence it is swept boldly upwards and across like a curlicue in a work by Aubrey Beardsley . . . The whole effect is breathtaking, and I have it on higher authority than my own that the tension between the sophisticated artifice of the hairdo and the contrasting unforced naturalness of Robert's discourse is the reason for his enduring appeal.

Paint Ain't the Answer

According to an old joke, if you paint rabbits on your bald head, they will look like hares from a distance. Rather more amusingly, many people have indeed used paint in a serious attempt to hide their baldness. An acquaintance of the poet Martial tried this, but was ruthlessly exposed:

> You use ointment to pretend you have hair, Phoebus, and your bald and dirty head is covered with painted-on locks. There is no need to summon a hairdresser to shave your head; a sponge, Phoebus, would do it better for you.

Paint is still used today, though it comes in the form of aerosol sprays and is generally called 'hair thickener'. The product description usually claims that it enhances the fine hairs which remain on the bald scalp, but one would have to be using large doses of head thickener not to realise that this is pate-painting by another name. After the bare patch has been overcome with emulsion, the remaining hair is combed over to cover it.

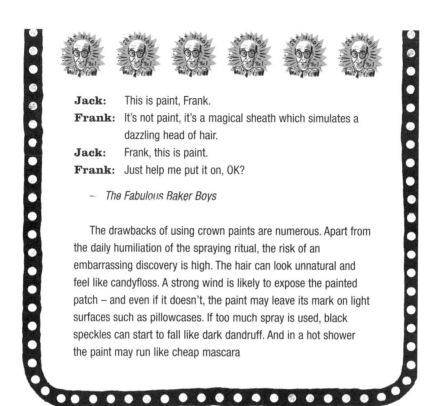

Jack: This is paint, Frank.

Frank: It's not paint, it's a magical sheath which simulates a dazzling head of hair.

Jack: Frank, this is paint.

Frank: Just help me put it on, OK?

— *The Fabulous Baker Boys*

The drawbacks of using crown paints are numerous. Apart from the daily humiliation of the spraying ritual, the risk of an embarrassing discovery is high. The hair can look unnatural and feel like candyfloss. A strong wind is likely to expose the painted patch – and even if it doesn't, the paint may leave its mark on light surfaces such as pillowcases. If too much spray is used, black speckles can start to fall like dark dandruff. And in a hot shower the paint may run like cheap mascara

One begins to see why Nettles thought that a wig would be a good idea.

A combover is particularly inadvisable for anyone involved in politics. As well as looking ridiculous, the wearer can appear misguided and even dishonest. To quote Philip II of Macedon: 'I could not think that one who was faithless in his hair could be trustworthy in his deeds.' Miners' leader Arthur Scargill found his combover to be the target of scorn from Frank Johnson of *The Times* during the 1983 TUC conference. On 6 September, Johnson considered the idea that his style was not just a sign of delusion but of scorn towards the general public: 'What it signifies is that a man who believes that he and his friends should plan our entire economy thinks the rest of us are too foolish, not just to plan our own personal economics, but to spot that he is bald.' The following day, Johnson wondered whether Scargill's Shredded Wheat might be symbolic of his socialist views:

He is satisfied that it is feasible, given good will on all sides, to start your parting a little above your left armpit and then somehow, with the new resources of strength thus created, to link up over the top of the exposed cranium with like-minded forces on the other side. By such sympathetic actions, he believes, the organised working class can smash baldness forever.

The sidewinder then being sported by Labour leader Neil Kinnock was also considered:

There is no doubt that he is trying to bridge the gap between left and right. He passionately wants unity. His parting is not as extreme as Mr Scargill's, but it is also designed to create enough backing to join up with the forces on the other side of his head. The trouble is that the two wings have little hope of meeting and finding a common cause . . .

Who's for Tattoos?

A permanent alternative to paint would be a tattoo on the scalp, but surely no one would be daft enough to . . . ah, apparently they would. In August 1992, a 58-year-old Blackpool man had hair tattooed on his head. He had tried wigs, tonics and transplants since going bald 35 years before, but eventually decided to spend four hours under the needle and have done with it. The tattooist was very proud of his work, claiming that nobody would be able to tell the hair was not real unless they got close.

The perfect solution, then – if you don't mind a bit of pain and can keep other people at least 20 yards away from you for the rest of your life.

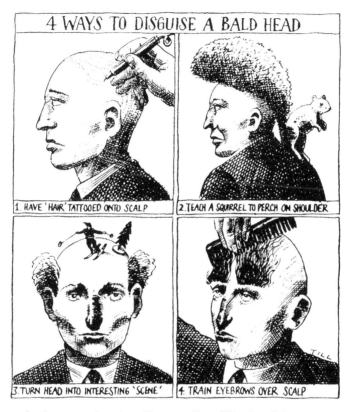

4 WAYS TO DISGUISE A BALD HEAD

1. HAVE 'HAIR' TATTOOED ONTO SCALP

2. TEACH A SQUIRREL TO PERCH ON SHOULDER

3. TURN HEAD INTO INTERESTING 'SCENE'

4. TRAIN EYEBROWS OVER SCALP

Sundry suggestions from illustrator Peter Till – though he meant tattoos as a joke

Kinnock eventually dispensed with the combover, but perhaps too late. He never did win a general election; could it be that the years of sweeping over those strands – and possibly the subconscious association of his combover with Scargill's in the minds of the electorate – harmed his chances?

If you think this unlikely, bear in mind that the same theory has been advanced on the other side of the Atlantic. The failure of an early bid by Rudolph Giuliani to become Mayor of New York was directly attributed to his combover by *New York Post* columnist Pete

Hamill. Giuliani's hair, he observed, looked like a rug – and not even a good rug at that, but more like an off-cut from a YMCA carpet.

Hamill went on to describe the candidate's coiffure as having the appearance of a vegetable burger and even a fur-bearing yarmulke – though there was no suggestion that Giuliani's look was intended as a subliminal appeal to New York's Jewish community.

Finally, a reminder that you do not have to be well known to have your sidewinder scorned. In May 1998, a 55-year-old man was awarded compensation of £950 by P&O Cruises after the fourth engineer on one of their ships deliberately messed up his Bobby Charlton barnet. It seems that the trouble started when the engineer began staring at him across a crowded bar on board and kept touching his temple. 'I ignored him' related the victim, 'but he suddenly came across, ruffled my hair with his hand and started laughing. My hair came down and I felt totally humiliated.' A P&O spokesman denied that the crew member was drunk, but added: 'We don't have a pollcy on how to deal with passengers who are losing their hair.'

CHAPTER SIX

Getting Scalped

Finot used the wonderful joke at the expense of Macassar Oil which made the audience roar at the Théâtre des Funambules, when Pierrot took an old horsehair broom, on the head of which only holes could be seen, and applied Macassar Oil to produce a thick growth of bristles. This ironic sketch made everyone laugh.

— Honoré de Balzac, *César Birotteau*

The huge number of men prepared to surrender their money and dignity to regain their hair provides fertile ground for con men, rip-off merchants, fly-by-night firms and quacks. These are just some of the cheeky charlatans parting coots from their cash on either side of the Atlantic in the last century and a half . . .

One of the earliest con men claiming to cure baldness who may be identified by name was an individual called Bartlett who operated in the late nineteenth century. He used a glass rod attached to a generator of static electricity, and when he moved this towards the hair of a client, it would stand on end. A prickling sensation would simultaneously run across the scalp. 'You can tell that it's growing,' Bartlett reportedly assured his clients. 'You must have felt it.' He travelled Europe for years with this device (no doubt realising that it would be safer to keep on the move) and made a fortune.

Another bogus practitioner of the day was Andrew Taylor Still, who declared in 1874 that all diseases are ultimately caused by the dislocation of small bones in the spine. In his autobiography, which proved to be full of fraudulent claims, Still declared that he had grown three inches of hair in a week on a patient's completely bald head, merely by rubbing his spine. The same method had also enabled him, he said, to cure malaria, yellow fever, diphtheria, diabetes, dandruff, obesity, piles and constipation. However, it was clearly no remedy for elephantiasis (enormous bollocks).

Since there were no regulatory bodies to call the con men to account during this period, it was left to assiduous investigators such as Arthur J. Cramp to expose their deceptions. He joined the staff of the American Medical Association in 1906 and went on to wage a personal campaign against charlatans of all kinds.

Among the establishments he investigated was the Professor Scholder Institute in New York. The institute claimed to have successfully treated the baldness of both Theodore Roosevelt and Harry Houdini – though since the two were dead, they could hardly deny this. Their advertisements invited prospective clients to send in a specimen of hair for analysis. Cramp sent in a few hairs taken from the cuff of a platinum fox fur coat belonging to a secretary. Before long, he received the following verdict from the institute: 'A microscopic examination discloses that the roots are in a seriously undernourished condition. You are in grave danger of continuous and increasing loss of your hair, but it can still be saved by prompt treatment.' Professor Scholder stated that he would be happy to take on the case and promised that he would 'positively restore your hair and scalp to a normal, healthy condition'.

Cramp then sent hairs from the collar of another coat, made of Siberian dog fur. The professor's reply was the same, word for word. Cramp followed up with yet more letters. He sent in short lengths of hair cut from the long, luxurious tresses of a girl, and on two occasions submitted strands of twine – in one case dyed black, in the other dyed brown. The diagnosis was identical each time, and the professor always promised a cure. Armed with his evidence, Cramp poured scorn on Professor Scholder in public and was able to drive him out of business. 'Seriously though,' Cramp observed, 'one wonders just how far it is possible to go in humbugging the bald and still keep out of jail'.

In 1909, the British Medical Association investigated the claims of a number of anti-baldness preparations. In the publication *Secret Remedies*, the Association looked at 'extracts from the statements made in regard to them by the proprietors, either on the labels or in circulars, letters, or newspaper advertisements' and revealed what customers were actually getting for their money. Among the products were:

Tatcho. The manufacturer claimed this to be: 'The certain, trusty, genuine, right, honest Hair-Grower. There is no other . . . It will bring back the hair of your youth, make a new being of you, and give you a new grip upon life'. Analysis revealed the principal ingredients to be borax, glycerine, alcohol and water, and

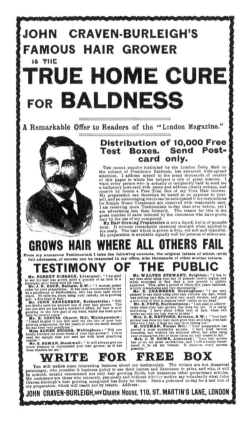

An inflated claim from Mr Craven-Burleigh. Or as Dr Spooner would have called him, Mr Brave 'n' Curly

estimated their cost to be $^1/_2$d for $5^1/_4$ fluid ounces, though the retail price for this amount was 2s 9d.

Edwards' Harlene. Supposedly, 'Harlene alone answers all requirements; it has the property of penetrating direct to the roots of the hair, stimulating them to renewed vigour . . . no other preparation can be successful'. Again, the chief ingredients proved to be borax, glycerine, alcohol and water – which rather undermines the claims of both this product and Tatcho to be the sole true remedy. Estimated cost of ingredients: 1d for 6 fluid ounces.

Does the bottom half of the young lady indicate an unfortunate side-effect?

Koko. The makers of this concoction at least acknowledged the hyperbole employed so often in this field: 'We often think that the public must be sick of seeing the eternal "This is the best" attached to every conceivable article which is offered for sale; and for this reason we usually refrain from saying much about Koko.' An admirable attitude – except that the line 'Undoubtedly the best dressing for the hair' was prominently featured across their advertisements. It will come as no surprise to the attentive reader that the main ingredients were borax, glycerine, alcohol and water. 12¹/₄ fluid ounces of this lotion sold for 4s 6d, yet the cost of the ingredients was estimated to be a mere 1d.

The BMA did not condemn the treatments explicitly, preferring simply to reveal their mundane contents (the Mexican Hair Renewer, for instance, was shown to contain the far from exotic sulphur, lead acetate and glycerine) and their true cost. Readers were left to draw their own conclusions about the value of such preparations. The effectiveness of such a restrained approach was unsurprising: it had none. 'Hair restorers' continued to be advertised in Britain for years.

During the 1920s, a US congressional committee analysed preparations such as Hair-A-Gain (a mixture of paraffin and lanolin), Hall's Hair Renewer (red pepper and borax) and Lucky Tiger (which contained arsenic as the hair-saving ingredient). This investigation had as much short-term effect as that of the BMA – but eventually, steps were taken to stop the worst excesses of misleading advertising and packaging.

Note the endorsement from 'popular authoress' John Strange Winter. Strange indeed

In March 1962, the US Food and Drug Administration seized over 750,000 vitamin capsules promoted by Basic Remedies Inc. of Monmouth, Oregon as being capable of causing new hair to grow on bald or thin areas, and helping existing hair to grow faster.

In 1970, 73-year-old radio evangelist Curtis Howe Springer of Ontario, California, was convicted on ten counts of false advertising concerning two of his products.

One of these was called 'Mo-Hair' – which, as the name suggests, was said to grow more hair. Springer claimed to have been given the formula by an unnamed German visiting his health resort, the Zzyxx Mineral Springs spa in southern California. (Presumably the last entry in the local phone book, unless there was a 'Zzzz Sleeping Pills Inc.' in the area.) On analysis, Mo-Hair proved to be a combination of mud and mineral oils.

In July 1975, Virgil Ganyard and Maryland Nance Jr of the National Hair and Scalp Clinic were convicted by a federal jury in the US for defrauding customers. The defence produced one witness who claimed to be a satisfied customer – but when he was forced to admit under cross-examination that his impressive head of hair was actually a wig which he had bought for $5 in a sale, the fate of the defendants was sealed.

In 1979, the FDA seized a shipment of a herbal potion being promoted by 74-year-old Ma Evans from Australia. She claimed the formula had been passed on to her by a gypsy in 1921, though strangely she had not used the potion until 1977, when she noticed that a friend's hair was falling out. 'I cried,' she professed. 'To think that the Lord could have given people bald heads.' The Lord had presumably been more generous in Ma's neighbourhood than in most, for her to have gone 56 years without noticing a single shiny pate.

Help Keep Your Husband
OUT OF THE BALDHEADED ROW
Ladies—if your husband's hair is getting thinner and thinner—buy him a bottle of Lucky Tiger—for Hair and Scalp—then see that he uses it. And here's a tip—he would like the soothing touch of your fingers if you would give his head a Lucky Tiger massage now and then.

A Simple Treatment
Apply Lucky Tiger two or three times weekly. Follow each time with a vigorous "muscle-loosening" scalp workout. Lucky Tiger eliminates clinging dandruff—stops itching —allays scalp irritations. The massage brings better muscle action and tone to the scalp. Just watch results.

Professional applications at any barber shop. Or get a bottle at your druggist.

Lucky Tiger
FOR HAIR
AND SCALP

In 1981 Bob Murphy of Reno, Nevada, was accused by the US Postal Service of using false representation through the mail to sell his 'New Generation' baldness cure. This treatment consisted of a shampoo and conditioner containing the magic ingredient Polysorbate 60, a standard emulsifier used in many bottled salad dressings.

When the case was heard, an army of New Generation users turned up to cheer Murphy and boo the prosecution. One hundred and seven people wanted to testify for him, but only 18 were allowed to. One of these, a Sacramento radio personality called Tony Russell, declared under oath: 'The experience of using New Generation has been like having sex and winning the Congressional Medal of Honor at the same time.' One wonders where they would hang the medal in such a situation, but that's by the by. Murphy claimed that Donny Osmond had also used New Generation (though apparently not even crazy horses could have dragged him to give evidence on the day).

Murphy lost the case, but claimed afterwards that this was because the lawyer representing him in court was bald. He duly appealed – and in 1985, a federal judge in Nevada reversed the decision in Murphy's favour. But a year after that, a US Court of Appeal overruled the Nevada judge's decision and again sided with the Postal Service. Not that Murphy lost out overall; it was estimated that he had sold nearly three million bottles of New Generation worldwide, grossing some $250 million.

A native American cure, according to Big Chief Spouting Bull

The principal target of the FDA around this time was an elusive multimillionaire called Glenn Braswell. He was king of the misleading mail-order cures, and constantly in trouble for making false claims. His products, such as Bioscala, Biogenesis and BioPrima II, were criticised by both the FDA and the US Postal Service, but on each occasion Braswell would move on, form a new corporation and put out a new product.

In 1992, a Chicago clinic was charged by the local State Attorney's Office with allowing staff who were not doctors to perform surgery on clients. It was claimed that one such member of staff was in fact a muskrat skinner who was first employed by one of the doctors running the firm to plant trees on his farm. It was also alleged that photographs of patients from other hair-loss clinics were being used in 'before' and 'after' pictures in their ads.

In 1994, a man was found guilty at Middlesex Guildhall Crown Court of defrauding balding clients at his Harley Street clinic. He used their credit cards to charge them twice for the same treatment and to order expensive shampoos and lotions without their consent. He figured that they would either not check their bills too closely, or would be too embarrassed to complain. Eventually, some clients became so angry that they tried to attack him with knives – and when they threatened to call the police, he closed the clinic and cleared off.

In 1996, the Advertising Standards Authority (ASA) stated that complaints about hair-loss treatments were on the increase. In many cases, companies cover themselves through clever wording which hints at hair restoration without explicitly promising it; nonetheless, there are numerous examples of over-claiming.

In January 1996, the High Court forbade Quest Hair Research from publishing advertisements for a book (*Natural Cure for Baldness*) and a formula called 'Restore'. The Director-General of the Office of Fair Trading, which sought the injunction after the ASA complained that Quest had broken its promise to stop publishing misleading ads, commented afterwards: 'Claims made for the book and the formula left consumers in no doubt that they would provide a cure for baldness. The "cure" outlined in the book amounted to standing on your shoulders for a short period each day.'

In 1997, the ASA asked newspapers and magazines not to accept an ad for the Nobel Clinic in Surrey which made the unsupported claim that: 'All our clients with thinning, receding hair or even very extensive hair loss experience NATURAL looking new growth within a few weeks.' Despite the ASA's action, the ad was still running the following year.

The topic of hair tonics was examined in July 1999 by *Which?*, the Consumers' Association magazine. This study concluded that the claims made for most products are even thinner than the hair they profess to save. Ten widely available preparations were considered by a panel of experts – and nine of these were judged to be, in effect, ineffective. In four cases, no supporting evidence was supplied by the manufacturers; in three more, the data provided was unreliable or unsatisfactory; and in another two, the research figures indicated that if there was any beneficial effect, it was minimal to say the least. The only treatment considered to produce any results was Regaine.

So, if you're intent on finding a baldness treatment, just be careful out there. If you have a bald head, it's very easy for them to see you coming.

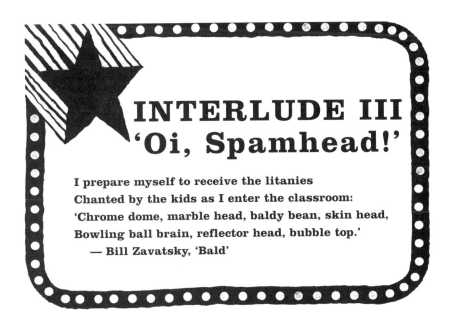

INTERLUDE III
'Oi, Spamhead!'

I prepare myself to receive the litanies
Chanted by the kids as I enter the classroom:
'Chrome dome, marble head, baldy bean, skin head,
Bowling ball brain, reflector head, bubble top.'
— Bill Zavatsky, 'Bald'

The exposed skin of the bald pate needs to become very thick to deal with all the insults aimed at it.

Baldy

Slaphead

Spamhead

Spoonhead

Shinehead

Melonhead (nickname of Colonel Hall in *The Phil Silvers Show*)

Egg-head

Cue-ball

Osram

Buttock-head

Mr Clean

Mr Sheen

Mr Pink

Fu Manchu

Daddy Warbucks

Kojak

Yul

Uncle Fester

Curly (ironic, obviously)

Polo

Wash 'n' go
Fly rink
Hairless coconut
Millennium Dome

Baldilocks
Keep your hair on!
Take that crash helmet off!

You bald-pated, lying rascal
— Shakespeare, *Measure for Measure*, V.i.356

Whoreson smooth-pates
— Shakespeare again, *II Henry IV*, I.ii.43

A pitiful bald crown
And again, *Henry IV Part I*, II.iv.385

You bald old saturnine poll-clawed parrot
— Robert Browning, *Old Pictures in Florence*

The jealous, the jealous old Baldpate
— John Keats, *Hush, Hush, Tread Softly, Hush, Hush My Dear*

Edward Lear scowls on being presented with a letter addressed to 'Mr Slappy'

Various gestures may also be employed, such as pretending to be dazzled by the glare of the pate, using it as a mirror, or rubbing the head and making a squeaky noise. Tapping the bald head with a spoon, as if about to eat a boiled egg, is also common.

And for wig-wearers:

Wiggy

Rugmeister

Carpet slipper

Carpetbagger

Astroturf

Axminster

Supertouper

Thatch

BMW ('Bald man's wig')

Walter (short for 'wall-to-wall carpet')

CHAPTER SEVEN

The Significance of Slapheadedness

Rimmer: Perhaps you'd like to explain to me why it is that every major battle in history has been won by the side with the shortest haircuts?

Kryten: Oh, surely not, sir.

Rimmer: Think about it, why did the US Cavalry beat the Indian Nation? Short back and sides versus girly hippy locks. The cavaliers and the roundheads . . . one-nil to the pudding basins. Vietnam, crew cuts both sides . . . no-score draw.

—*Red Dwarf*

The significance of a bald head varies considerably between, and within, different countries, cultures, centuries and sections of the community. The connotations are by no means exclusively negative.

A Sign of Ageing and Decay

Hair loss is part of the entirely natural process of ageing: 'We men are stripped bare, our hairs fall and are carried away by time, just as the north wind shakes down the leaves' (Ovid, *Ars Amatoria*); 'Men can have only a certain number of teeth, hair and ideas; there comes a time when he necessarily loses his teeth, hair and ideas' (Voltaire, *Dictionnaire Philosophique*).

Of course, people may try to deny it: '**Bald, adj**. Destitute of hair from hereditary or accidental causes – never from age' (Ambrose Bierce, *The Devil's Dictionary*). But the fact is that hair loss serves as a reminder of one's mortality. This provides one possible explanation for the mockery frequently aimed at the bald. Are those who jeer secretly scared of dying? Are they trying to suppress this fear by laughing at people they perceive to be closer to death? If so, their ridicule is a double-edged sword: if they pick on the wrong person, they could hasten their own demise.

A Sign of Weakness

Hair is symbolic of one's life-force in the way it is constantly growing and being renewed. The loss of hair therefore implies a loss of life-force.

The story of Samson is the best-known illustration of this: 'If I be shaven, then my strength will go from me, and I shall become weak, and be like any other man' (Judges 16:17). Legend also has it that a Fijian chieftain used to take the precaution of eating a man after every haircut to make up for whatever strength he had lost along with his locks. ('Someone for the weekend, sir?')

A Sign of Strength and Aggression

Throughout the centuries, soldiers have shaved their heads in order to appear tougher and fiercer. Alexander the Great ordered his whole army to have their hair cropped, though this was also to prevent the enemy from seizing them by their hair. (By contrast, Native American warriors used to leave one 'chivalrous lock' on their otherwise bald heads so that a conquering enemy would have something to hold when removing the scalp.) Head-shaving is partly a matter of shedding one's individuality to become part of an organised fighting unit, but at the same time the soldiers are rejecting the fripperies of everyday life. They have no time for politeness and gentility; they mean business.

If I were fierce and bald and short of breath,
I'd live with scarlet Majors at the Base,

And speed glum heroes up the line to death.
– Siegfried Sassoon, 'Base Details'

A Sign of Virility

Although bald men do not necessarily produce more testosterone than those with a full head of hair, a bald head does prove that some testosterone is being produced. One can never be as sure with a man who has plenty on top, however; eunuchs do not go bald. Furthermore, Dr E. William Rosenborg of the University of Tennessee suggested in 1981 that there may be some truth in the description of a bald pate as 'a solar panel for a sex machine'. He claimed that sunshine on the head affects the pineal gland, which in turn affects the endocrine system and the amount of testosterone produced.

A Sign of Sexual Suppression

From the traditional story of Rapunzel to *The Rape of the Lock* by Alexander Pope, female hair has long been a powerful sexual symbol. Its removal can thus represent a disavowal of this sexuality, or can symbolise humility. Brides in ancient Greece, for instance, would cut off their hair on their wedding day as a renunciation of personal vanity. Orthodox Jewish brides have traditionally done the same, to show symbolically that they are no longer free to be courted.

The absence of hair can also be a sign of piety and chastity in men. The tonsure of the monk in the *Canterbury Tales* is noted in Chaucer's Prologue (line 198): 'His heed was ballid, and schon as eny glas'. The precise symbolism of the tonsure varies. It may represent a return to the newness and bare innocence of a baby. It may be a metaphorical (as well as literal) reflection of the sun. In Christianity, it suggests the crown of thorns worn by Jesus on the cross, and also hints at an angel's halo. Above all, however, the tonsure denotes the renunciation of the world's physical pleasures.

Hare Krishna devotees shave their heads, but leave a top knot of hair – which, they believe, Krishna will use to pluck them up when they die or at the deliverance of the world. Buddhists in Thailand similarly leave a tuft of hair for Buddha to grab so that he may lift them up to Heaven.

A Sign of Cleanliness

Hairlessness and cleanliness are expressly linked in the book of Leviticus. First the point is made that there is nothing wrong with baldness per se: 'And the man whose hair is fallen off his head, he is bald; yet is he clean. And he that hath his hair fallen off from the part of his head toward his face, he is forehead bald: yet is he clean' (13:40–41). Removing the hair is then recommended as a means of cleansing:

> And he that is to be cleansed shall wash his clothes, and
> shave off all his hair, and wash himself in water, that he may
> be clean: and after that he shall come into the camp, and
> shall tarry abroad out of his tent seven days. But it shall be

on the seventh day, that he shall shave all his hair off his head and his beard and his eyebrows, even all his hair he shall shave off: and he shall wash his clothes, also he shall wash his flesh in water, and he shall be clean.

– Leviticus 14:8–9

A Sign of Intelligence and Wisdom

If a bald head creates an older appearance, it is widely assumed that the cerebral benefits of age have been acquired. In addition, the misguided but once common theory that strenuous mental activity causes hair loss has contributed to associations of intelligence. In Elizabethan times, the view that baldness was a sign of brains was so prevalent that women as well as men shaved their heads at the front.

The connection was also given serious consideration by the US Army in 1938. Major Witton B. Persons and Captain Lawrence J. Carr put forward the suggestion in a letter entitled 'Brain Directive' that promotions should be made from the ranks of bald soldiers, since these were the brightest men in the army. To illustrate their point, they enclosed photographs of themselves with their hair painted out, along with instructions for measuring bare pates.

The document was passed to Secretary Woodring by the Chief of Staff, General Malin Craig, who attached his own letter entitled 'Brain Detective'. General Craig commented: 'For some time I have been conscious of the necessity of developing a method by which we could be assured of brains on the General Staff. The enclosed proposal is not without merit.' Secretary

> **Bald heads forgetful of their sins,**
> **Old, learned, respectable bald heads**
> **Edit and annotate the lines**
> **That young men, tossing on their**
> **beds,**
> **Rhymed out in love's despair**
> **To flatter beauty's ignorant ear.**
>
> **—W. B. Yeats, 'The Scholars'**
>
> **Learned, we found him.**
> **Yea, but we found him bald too, eyes**
> **like lead . . .**
>
> **—Robert Browning, 'A Grammarian's**
> **Funeral'**

Woodring replied – in a letter headed 'Brain Dissected' – that extensive tests would need to be carried out before any new method of selection was adopted.

A Sign of Misfortune or Illness

According to one superstition, 'a bald-headed man at the altar, whether he be minister, groom, or bride's father, foretells the advent of marriage squalls'. A sudden loss of hair has also been thought to presage a decline in health, the loss of property or failure in business, or even the death of a closely related child. Baldness may certainly be a sign of illness, not least because some treatments – most notably chemotherapy – can have this effect.

According to C. J. S. Thompson's *Magic and Healing*, removing the hair was once a common treatment in its own right:

> In the northern counties, a cure for a cough was to shave the patient's head and hang the hair on a bush, so the birds could carry it away and with it the 'cough' to their nests. In Devonshire and Cornwall the procedure was varied by placing the hair cut from the person's head between two slices of bread and butter which were then given to the dog to eat.

If the person thus shorn chose to cover his baldness, the wig would presumably be known as a cough syrup.

Tobias Smollett refers in *Travels through France and Italy* (1766) to a similar practice on the other side of the Channel, though it was evidently welcomed with rather less enthusiasm:

> A Frenchman will sooner part with his religion than his hair, which, indeed, no consideration will induce him to forego. I know a gentleman afflicted with a continual head-ach, and a defluxion on his eyes, who was told by his physician that the best chance he had for being cured, would be to have his head close shaved . . . He dismissed his physician, lost his eye-sight, and almost his senses, and is now led about with his hair in a bag, and a piece of green silk hanging like a screen before his face.

A Sign of Belonging to a Social Group

Baldness has expressed the opposing ideologies of social movements as early as the English Civil War. In the seventeenth century, the Cavaliers considered the Roundheads to be as lacking in wit, wisdom and virtue as they were in hair; the Puritan Roundheads, meanwhile, believed that all sorts of vices dwelt in the luxurious curly locks of the monarchists.

For the hippies in the 1960s, long hair was an expression of personal freedom and their rejection of the straight-laced mores of bourgeois society. The title song from the musical *Hair* shows just how powerful a symbol it was, and how the hippies revelled in it:

> Darlin', give me a head with hair,
> Long, beautiful hair,
> Shining, gleaming, steaming, flaxen, waxen,
> Give me down to there hair,
> Shoulder length or longer,
> Here, baby, there, momma, ev'rywhere, daddy, daddy.
> Hair, hair, hair, hair, hair, hair, hair, hair.

By the late 1960s, the hippies were increasingly resented by other youths, who saw them as middle-class poseurs. Their talk of 'dropping out' of comfortable society did not go down well with those who had never had a chance to 'drop in' in the first place. In rejecting the hippy lifestyle, many of the less well-off youngsters rejected the hippy hairstyle – and the skinhead cult was born.

The severity of the skinhead crop could vary, and different styles were soon given numbers depending on which attachment was applied to the hair clippers. A 'Number 1' leaves little hair on the head; a 'Number 2' leaves slightly more (if you're not too embarrassed to ask for it.)

In its early years, the skinhead movement was closely linked with ska, a form of music which has its roots in reggae. As the 1970s and 1980s progressed, however, the skinhead look was adopted by extreme right-wing groups and became associated with loud, rowdy, 'Oi!' music. Eventually it reached the point where anyone with a shaven head was suspected of being a racist thug.

During the 1990s, the shaven head became widely popular, and the right-wing connotations faded. Once again, the style appeared to be a reaction against a particularly 'hairy' period; it symbolised a turning-away from the excesses and tackiness of the 1980s – 'Flock of Seagulls' haircuts and all – and in some cases was a conscious rejection of the short-lived and now unfashionable 'grunge' look. The look may also be seen to reflect the general paring-down of contemporary society: cutbacks intended to increase the efficiency and profitability of businesses, awareness of the environmental need to reduce waste, and general disdain for bragging and ostentation.

A Sign of Mourning

The loss of a loved one has driven people in many cultures to lose their hair. In Homer's *Iliad*, Agamemnon displays his grief with a bout of hair-tearing. In Phoenicia, women were obliged to sacrifice their hair in the annual mourning of Adonis – and if they refused, they were forced to sleep with strangers, with the money earned being devoted to the goddess Aphrodite. In the Book of Micah, God issues these instructions on mourning: 'Make thee bald, and poll thee for thy delicate children; enlarge thy baldness as the eagle; for they are gone into captivity from thee' (1:16). By contrast, Cicero sounds a note of reason, quoting Bion of Borysthenes: 'It is foolish to tear out one's hair in grief, as if sorrow could be assuaged by baldness.'

A Sign of Solidarity and Comradeship

The friends and family of those undergoing chemotherapy sometimes shave their heads to show their support, especially if the patient is a young child who may be alarmed at suddenly losing their hair. (In an episode of the sitcom *Frasier* titled 'Author, Author', Frasier Crane tells his brother Niles that he would be prepared to make such a sacrifice in such circumstances. Niles fixes his gaze on Frasier's receding hairline and comments that the significance of this gesture is diminishing by the year.)

A similar principle has been used to forge team spirit in various sports. In the 1997 Confederations Cup in Saudi Arabia, every player in the Brazilian football team shaved his head to match that of star striker Ronaldo. During the 1995 Rugby Union World Cup, most of the French backs shaved their heads. And at the 1992 Olympics in Barcelona, the entire US volleyball team wielded their razors in support of their bald team member Bob Samuelson, following a controversial ruling by FIVB, the sport's governing body – even though one of them, Steve Timmons, had a distinctive high red flat-top haircut, which was the trademark of his beach-clothing company and therefore extremely valuable to him.

In 1998, the players of Polish football club LKS Lodz shaved their heads, though their motivation was financial rather than fraternal. The club sponsors paid each of them £2,000 to advertise a glue specially formulated to keep wigs on in the strongest winds.

A Sign of Shame

A shaven head has often been a mark of punishment and humiliation, especially for women:

> Moreover the Lord saith, Because the daughters of Zion are haughty, and walk with stretched forth necks and wanton eyes, walking and mincing as they go, and making a tinkling with their feet: Therefore the Lord will smite with a scab the crown of the head of the daughters of Zion . . . And it shall come to pass, that instead of sweet smell there shall be stink; and instead of a girdle a rent; and instead of well set hair baldness; and instead of a stomacher a girding of sackcloth; and burning instead of beauty.
> —Isaiah 3:16–17, 24

Nature herself abhors to see a woman shorn or polled; a woman with cut hair is a filthy spectacle, and much like a monster.

—William Prynne, *Histrio-mastix* (1633)

A bull without horns is unsightly, as is a field without grass, a bush without leaves, and a head without hair.

—Ovid, *Ars Amatoria*

In ancient Greece and Rome, it was common for a jealous husband to shave his wife's head if he believed that she had been unfaithful. The practice continued into the twentieth century; in World War II, French women believed to have collaborated with German troops were taken out into the streets and shaved before an angry crowd.

It has also been a method of punishment and humiliation applied to men. Julius Caesar ordered that prisoners from Gaul should be shorn. Those held in Nazi concentration camps also had their hair removed. In 2003, some football clubs in Bulgaria took to punishing poorly performing players by forcing them to shave off their hair. And in 1997, a New York man sought similar redress from his hairdresser. Furious that his highlights had been overdone, turning his Afro peroxide white and giving him a bald patch, the man kidnapped his barber, shaved his head, painted it silver and superglued him to his shop window.

A Sign of Attractiveness

. . . And not just in men: in some societies, women would remove all the hair from their heads in order to appear more attractive. In some African tribes, such as the Masai and the Dinka, a bald head is seen as a perfectly normal style for a woman. And in his *Anthropometamorphosis* (1653), John Bulwer listed several more communities and regions in which women commonly shaved their scalps.

These women, according to Bulwer, regarded hair as 'a most abject excrement, an unprofitable burthen and a most unnecessary and uncomely covering'. However, he declared that all those – male or female – who shave themselves in this way 'doe not only bring a deformitie upon Nature, but affoord an occasion to defluxions'. Indeed, the practice is 'servile, ridiculous, and proper to Fooles and Knaves, an infamous blot of effeminacy, an index of ignominy, calamitie and damage, uncomely . . . not to mention how repugnant it is to divine writ'. He was, it seems safe to assume, against it.

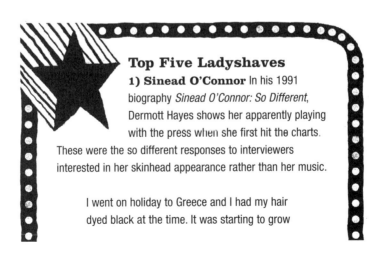

Top Five Ladyshaves

1) Sinead O'Connor In his 1991 biography *Sinead O'Connor: So Different*, Dermott Hayes shows her apparently playing with the press when she first hit the charts. These were the so different responses to interviewers interested in her skinhead appearance rather than her music.

I went on holiday to Greece and I had my hair dyed black at the time. It was starting to grow

out and I went to an Italian barber and asked him to remove the dyed bits. He didn't have a clue what I was saying and just shaved away. I loved it and haven't looked back since. The record company loves it too – it gets a laugh.
– *Hot Press*, 4 December 1986

The reason I cut it sounds really boring but there was this geezer in London who I really fancied and who had the same hair style. So I thought if I cut my hair off I might have a chance. It didn't work but I liked the hair cut so much I kept it.
– *Fresh*, November 1987

A while back when these people from a record company were telling me to look more feminine, giving me all this advice, I just thought, 'Fuck you' and had it all shaved. It was good for me because it lets me play around with conventional ideas of masculinity and femininity. I'm much happier with androgyny.
– *Melody Maker*, November 1987

People always ask me if I shaved my head to look aggressive but I shaved my head because I didn't want another boring hairdo. I did it because I'd done everything else that I could possibly do to my hair.
– *Q Magazine*, March 1990

2) **Sigourney Weaver** When, in *Alien³*, her character Lieutenant Ripley had to shave her head after landing on a lice-infested planet, Ms Weaver turned the storyline to her own advantage: she reportedly demanded a higher fee to compensate for going bald.

3) **Skin**, formerly lead singer of the band Skunk Anansie.

4) **Persis Khambatta**, who played Ilia in *Star Trek*. She held the record for the least hair on a cast member until Patrick Stewart joined.

5) **Demi Moore** had less for her role in the 1996 film *GI Jane*. This echoed the experience of 19-year-old Shannon Faulkner of Charleston, South Carolina, who hit the headlines – and whose hairline was hit – in 1994. Faulkner was the first female student to be admitted by the Citadel military college in its 152-year history, but did not want to have her head shaved like the men. She took her case to a federal court, where her lawyer argued that she would 'look like a freak' if she lost her long blonde locks. The college replied that the clipping symbolises the 'relinquishment of individuality' and pointed out that Faulkner had wished to receive 'the full cadet experience'. The issue became a *cause célèbre* in Charleston, where bumper stickers proclaiming 'Shave Shannon!' became very popular. A poll carried out by the local radio station showed a huge majority in favour of her losing her hair. The judge finally ruled that she should be shorn, which she accepted.

If Ligeia has as many years as she has hairs on her entire head, she is three years old.
   —Martial, *Epigrams*

Be she bald, or do's she weare
Locks incurl'd of other haire;
I shall find enchantment there.
    —Robert Herrick, 'Love Dislikes Nothing'

He was introduced to all the people. They were all
shorter than he was, and bald. The few women there
were bald even on their heads; he realised at last that
they must shave off all their hair, the very fine, soft, short
body-hair of his race, and the head-hair as well.
    —Ursula K. Le Guin, *The Dispossessed*

Baldness Anxiety: The Sub-Waist Subtext

It is not just baldness itself that is open to interpretation; worrying about baldness has also
been ascribed a deeper meaning. According to the Freudian psychiatrist Charles Berg, the
reasons go far deeper than thoughts of ageing or vanity. In his 1951 book *The Unconscious
Significance of Hair*, Berg begins by establishing a link between pubic hair and the hair on
the head; he terms this 'the operation of the mechanism of displacement upwards', which
gives a fair idea of the terminology he uses throughout. He argues:

> It is as though the hair which we display in our clothed
> social state were the only phallus permitted us by society –
> the only phallus we are permitted to reveal. There is the
> tendency to show how fine it is, to be proud of it and sue for
> its approval, alternating with a fear lest it should not be
> approved.

Berg reinforces the link by detailing a number of cases. For example, one patient's dream about going to an important social function and not being able to get his hair to lie flat is interpreted as a fear of the embarrassment which would ensue if he had a visible erection in public. From here, it is only a short step to Berg's central contention: 'The normal concern or anxiety about the hair becoming thin or falling out, alopecia, or becoming grey, are displacements of castration anxiety' – odd when you consider that this is the one sure-fire method of preserving the hair.

He goes on to recount the following discussion of a patient's dream:

PATIENT: I looked at the back of a man – a musical comedy actor – and noticed the back of his head, and I saw the hair was going thin in streaks. He had not got alopecia but thin strands of hair and baldness. I thought 'What a pity' and then I worried as though it were my hair and it was me . . . Sometimes I feel I have not any eyebrows, and this baldness . . . is like being naked and walking about naked with the penis cut off to the hilt . . . In public I would feel unimportant as if I had no penis.

ANALYST: This tall and handsome musical comedy actor?

PATIENT: Perhaps he was my penis, and that is why I could see him and was worried about his hair. What I was really worried about was the length of my penis that was cut off. Then I think of those terrible things before I had my penis cut off – before the nurse's masturbation when I wanted to go inside my mother. I wondered if I then decided to cut off my penis. I did not want to do it and yet I felt it was either the penis or me . . .

Men with plenty of hair may be inclined to seize on Berg's theories, since being well-endowed in the symbolic-phallus department would mean they are free from fears of castration. But before rushing to espouse his views, they should take note of his caveat:

> Long hair can obviously have two opposite meanings: (a)
> (probably primary) masculine – where long hair means much
> penis, and (b) feminine; because by social convention women
> have for many years worn longer hair than men. Hence the
> secondary association to long hair, brought about by social
> usage is feminine – i.e. no penis.

Berg also quotes from *On the Nightmare*, a work by a Dr Ernest Jones. Jones suggests that constant fussing with the hair is a sign of anxiety that a guilty secret might be seen in public:

> Hair itself has several sexual meanings, being indeed
> biologically a secondary sexual characteristic. One that I do
> not remember having been pointed out but which I have
> several times found during psycho-analysis, is an association
> with faeces.

So there you have it. Hair is shit.

CHAPTER EIGHT

10 Disadvantages of Depilation

A ram had been trained by its owner to butt a discus for fun. One day the man, who was bald and in his cups, took off his wig and lay down on the ground to sleep. The ram noticed this, and thought that his master was inviting him to butt the discus – so he struck his bald head and killed him.

— Anon, *The Ram and his Bald-headed Master*

1

Bald men tend to look older than they really are. Thomas Cash, a professor from Norfolk, Virginia, suggested in his 1988 work *The Psychosocial Effects of Male Pattern Balding* that a balding man was usually reckoned to be five years older than someone the same age with a full head of hair.

He looks about forty, as he is beginning to be bald, but he is, in reality, just twenty-two.
—Rudyard Kipling, described by his friend Edmonia Hill in 1888

Of course, there are occasions when looking older can be an advantage, such as getting served in pubs, or getting Anna Nicole Smith to marry you, but in cultures or environments in which youthfulness is worshipped, a bare scalp could be considered a real drawback.

2

Many women find a bald head unattractive. In some cases, it is the lack of self-confidence caused by the lack of hair which puts them off, but it must be conceded that the pink pate itself can be a problem. It is not unknown for personal ads to state the need for a FHOH (Full Head Of Hair) as well as the obligatory GSOH. In 1996, Dr David Przybyla of Denison University in Ohio announced the results of three studies which showed that bald men were generally considered to be less attractive than men with hair, as well as less socially skilled and less successful. This survey is unlikely to have been slanted to produce such conclusions; Dr Przybyla himself is bald.

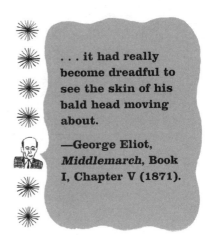

... it had really become dreadful to see the skin of his bald head moving about.

—George Eliot, *Middlemarch*, Book I, Chapter V (1871).

3

A hairless head may prevent you from getting ahead in a regular job, as Dr William P. Cunningham observed in the *Medical Record* in August 1915: '[Bald heads] are a detriment to the seeker for employment . . . In general terms, it is admitted that the possession of a bald head is in most of the paths of industry a very undesirable asset.'

A completely bald head was even said to have been a drawback when it came to playing football for England under Glenn Hoddle. West Ham's shaven-headed full back Julian Dicks claimed in February 1997 that he had been told he would not be picked for the national squad unless he let his hair grow – though this was later denied.

The Bald Bishop

One of the most remarkable works on the subject of baldness is *De Calvitii Encomium*, written by Synesius, Bishop of Cyrene (now Shahhat in Libya) in the early fifth century. Fortunately for us, it was 'Englished' in 1579 by Abraham Fleming as 'A Paradoxe, proving by Reason and Example, that Baldnesse is much better than Bushie Haire, &c'.

Synesius begins by acknowledging that baldness has its drawbacks. He is mocked at 'great banquets and solemne feastes, when baldnesse is called in question' – and even his family poke fun: 'But my mother which bare me, and my sisters which sucked of the same milke, what say they? Their words are these, that beautie and wellfavourednesse standeth much upon the haire.' Women find his pate unattractive: 'And what offence have I committed, that I should become so unsavourie and unsweete a morsell unto women kinde?'

So vexed is he by the injustice of it all that he doesn't stop to explain why appearing unattractive to women should be of such concern to a devoted bishop.

Perhaps you think the way to prevent your pate from precluding your progress is to head your own company? Wrong. In 1993, a New York lawyer found that 70 per cent of his business fell off when his hair suddenly did the same. His long and flowing white locks, which had given him something of an Albert Einstein look, disappeared through alopecia generalis – but because he never talked about it, his clients assumed that he must be having chemotherapy treatment for cancer. Worried that he might soon be joining that great law firm in the sky (or down below, depending on St Peter's views on lawyers), they took their business elsewhere. He then had to go around telling everyone the real reason for his hair loss. Some of his clients returned. By the middle of the following year, his hair still hadn't.

4

Baldness entails a number of practical drawbacks. It takes longer to wash your face, since there is more of it – and if you have your face painted when attending a football match, it will cost you twice as much as a person with hair.

A lack of loft insulation will make you feel colder in winter, and during the summer there is an increased risk of sunburn. You are faced with the choice of spending money on hats and sunblock, or having a head as luminous as a Belisha beacon. Plato recognised the year-round value of hair in around 400 BC:

> Our Maker designed the head to have an abundance of hair, intending that, instead of flesh, the hair should serve as a light covering for the part surrounding the brain. This is for safety reasons; it provides ample shade and protection in summer and in winter, and yet does not impede one's field of vision.

An ad apparently suggesting that one should try to keep one's hair in order to pick up schoolgirls. At least the girls have armed themselves in order to whack any hairy lechers in the Pinaud's

A lack of hair means a lack of protection from impacts to the head. It is reckoned that a bald head feels a blow 3–5 per cent more acutely than a head covered with hair – and of course, any resulting bumps or scratches are visible long afterwards. A bald head can even lead to death. According to legend, the Greek tragedian Aeschylus was killed by an eagle dropping a tortoise on to his head from a great height. The bird had been looking for a way to smash the shell of its prey and, looking down, it mistook Aeschylus' bare pate for a rock.

5

There are also particular health risks associated with baldness. In *The Golden Bough*, Sir James George Frazer describes a remedy for a fever which involved embracing a bald-headed Brahman widow first thing in the morning. The fever was supposedly transferred to the unfortunate woman, as if she didn't have enough to be unhappy about.

More recently, it has been suggested that a bald head can indicate a higher than average risk of heart disease. In February 1993, a Boston University report in the *Journal of the American Medical Association* claimed that men experiencing mild or moderate baldness on the crown of the head are 40 per cent more likely to have a heart attack than men with a full head of hair, while those with severe baldness in that area are 340 per cent more likely. A study published in the *American Journal of Epidemiology* two years later argued that it is the speed of hair loss on the crown, rather than the degree, which points to a greater chance of heart disease, but the general principle is clear. (However, this increased risk does not apply to those losing their hair from the front; and those with severe baldness on the crown are still in less danger than those who smoke or have untreated high blood pressure.) This does not mean, of course, that baldness is the cause of heart attacks; what the studies indicate is that baldness on the crown may be a warning that all is not well with the heart. It could be that both conditions share a common cause, perhaps linked with testosterone.

A study published in the US in 1990 had already suggested that men with male pattern

> I don't advise a haircut, man. All hairdressers are in the employment of the government. Hairs are your aerials. They pick up signals from the cosmos, and transmit them directly into the brain. This is the reason bald-headed men are uptight.
>
> —*Withnail and I*

baldness are likely to develop higher cholesterol levels and higher blood pressure than those who have more hair. The blood pressure problem may result from continual taunting, but it would appear that the bald should be especially prudent with regard to their diet, weight, level of exercise and smoking habits.

6

A bare pate may get you barred from certain places. In 1995, a nightclub in Newcastle-upon-Tyne turned away a 30-year-old man – not because he had no tie or smart shoes, but because he had no hair. On another occasion, a man was refused entry to the US because he did not have enough hair to declare. In June 1921, Antonio Ippolito of New York obtained a writ of habeas corpus to prevent the Ellis Island authorities from deporting his 17-year-old brother Salvatore. According to the petition, Salvatore was detained by the immigration inspectors on his arrival from Italy because 'he had a bald spot on his head'. Antonio argued that a bald spot did not constitute proper grounds for excluding his brother from the US, and asked why bald-headed men were not being deported from the country if it did. The *New York Times* viewed the case with some concern, fearing that if Salvatore's deportation went ahead, this might lead to further forms of discrimination against 'those with negligible hirsute decoration'.

7

The most common discrimination against the bald takes the form of jokes and taunts. It is no longer acceptable to laugh at people because of their colour, sexual orientation, height

No Home for a Dome
Baldness has even been known to lead to eviction. In his poem 'The Penalties of Baldness', Sir Owen Seaman referred to a court case brought by a man against a landlady, who had turned him away because she claimed his head would be considered unsightly by her younger lodgers.

Tis not that both my eyes are black,
My legs arrayed in odd extensions;
Not that I wear, like *Bergerac*,
A nose of rather rude dimensions . . .

But just because above my brow,
That still preserves a certain lustre,
The locks of youth no longer now
Promiscuously cling (or cluster);

Because, in fact, I chance by some
Design of Providence, it may be,
To have my pericranium
Bald as the surface of a baby;

For this, although my state is due
To no specific sin or error,
Woman, I understand you view
My form with unaffected terror.

I that was pleasing in your sight,
When first you saw me with my hat on,
Soon as my top is bathed in light,
Am, metaphorically, spat on!

My presence, so you say, would jar
Upon your younger lodgers' joyance;
To such the hairless ever are
A source, you think, of deep annoyance . . .

But you, who should have probed beneath
The rusty rind, the faded gilding –
You threw my baldness in my teeth,
And me myself outside the building!

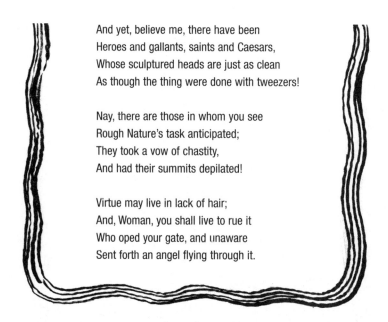

And yet, believe me, there have been
Heroes and gallants, saints and Caesars,
Whose sculptured heads are just as clean
As though the thing were done with tweezers!

Nay, there are those in whom you see
Rough Nature's task anticipated;
They took a vow of chastity,
And had their summits depilated!

Virtue may live in lack of hair;
And, Woman, you shall live to rue it
Who oped your gate, and unaware
Sent forth an angel flying through it.

or weight, but for some reason the PC police have not clamped down on anti-hairless humour. Perhaps baldness is seen as a trivial concern, and jibes on the subject are not thought to be taken seriously. However, the barbs may be keenly felt. As the American journalist Helen Rowland observed in *Reflections of a Bachelor Girl* (1903): 'The tenderest spot in a man's make-up is sometimes the bald spot on top of his head.' Even if a bald man is not hurt by the mockery, he is likely to be wearied by it. After all, it goes on all the time . . .

Baldness gags can feel as much a part of the daily grind as a nine-to-five job. One man, for instance, whose work involved frequent telephone conversations with contacts in Germany, often returned to his desk to find a message asking him to call Herr Loss, Herr Orff or Herr Piess.

A simple visit to the hairdressers can bring its own humiliation. There you are, sitting in the chair, when the barber turns to a hesitant customer at the door and declares, 'Come in, this won't take long!'

A meal in a restaurant may not go undisturbed either. Groucho Marx was once refused entry to the dining room of a high-class hotel in Los Angeles because he was not wearing a

The nineteenth-century dramatist J. R. Planché was the butt of a joke made by journalist Theodore Hook. The latter described him as 'short and bald – he used to cut his hair, but now his hair has cut him'.

tie. Spotting a bald man inside, Groucho took issue with the head waiter. 'Look at him!' he shouted. 'You won't let me in without a necktie, but you let him in without his hair.'

"I WASN'T GOING AS FAST AS YOUR HAIR'S GOING"

The actress Mrs Patrick Campbell could be equally tactless. Towards the end of her career, she was introduced to a distinguished bald man she had met several times before, but whom she had always failed to recognise. When her memory failed her yet again, the man muttered something in annoyance. She replied, 'I'm so sorry. I think it's because you do your hair differently.'

If you become involved in a heated argument, it is only a matter of time before your pate becomes a target. This was the case even in the fourth century BC. When the Athenian philosopher Diogenes had a disagreement with a bald man, he declared: 'You have no right to insult me, heaven knows. No, I commend the good sense of the hairs which have left your miserable head.'

You are obvious prey for stand-up comics. One in Las Vegas had bald men brought to the front row when he performed. He would then talk about how he invariably found hair in the soap at service stations and put forward his own theory as to why this was. 'I've always suspected that one guy was leaving his hair in soap all over the country – and I've just found him. There he is!' At this point, a spotlight would shine on a bald pate in the front row, much to everyone else's amusement.

Then there are the practical jokes. In 1924, a ticket seller at a theatre in Gdansk drew a picture on his seating chart, then sold certain seats in the stalls to bald men only. As the stalls filled on the night in question, and the bald men took their allotted seats, the outline was completed. Just before the curtain rose, the audience in the galleries above could clearly make out the outline of a bird formed by the pink pates below.

It's not just cheeky humans you have to watch out for. According to the *New York Times* in November 1889: 'It is recorded that an ostrich once sat down upon the bald head of an Englishman, under the impression that it was an egg which required hatching.'

8

Hair loss is often a matter of regret, as the American writer Gelett Burgess remarked in his poem 'On Digital Extremeties' even before it happened to him:

> I'd rather have fingers than toes,
> I'd rather have eyes than a nose;
> And as for my hair
> I'm glad it's all there,
> I'll be awfully sad when it goes.

Feelings about baldness can go way past mere regret; losing one's hair can cause severe psychological damage. A 1984 study published in *Personality and Individual Differences* (Vol. 5) showed that bald men scored significantly higher than average on psychoticism and neuroticism scales.

In August 1995, the *British Journal of Psychology* published a paper titled 'Does Fortune Favour the Bald?', which considered that 'far from being a laughing matter, male hair loss is clearly associated with a marked decrease in psychological well-being'. The paper concluded

The Bald Bishop

Bishop Synesius on the distress caused by the loss of his hair:

When this ornament of haire decaieth and falleth, it striketh sore torments into the heart. Heereupon I thought that my luck was to suffer far more greevous inconveniences, than the Atheniens did at the hands of Archidemus, in the cutting downe of the trees of Acarnania.

that 'hair loss in males is associated with depression, low self-esteem, neuroticism, introversion and feelings of unattractiveness, independently of age; and in the case of self-esteem, introversion and feelings of unattractiveness, the effect is especially pronounced in younger males'.

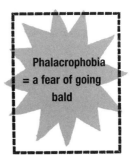

Phalacrophobia = a fear of going bald

It is possible that the low self-esteem of bald men in fact springs from another source; they may make baldness a scapegoat, whereas the real problem lies elsewhere. This was the view of a dermatologist quoted in *Focus* magazine in 1969:

> Many of them [i.e. bald men] are pathetic. They come to tell me they fear they are going bald. Many of them have become neurotic about it. They are all in an anxiety state. They tell me they have failed in life; failed with girls; failed with jobs. They believe their baldness is the cause of their failure.

The real reason for their failure, claimed Dr Sympathetic, was not baldness, but the fact that they were losers. This view was echoed by Thomas Cash in his 1988 study; he remarked that men who are particularly troubled by losing their hair tend to believe that their lives are controlled by external forces.

9

Baldness has been blamed for many extreme actions. In 1993, a 43-year-old civil servant from Hitchin in Hertfordshire took a cocktail of drugs and alcohol before gassing himself with car exhaust fumes – most probably, the coroner's inquest was told, because he could not arrest his hair loss. He reportedly talked of little else. However, the motive was in no doubt at all in a 1958 case, when a 17-year-old student at Leeds University poisoned himself with coal-gas. A note left at the scene read: 'Subject: suicide. Reason: permanent loss of hair which is still continuing to go.'

When New Labour pledged to be 'tough on the causes of crime', they probably didn't have hair loss in mind. Nevertheless, this has been cited as the motivation for a number of offences:

A man in Cheshire committed burglary and assault to obtain the money for a new hairpiece. He had previously left a number of jobs, as he could not bear to stay at any workplace where he felt his baldness had been spotted.

Similarly, a 31-year-old Yorkshireman accused of theft claimed in court that his hair was thinning and that this had 'unsettled' him. The judge considered this to be a valid point in his defence and awarded him only a suspended sentence.

In 1993, a 25-year-old Londoner hijacked a lorry full of leather jackets to fund a £5,000 hair transplant. He was sent down for a year.

In April 1998, a West Midlands man was jailed for five and a half years for the manslaughter of his wife after she teased him about his hair loss. Strangely, he was generally thought by others to have a full head of hair – and even stranger, he shaved it all off after he was arrested.

10

Finally, baldness can prove to be a danger to others. In 1973, a court of enquiry in the UK found that the driver of a goods train was so preoccupied with thoughts about his hair loss that he missed a signal and ran into the back of a stationary guard's van. And the pilot of a helicopter had to radio down before he could land safely on a US Navy aircraft carrier: he complained that the bare pate of a chief petty officer on deck was causing too much glare, and told him to put a hat on.

INTERLUDE IV
Slapping Back

Ide rather be a balde Gentleman than a hairy; for I am sure the best and tallest Yeomen in England have balde heads: me thinkes haire is a scurvie lowsie commodity.
— Thomas Dekker, *Satiromastix* (1602)

The best response to an anti-bald insult is simply to ignore it. However, should you find it impossible to remain silent in the face of provocation, it shouldn't be difficult to respond with more wit than your antagonist. The following retorts are a starting point; once you have them in your repertoire, you can go on to develop original responses of your own.

- I'd rather be a slaphead than a dickhead.
- Better to be thin on top than fat on the bottom.
- At least I'm only deficient on the outside of my head.
- Better a bald head than an empty one.
- Grass doesn't grow on a busy street.
- Do you know how I lost my hair? Through standing on my head so people like you can kiss my arse.
- A turbo-charged brain needs air-cooling.
- Better hairless than harebrained.
- A receding hairline is better than an advancing one.
- They don't put marble tops on cheap furniture.
- Well, we can't all be dense like you.

Responding to accusations that you are wearing a wig is more difficult, though American entertainer Steve Allen offered one suggestion:

> The hair is real – it's the head that's a fake.

If the insult is as unimaginative as 'Slaphead!', you could try following the example set by Cyrano de Bergerac in Edmond Rostand's play of the same name. When a man remarks on the size of his nose, Cyrano belittles him by demonstrating at length how much more inventive and witty the insult might have been. The technique might be adapted thus:

> 'Slaphead'? Is that really the best you can do? Confronted with a bare pate of such magnitude and luminosity, all you can come up with to insult me is 'slaphead'? There are so many cleverer things you could have said. Allow me to offer you a few examples . . .

Physiognomical: 'When you wash your face, where do you stop?'
Entomological: 'Ah, you love ladybirds so much, you've provided a landing-strip for them.'
Ecclesiastical: 'Look, it's St Paul – oh no, it's his cathedral.'
Financial: 'Are you buying that hair in instalments?'
Celebratory: 'Hurrah! The neighbourhood's got its own Millennium Dome!'
Valedictory: 'Some people have wavy hair; yours is just waving goodbye.'
Mock-sympathetic: 'Tell me, were you terribly attached to your hair?'
Wildean: 'To lose half one's hair may be regarded as a misfortune; to lose it all looks like hairlessness.'
Televisual: 'How long have you suffered from premature Kojakulation?'
Horticultural: 'When you see a gooseberry, do you feel jealous?'
Ablutionary: 'Which brand of shampoo do you use? "Shoulders"?'

Now you have an idea of what may be achieved if you are more
than halfway to being a wit. Might I suggest that you go and
practise before insulting me again?

Edmond Rostand, incidentally, was bald. It is tempting to imagine
that his interest in the story of Cyrano was piqued by having his own
abilities overlooked for a more conspicuous, physical feature.

In a *Roseanne* episode titled 'Homecoming', Dan Conner mocks
Barry, an old football team-mate who has turned bald in the years
since they last saw each other, by stroking his own hair and
remarking on how quickly it grows. Unfazed, Barry looks around at
the unsophisticated surroundings of the Conner household and says
that he can see why Dan's hair is so important to him.

Perhaps the most famous verbal retort to a quip about baldness
was delivered by American playwright Marc Connelly at the
Algonquin Round Table, where the great wits of New York gathered
during the 1920s and 1930s. An acquaintance of Connelly reputedly
came up behind him while he was playing poker, gently stroked his
hairless head and said, 'Mmm, feels just like my wife's ass.' Connelly
reached up, rubbed his own head and replied, 'So it does.'

The ultimate form of retaliation, however, is to be found in the
Bible. Our reading concerneth the prophet Elisha:

> And he went up from thence unto Bethel: and as
> he was going up by the way, there came forth
> little children out of the city, and mocked him,
> and said unto him, Go up, thou bald head; go up,
> thou bald head. And he turned back, and looked on
> them, and cursed them in the name of the Lord.
> And there came forth two she bears out of the
> wood, and tare forty and two children of them.
> —2 Kings 2:23–4

It isn't easy to get hold of a couple of she-bears, let alone train them
to kill on command, but it's a nifty trick if you can pull it off.

CHAPTER NINE

40 Advantages of Alopecia

There's one thing about baldness: it's neat.
— Don Herold

Don't feel too dispirited by the list of disadvantages. There may be ten drawbacks, but there are more advantages than there are hairs on your head. Well, forty anyway.

1

You can never have a bad hair day if you don't have any.

2

A completely hairless head makes for a timeless appearance. No one else can be sure of exactly how old you are. And you cannot turn grey if you have already gone pink or brown.

3

If you choose to see baldness as a sign of mortality, a reminder that life is finite, it can spur you on to make the most of it while you still can. You have no time to lose.

4

Once you have realised the futility of worrying about hair loss, the acceptance of the situation makes you a stronger and wiser person. You are less likely to waste time fretting over petty concerns, less likely to judge people by their appearance and you become much better at shrugging off the strictures of others. You will come to realise that your personality is much more important than the way you look.

'Even such a thing as this,' said Mr Pecksniff, laying the forefinger of his left hand upon the brown-paper patch on the top of his head, 'slight casual baldness though it be, reminds us that we are but' – he was going to say 'worms', but recollecting that worms were not remarkable for heads of hair, he substituted 'flesh and blood'.
— Charles Dickens, *Martin Chuzzlewit* (1844)

I might never have made anything of my life, certainly wouldn't have got to the top in sport, if it hadn't been for that change in outlook.
— Duncan Goodhew, Olympic champion swimmer

5

Baldness doesn't have to imply barrenness in one's life. It can indicate a time of maturity and richness. As Logan Pearsall Smith remarked in 'Afterthoughts' (1931): 'There is more felicity on the far side of baldness than young men can possibly imagine.'

6

Bald men are frequently considered to be more intelligent than average. In Act II of *The Comedy of Errors*, Shakespeare remarks of Time that 'what he hath scanted men in hair, he hath given them in wit'.

Hair is 'a blessing that he bestows on beasts'. The fact that Shakespeare was bald is obviously coincidental.

> **The Bald Bishop**
>
> For whie, having a smooth head, and a thinne: he hath wisdome enoughe both for him selfe and his freend.

> Respectability, n. The offspring of a liaison between a bald head and a bank account.
> — Ambrose Bierce, *The Devil's Dictionary*

7

According to a report published in the journal *Ethology and Sociobiology* in January 1997, bald and balding men are generally perceived as being more even-tempered than men with a full head of hair. In the study, the bald were more frequently identified as leaders and were considered to be of greater social standing.

8

William Makepeace Thackeray was apparently of the opinion that the loss of one's hair could give rise to a new clarity of thought:

Forty times over let Michaelmas pass,
Grizzling hair the brain doth clear —
Then you know a boy is an ass,
Then you know the worth of a lass,
Once you have come to Forty Year.

9

A bald head would seem to be particularly advantageous in the medical field, according to nineteenth-century American doctor Oliver Wendell Holmes:

> He had, in fact, an ancient, mildewed air,
> A long gray beard, a plenteous lack of hair, –
> The musty look that always recommends
> Your good old Doctor to his ailing friends.
> Talk of your science! After all is said
> There's nothing like a bare and shiny head;
> Age lends the graces that are sure to please;
> Folks want their doctors mouldy, like their cheese!

The Bald Bishop

And as before the fall of the leafe, the fruite is not come to full perfection: no more is understanding setled in the head, untill suche time as all superfluities are fanned awaie. When therefore you see a baldpate, suppose streight way that the fruit there hath attained perfect ripenesse.

This view was endorsed by a London doctor who complained in 1889 that his career was not going as well as it should because his hair was 'inconveniently thick':

> Incipient baldness gives the appearance of a 'high and dome-like forehead', and inspires the ladies with confidence. The fortunate possessor of this beautiful feature is pronounced 'very clever', which settles the matter. Besides, it is almost indispensable for a 'good bedside manner'. All my medical friends who are getting on well have either money or bald heads; most of them have both.

His view was published in the *Medical Press and Circular*, which agreed: 'It is, no doubt, very much to the advantage of a young practitioner to exhibit a "modern antique" appearance, and nothing contributes so greatly to this end as a head which is innocent of hair.'

Repeat after me: 'I am not bald, I am innocent of hair.' What a wonderful expression.

10

Though baldness does not necessarily indicate a higher level of testosterone than in men with hair, there are enough people around who believe the virility myth to make this an advantage which may be usefully exploited. While you're at it, wear a large pair of shoes too; you know what they say about men with big feet.

11

Many women find baldness attractive, even if a few profess to dislike it. Consider the following ten pleasure domes:

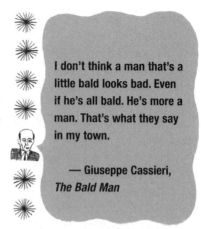

I don't think a man that's a little bald looks bad. Even if he's all bald. He's more a man. That's what they say in my town.

— Giuseppe Cassieri, *The Bald Man*

1) **Sean Connery** Voted 'Sexiest Man Alive' by the US magazine *People* in 1989, and top of many similar polls, Connery has been known to pass praise on to a less obvious pin-up: Mikhail Gorbachev. 'I can't answer for women,' said Sean in 1999, 'but I find him very attractive as a man's man. He has an extraordinary combination of intelligence, baldness and serenity. Almost Buddha-like.'
2) **Patrick Stewart** Once voted 'Sexiest Man on TV' in America – which William Shatner, his rugged predecessor as the captain in *Star Trek*, never managed.
3) **Pablo Picasso** Reputedly slept with hundreds of women during his lifetime.
4) **Pierluigi Collina** Football referee, once voted the sexiest man in Italy.
5) **Michael Jordan** Named in the top ten of *People* magazine's 50 Most Beautiful People of 1991.
6) **Andre Agassi** These days, a lot less hairy than the balls he hits.
7) **John Malkovich** Named in *Empire* magazine's 1995 list of the 100 sexiest film stars of all time (men and women).
8) **Ed Harris** Number seven in *People* magazine's 50 Most Beautiful People of 2001.
9) **Vin Diesel** Made the top 20 in *Company* magazine's Sexiest Men of 2003.
10) **Telly Savalas** Once quoted as saying: 'There are times when I think I'm absolutely beautiful. Look at that classic nose! There's a definite pleasantness about me. My mother used to say to me: "Aristotle, you're the most attractive man in the world. And you've been attractive for 2,500 years. You are the image of the Hermes statue done by Praxiteles."' Mind you, all mums say that, don't they?

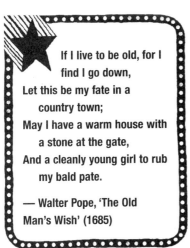

If I live to be old, for I
find I go down,
Let this be my fate in a
country town;
May I have a warm house with
a stone at the gate,
And a cleanly young girl to rub
my bald pate.

— Walter Pope, 'The Old
Man's Wish' (1685)

12

If the allure of your bald head should lead to a steamy session, you are not left with incriminating ruffled hair afterwards. At the same time, your partner will not have any of your stray hairs on their clothing to give the game away. Having no hair also helps you make quicker U-turns between the sheets.

13

It also saves your partner time when they feel affectionate. Instead of coming round to the front to kiss you, they can simply plant a smacker on your pate.

14

A bald head makes you look happier, at least according to heavyweight boxer George Foreman, who chose to remove all his hair in 1977 after a haircut went wrong: 'People think I'm smiling even when I'm not. Even my eyes look like they're smiling.' Well, would you want to disagree with him?

15

On the other hand, Tommy Lee of the band Mötley Crüe said of his shaven look in the early 1990s: 'It looks scary. There's a psychotic side to it, like I'm going to kill someone. I like it.' Hmm. Disagreeing with him probably wouldn't be a good idea either. Suffice it to say that a completely bald head will accentuate whatever sort of image you are trying to convey.

16

Baldness makes you less servile. After all, how can you touch your forelock If you don't have one?

17

If your bare pate is displayed to the world, there is no chance of being accused of being a rug-wearer. This indignity is not confined to the bewigged; the finger of shame may also be pointed at the naturally hirsute. When Brendan Bracken became Minister of Information during the Second World War, a journalist told him: 'I don't believe a word you say, Brendan. Everything about you is phoney. Even your hair, which looks like a wig, isn't.'

18

The bald can claim to be higher up the evolutionary ladder than those with a full head of hair. At a convention in Miami Beach in December 1966, a Dr Arthur C. Curtis argued that hair was becoming less important to man and that in a few centuries all men and women would be hairless. This view was echoed in 1997 by Loring Brace, professor of anthropology at the University of Michigan. He claimed that a higher incidence of baldness indicates an evolutionary shift away from man's early role as hunter-gatherer, when hair was important: 'Hair is a cushion. Get whacked on the head while hunting, go all woozy, you've lost your meal.'

The Bald Bishop

Beastes therefore which are farre from understanding and reason, have all their bodie overgrowne with haire: but man, for that he is partaker of a more excellent estate of life, appeareth more naked and bare . . . Wherby it commeth to passe, that howe much the lesse haire any one hath about his bodie: so much the more doeth he excell other, even as farre as a man is to be preferred before a beast . . . A sheepe of all living things, is the foolishest, because there is no part of her bodie without haire.

19

A smooth pate is far easier to maintain than a full head of hair; there's no need to worry about split ends if all of your hair has split. In April 1988, a Tunbridge Wells man in his seventies wrote to a national newspaper to moan about his troublesome locks: 'Not only is this condition costly in time, money and temper, but we unfortunates always appear unkempt. How I yearn for a tidy head of flesh.'

20

One many-layered advantage to being bald is that of trimming time at the barber's. Over the years, many have complained about their over-talkative hairdressers. Plutarch, writing in the first century AD, records an example from around five centuries earlier:

> It was a witty retort, for example, that King Archelaus [*of Macedonia*] gave to a talkative barber. As he wrapped a towel around him, he asked, 'How shall I cut your hair, Sire?'
> 'In silence,' said Archelaus.

The usual topics of conversation – holiday plans, the fortunes of the local football team – become irritating enough, but when they start chattering at length about your hair, they can be downright annoying. American poet Robert Frost: 'Now see here! I cut my own hair. I got sick of barbers because they talk too much. And too much of their talk was about my hair coming out.'

Less time is wasted if you have less to cut. In 1993, Bill Clinton was strongly criticised after he had a haircut on the presidential plane while it was parked on the runway at Los Angeles international airport. Two of the airport's four runways had to be closed down while he was given good head treatment, and many other planes were delayed.

When you do go to the hairdresser, baldness is a money saver. Former Conservative leader William Hague once remarked: 'The most expensive haircut I ever had cost a tenner. And nine pounds went on the search fee.' Of course, you save even more when you don't go at all. The poet Philip Larkin, in a letter dated 24 March 1949:

> My baldness seems to be keeping its end up well. I don't go to the barbers now: I have bought a pair of clippers & just clip & shave my neck. Well, damn it! The sods charge 2/-, & then expect a tip. I think it's excessive.

Recognising the loss of trade, some hairdressers have made efforts to attract the custom of the bald in other ways. In August 1891, a Brooklyn barber set up a sideline in 'bald-head burnishing'. The *New York Times* described the procedure involved:

> After the bald-headed man is seated, a bucket-shaped

contrivance is placed on his head and fitted to the cranium by means of a screw. Then the attendant produces a pair of tweezers and pulls out the superfluous hairs that grow on all bald heads. The scalp is then sponged with alcohol, and then covered with glycerine. This is rubbed in vigorously, after which a coat of what looks like varnish is applied with a camel's hair pencil. The victim is let alone for a while after that operation, presumably to enable him to recover from its effects, but the barber soon returns to the charge armed with a piece of chamois and several brushes varying in size. The bald pate is then rubbed vigorously, after which the scalp is too slippery even for flies to tread upon.

21

More than saving you money, a lack of hair could even save your life. In February 1995, after crashing his car near the harbour, a man in Shoreham, Sussex, staggered out and fell into the cold water. Thirty minutes later, a fire officer at the scene shone his torch out to sea and spotted a shining object some distance away. At first, he thought it was a buoy – but then realised that it was the man's bald head. Two other officers swam out and reached him just as he was about to disappear below the surface. One of his rescuers remarked afterwards that only his bald head saved him: 'If he'd had a full head of hair he wouldn't have been noticed.'

The Bald Bishop

The sight is the quickest, the liveliest, the most necessarie [*of the five senses*], and (you knowe) the eies have their smoothnesse and baldnesse. That therfore which in man is of this kinde, deserveth most honour. So it followeth in conclusion, that the verie best things are bald.

22

A completely hairless head is the simplest and cheapest way to achieve a bold and striking look. Male pattern baldness, with hair remaining at the back and sides, admittedly less trendy – but it was once all the rage in Tahiti, as Charles Darwin noted in *The Voyage of the Beagle* (1839):

An unbecoming fashion in one respect is now almost
universal: it is that of cutting the hair, or rather shaving it,
from the upper part of the head, in a circular form, so as to
leave only an outer ring of hair. The missionaries have tried to
persuade the people to change this habit: but it is the
fashion.

Darwin's disapproval may seem strange, given that he went bald himself – unless he
suspected the Tahitians of taking the mickey.

23

A bald head can make you more memorable. A man from Allentown, Pennsylvania, had the
honour of having a sandwich named after him at his favourite deli. His usual was described
on the menu as the 'Bald Man's Special'.

24

Baldness has been claimed to bring a number of health benefits. One of Hippocrates'
Aphorisms states 'People who are bald do not get varicose veins; if anyone bald should
develop varicose veins, his hair will grow again.' A contribution to *Notes and Queries* in
January 1918 suggests another advantage:

A heavy crop of hair is often regarded as being the cause of
headaches. One of my brothers had his thick thatch thinned
in order to prevent his suffering from the pain; and I think
long or heavy hair is considered exhausting to the system of
weedy little girls.

Even madness has been treated by baldness, according to H. P. Truefitt:

A friend of Valsalva, Morgagni says, dispelled a maniacal
affection by having the patient's head shaved; and beneficial
results from the same process are frequently seen in the
lunatic asylums – results which, it must be confessed, lend
some force to the injunction so frequently conveyed to

demented persons, although not showing very clearly why
they should proceed to Bath to act up to it.

The injunction to which Truefitt alludes is 'Go to Bath and get your head shaved' – not,
as you might think, a slogan of the West Country Tourist Board, but a common cry of the
day. A modern equivalent would be 'Go boil your head.'

More believably – and more seriously – it seems that bald men are much less prone to
cancer of the bronchus. Statistics suggest that those with a full head of hair are four times
more likely to contract this form of cancer than those losing their hair, though the reason for
this has not yet been firmly established.

25

If you have no hair, it cannot be used in magic spells to harm you. In ancient Egypt, it was
widely believed that shorn hair could be used, with suitable incantations, to harm the
original possessor; great care was taken to dispose of the severed locks after every haircut
to prevent this from happening. As recently as 1946, C. J. S. Thompson reported in *Magic
and Healing* that similar beliefs still existed in parts of Indonesia.

Lucius Apuleius refers to the belief in *The Golden Ass*, though in his story things do not
work out quite as planned. A maid is sent by her mistress to fetch a man's hair from the
barber's so that she may cast a spell – but after the barber catches the maid and
reproaches her, the latter takes some goat hair back to her mistress instead. When this hair
is burned, the goat skins from which it was taken spring back to life and come knocking at
the door.

26

The attentions of hair-snipping fiends may also be avoided with a bare pate. This
phenomenon crops up from time to time, with one of the most serious cases occurring in
Boston, Massachusetts, in 1911. A man nicknamed 'Jack the Snipper' cut the hair from
around a dozen girls and young women in the street, often so surreptitiously that they did
not notice until they returned home. The police advised victims to get new locks fitted as
soon as possible.

27

A bald head may be used to ward off muggers – and not necessarily with a head-butt. American Senator William Proxmire (the man who wore a turban in the senate after having a hair transplant) was once held up at gunpoint while out walking. 'Go ahead and shoot!' he yelled at the robber. 'I'm going to die of cancer in three months anyway.' His would-be assailant fled.

28

You cannot get bats caught in a bare pate – an inconvenience described by a *Notes and Queries* correspondent in February 1931:

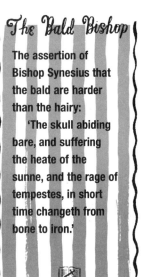

The Bald Bishop

The assertion of Bishop Synesius that the bald are harder than the hairy:

'The skull abiding bare, and suffering the heate of the sunne, and the rage of tempestes, in short time changeth from bone to iron.'

> In the summer of 1908, I witnessed the following incident in Heath Street, Hampstead.
> A lady, evidently on her way to a theatre, without a hat, was walking along the street, when a bat flew against her head and became entangled in her hair to such an extent that a passer-by, who went to her assistance, found it necessary to let the hair (which was very long) down, before she could be released.

29

Bats are not the only creatures to be found in hair. On 23 January 1669, Samuel Pepys found more than 20 lice in his hair and promptly shaved it all off: 'How they came, I know not; but presently did shift myself, and so shall be rid of them, and cut my hayre close to my head.'

The danger of infestation was apparently just as great a century later. In a letter of 1767, the Countess of Suffolk mentions a remark made to Lord Chesterfield about the women at Bath who were wearing their hair 'three or four storeys high'. 'Yes,' Lord Chesterfield replied, 'and I believe every storey is inhabited, like the lodging houses here, for I observe a great deal of scratching.' Standards of hirsute hygiene may have risen since then, but a hairless head is still clearly cleaner.

30

Keeping the scalp clean costs much less when you have no hair. Take two bottles into the shower? Take none.

31

You also save money on combs, hairbrushes and hairdryers. Furthermore, you don't have to remember to pack them when you travel anywhere. The same goes for those silly-looking swimming and shower caps.

32

The elements are of less concern to you if you are bald. If it is windy, you will not be worrying all the time about how your hair looks. (William Hague again: 'It makes life very simple actually. You could be giving a TV interview in a howling gale and it no longer matters.') If it is raining, it is easy to dry your head. And should you wish to take cover, you will feel the first spots of rain before anyone else.

33

Since you do not have to worry about how your hair looks, you are less likely to be accused of vanity. You will never get caught checking your hair in a shop window, unless you are thinking of buying some.

34

A bare pate may prove useful for advertising purposes. Duncan Goodhew has found it most profitable – for example, he was once featured on a poster with the strapline 'Heineken refreshes the pates other beers cannot reach'. And in 1996, a man from Welling in Kent used his head to publicise his local snooker club. When his pass was stolen and the club was slow to replace it, he had one tattooed on his shaven scalp. This ensured that he could never forget to bring it along with him – and the club was delighted at the free advertising it provided.

The marketing possibilities of baldness have been exploited to the greatest extent in the US in the early 1970s.

In the early 1970s, Republican Senator Jake Garn of Utah campaigned for election by plastering the state with posters which read: 'Garn-candid. Garn-decisive. Garn-aware. Garn-bald.' He won by 25,000 votes.

During the 1980s, the hairless owner of a tyre-retreading business in Tega Cay, South Carolina, put a sign outside which said: 'Baldness can be cured here'. He received a lot of TV coverage as a result.

At the same time the proprietor of a Miami lighting business was advertising on the radio by calling himself 'Lightbulb Head'.

The bald manufacturer of a hot barbecue sauce in Tallahassee, Florida, claimed: 'Eat my sauce and it will take the hair off your head.'

The bare-pated owner of a commercial cleaning company chose the name 'Mr Clean and his Machine' – and duly cleaned up.

35

Being bald could bring you a special discount at some establishments, and not just the hairdresser's. In the 1980s, the owner of the Old Mill Inn in Basking Ridge, New Jersey, started holding 'Bald is Beautiful' nights on which bald men could eat in the restaurant for half price. And in 2000, a Houston sandwich shop called Neptune Subs designated the first Monday in every month as 'Bald Monday'. Any bald or balding customer got money off their meal, proportionate to their hair loss. Or as the menu put it: 'The more you shine, the cheaper you dine!'

36

You may even be entitled to freebies. In March 1993, the Houston Rockets basketball club offered free admission to their match against the Phoenix Suns (featuring the bald star Charles Barkley) to anyone with a shaven head. All the Barkley boncealikes also became eligible to take part in a draw to win a trip to Phoenix for a later game between the two teams. In addition, the Rockets said they would give two free tickets to every remaining home match that season to any female fans who turned up with no hair. Twelve women took them up on their offer – though one wonders how many had had their heads shaved by basketball-mad partners while they were asleep.

37

On several occasions (albeit in the nineteenth century), pensions have been granted because of baldness. In June 1893, it was revealed that a former soldier, Allen G. Peek of the 1st Rhode Island Light Artillery, had been awarded a pension in October 1891 for 'loss of hair' resulting from typhoid fever. The pension, worth four dollars a month, had been backdated to March 1884 – giving Peek a tidy lump sum. A fuss had been made earlier in 1893 in the House of Representatives when it had first been claimed that pensions were being granted on account of baldness. This was officially denied at first, but later proved to be true.

38

A shorn bonce may bring *bonne chance* on a football field. During the 1998 World Cup finals in France, the French captain Laurent Blanc kissed the pate of goalkeeper Fabien Barthez just before the start of every match. The team progressed through stage after stage, including a penalty shoot-out against Italy. Blanc, however, was suspended for the final and there was much speculation as to what would happen to the lucky ritual. Would Barthez remain unkissed? Would someone else – possibly the bald defender Franck Leboeuf – take over Blanc's osculatory duties? In the end, the French decided that they could not risk any change; Blanc briefly came on to the pitch to kiss Barthez before the kick-off. France went on to beat Brazil 3–0.

39

The bald escape the disapproval of religious leaders, who have frequently condemned men for having long hair. St Paul describes it as a disgrace on a man (1 Corinthians 11:14), and an eleventh-century Pope decreed that all those with luxuriant locks should be excommunicated. St Anselm, Archbishop of Canterbury at around the same time, would not allow anyone with long hair inside his cathedral.

St Wulstan, Bishop of Worcester from 1062 to 1095, always carried a small knife in his pocket, which he would produce whenever a long-haired man knelt before him to receive his blessing. He would cut off a handful of hair, throw it in the man's face and tell him to cut off the rest or he would go to hell.

The Bald Bishop

In Bishop Synesius' opinion, the hirsute are for the most part 'adulterers and lascivious livers', 'a kinde of people given to the spoile, voide of hope, without grace, destitute of trueth'. In particular, the long-haired Paris, Clisthenes and Timachus of legend were just a bunch of big girls' blouses: 'What are they but effeminate fellowes, womanlike wantons, and hucksters of their own honestie?'

40

If you are bald, you are immune to the discrimination suffered by long-haired men.

Harvard College condemned long hair as long ago as 1649: 'Wee the magistrates . . . doe declare and manifest our dislike and detestation against the wearing of such long haire, as against a thing uncivil and unmanly whereby men doe deforme themselves, and offend sober and modest men, and doe corrupt good manners.'

In 1967, the military regime in Greece banned long hair and beards. Greek citizens were given a choice between prison and a haircut.

In 1970, police in Saigon (now Ho Chi Minh City) seized long-haired youths in the streets and sheared them with bayonets.

Two years later, Singapore began to refuse entry to men with 'hair reaching below an ordinary shirt collar; or hair covering the ears; or hair falling across the forehead and touching the eyelashes'. Through the imposition of such conditions, dangerous subversives such as Dave Brubeck, Joe Cocker and Cliff Richard were kept out of the country. (Cat Stevens was allowed in, but only after lengthy consideration.)

Also in 1972, Kenya barred visitors with long hair and Chile forbade its students from following the fashion.

In 1973, the South Korean President Park Chung Hee banned it – and in the first days after the law was enacted, the Seoul police rounded up more than a thousand youths. In March of the same year, the state of California cut jobless benefits to men with long hair.

In February 1974, the Bavarian State Interior Ministry banned public appearances by long-haired male entertainers, and the police ordered young men in the street to get a haircut.

In 1979, Albania prohibited the hirsute from entering the country. 'Should the authorities not be satisfied in this respect,' the government declared, 'the hair will be cut by the airport barber on arrival.' Ten years later, the law was still in force and caused the mulleted footballer Chris Waddle some concern before an England match there. 'If they won't let me in, I'll pack my bags and go home,' he said. 'I'm not getting my hair cut for anybody . . . If the worst comes to the worst, I'll wear a hair net and put a swimming cap on top so they won't see it.'

If Waddle had been an Argentinian player during the 1990s, he probably wouldn't have been picked in the first place. In 1995, the Real Madrid midfielder Fernando Redondo was dropped by national coach Daniel Passarella for refusing to lose his shoulder-length locks. Passarella's view was that long hair 'often impedes vision'. The following year, his compatriot Leonardo Ricatti was told by Italian Serie B club Avellino that he would have to get his hair cut before they would consider signing him. 'We've never had room for people with long hair here,' said a club spokesman.

Now that you have counted the blessings of baldness – a catalogue, it is worth repeating, four times longer than the negatives of having no hair – this much should be clear: even if your hair is going from you, you still have an awful lot going for you.

INTERLUDE V
'As bald as . . .'

His hat and wig were hanged upon a knob behind him, his head as bald as a bladder of lard, and his expression very shrewd, cantankerous, and inquisitive.
— Robert Louis Stevenson, *St Ives*

If you are looking for a way to describe a hairless head, here is a list of similarly expressive similes to choose from.

As bald as . . .

a coot (One of the oldest and most common similes. The fifteenth-century poet John Lydgate uses it in his *Troy Book*: 'He was ballid as a cote'.)

a billiard ball (Common usage)

a cueball (Ed McBain)

a cannon ball (William Makepeace Thackeray)

an electric lightbulb (David Lodge, *Therapy*)

a grapefruit (Raymond Chandler)

a Crenshaw melon (Used in an episode of the sitcom *Frasier* – ironically, by the balding lead character to describe a bald female artist.)

a pumpkin (Apuleius, *The Golden Ass*: 'Whereas I, poor and wretched as I am, have married a man older than my father, balder than a pumpkin and weaker than a boy'.)

an egg (Alfred, Lord Tennyson, *Harold*: 'I

may give that egg-bald head the tap that silences'.)

a balloon (Percival Wilde, *Tinsley's Bones*)

a cucumber (Used at some time in Cornwall, apparently; do they also say 'as cool as a coot'?)

a lizard (An expression from Texas)

Heaven (Another simile from the States, the point being that there is no parting from Heaven – geddit?)

a lunar sea of senility (Albert Morris)

a monk (Chaucer hints at this when he says: 'For I am shave as nye [*closely*] as any frere [*friar*]', *Complaint to his Purse*)

an ape (Chaucer again: 'As piled [*bald*] as an ape', *The Reeve's Tale*)

a cow (The song *The Hunting of the Hare*, dating from around 1500, contains the line: 'Sym, that was balyd lyke a cow'.)

a badger's bum (This derives from the use of badger bristles to make shaving brushes.)

a baby's bottom (cf. Cybill Shepherd's observation on Bruce Willis, p.175 below)

is the winter tree (William Morris)

the palm of your hand (R. H. Barham)

a looking-glass (Chaucer yet again: 'His heed was balled that shoon as any glas', *Prologue to the Canterbury Tales*)

Time (See 'The Divine and the Abstract', p.167 below)

fine weather (Sophron, *Mimes*, c.450 BC)

a Mykonos (It was said that all inhabitants of this Greek island were bald. John Bulwer in his 1653 work *Anthropometamorphosis*: 'The Miconii also are born without Haire, and baldnesse is lovely and Nationall to them, wherefore they are wont to call bald men Myconians. And it is likely that this which now is naturall unto them, proceeded at first from some affectation & endeavour of Art, which in time, through the indignation of Nature, made the heads of their off-springs Naturally barren of Haire'.)

CHAPTER TEN

A Hairless History of the World

Many a crown covers bald foreheads
— Elizabeth Barrett Browning, *Aurora Leigh*

Many world leaders and influential figures have been bald, including the head-shaving Pharaohs of ancient Egypt, Roman Emperors (somewhat ironic considering that the title 'Caesar' comes from the word 'caesaries', which denotes a thick head of hair), monarchs, warriors, and politicians. Here is an advancing timeline of the most prominent receding hairlines of the last 2,000 years or so.

49 BC Julius Caesar becomes dictator of Rome. The historian Suetonius described him thus in 'De Vita Caesarum': 'His baldness was a disfigurement which displeased him greatly, since it was often the subject of jibes from his detractors. For this reason, he used to comb the thin strands of hair forward from his crown. And of all the honours bestowed upon him, there was none he accepted so gladly as the privilege of wearing a laurel wreath on all occasions.' Veni, vidi, wigi.

AD 37 Caligula becomes Roman Emperor. Suetonius again: 'His hair was thin and he had none on the top of his head, yet the rest of his body was hairy. For this reason, looking down on him from a higher place as he passed by or mentioning goats for any reason whatsoever was considered to be a capital offence . . . Whenever he came across any good-looking men with a fine head of hair, he disfigured them by having the backs of their heads shaved.'

AD 68 Galba becomes Roman Emperor. A year later 'he was murdered beside the Lake of Curtius, and was left lying just as he fell, until a private soldier returning from a distribution of grain set down his load and decapitated the body. Since he could not take hold of Galba's head by the hair (as there was none) he stuffed it inside his cloak, and brought it to Otho with his thumb thrust into the mouth.'

AD 69 Otho becomes Roman Emperor. 'His body had been depilated, and because his hair was so sparse, he wore a wig so well shaped and fitted that no one suspected it.'

AD 81 Domitian becomes Roman Emperor. 'He was so sensitive about his baldness that he took it as a personal insult if any other bald men were targeted, either in fun or in earnest; yet in his book on the care of the hair, which he published with a dedication to a friend, he wrote by way of mutual consolation: "Can you not see that I too am tall and fine to behold?"'

c. 250–850 The Dark Ages for baldness in Europe, with the rise of the Goths and Franks. The Goths mistrusted anyone who did not have long hair, as short hair was the Roman style. The Franks chose their leader from the most hirsute warriors. Their king was known as 'rex crinitus' (hairy king) – and if he failed in his duties and was deposed, he would have his head shaved. This was a humiliation which, it was thought, no ruler could survive.

832 Chinese poet Po Chü-I writes 'On His Baldness' (translated by Arthur Waley in his 1946 collection *Chinese Poems*):

> At dawn I sighed to see my hairs fall;
> At dusk I sighed to see my hairs fall.
> For I dreaded the time when the last lock should go
> [. . .] They are all gone and I do not mind at all!
> I have done with that cumbrous washing and getting dry;
> My tiresome comb for ever is laid aside.
> Best of all, when the weather is hot and wet,
> To have no top-knot weighing down on one's head!
> I put aside my messy cloth wrap;
> I have got rid of my dusty tasselled fringe.
> In a silver jar I have stored a cold stream,
> On my bald pate I trickle a ladle full.
> Like one baptised with the Water of Buddha's Law,
> I sit and receive this cool, cleansing joy.
> *Now* I know why the priest who seeks repose
> Frees his heart by first shaving his head.

843 Charles the Bald becomes King of France. It may not sound like the most flattering epithet, but it could have been worse. Charles the Fat became Holy Roman Emperor in 877, and Charles the Simple became King of France in 893. Charles the Bad was King of Navarre from 1349, and Charles the Mad reigned in France from 1380 to 1422, despite losing the royal marbles in 1392. Charles the Bald was succeeded by his eldest son, Louis the Stammerer. He reigned for only two years – probably just enough time to complete his coronation address.

916   Idwal the Bald (or Idwal Foel) becomes ruler of Wales.

Early   Baldwin the Bald (an epithet which sounds strangely familiar to the author)
900s   vigorously defends Flanders against the Norsemen.

1100   Henry I becomes King of England. His chaplain preached a sermon on the torments which awaited him if he did not lose his locks, and the King reluctantly complied. When his hair grew back, Henry was greatly disturbed by visions of bishops, abbots and monks threatening him, and on more than one occasion he leapt up and tried to attack these illusions with his sword. This time his doctor advised him to shave his head and to offer alms and prayers. He was still loath to follow such a course of action, but finally consented again when he almost drowned in a storm at sea.

1137   King Louis VII becomes King of France. When he cropped his hair like a monk, his queen, Eleanor of Guienne, was less than impressed. She tried without success to dissuade him from his hairstyle (and his asceticism), and eventually she was unfaithful. They divorced, and so Louis lost the rich provinces of Guienne and Poiton which were her dowry. Eleanor soon gave her hand – and her land – to Henry, Duke of Normandy, who later became Henry II of England. The English monarchy thereby acquired a strong foothold in France, which became the cause of bitter conflict between the two countries for centuries. The bare French crown had a lot to answer for.

c. 1300   The future King Edward II of England loses most of his hair at the hands of his father, Edward I. He wanted to give away Pontieu to Piers Gaveston, his catamite, and his father was so infuriated that he seized a tuft of the prince's hair in each hand and tore out as much as he could until he was exhausted.

1399   Henry IV becomes King of England. He lost his hair in particularly unpleasant and inauspicious circumstances, according to the contemporary chronicler Adam of Usk: 'Henry the fourth, after that he had reigned with power for fourteen years . . . fell sick, having been poisoned; from which cause he had been tormented for five years by a rotting of the flesh, by a drying up of the eyes, and by a rupture of the intestines . . . That same rotting did the anointing at his coronation portend; for there ensued such a growth of lice, especially on his head, that he neither grew hair, nor could he have his head uncovered for many months.'

c. 1430   Prokop the Bald, a Bohemian warrior priest, is a leading figure in the later period of the Hussite Wars.

1558   Elizabeth I becomes Queen of England. Late in life, she became almost totally bald and had a collection of more than 80 wigs. The German tutor Paul Hentzner describes her thus in *Journey into England* (1598): 'Next came the Queen . . . her face oblong, fair but wrinkled; her eyes small, yet black and pleasant; her nose a little hooked, her lips narrow and her teeth black (a defect the English seem subject to from their too great use of sugar) . . . She wore false hair and that red.'

1564   William Shakespeare is born. The bald bard's fullest examination of baldness is to be found in Act II, Scene ii of *The Comedy of Errors* (c.1591). The character Dromio of Syracuse declares baldness to be a natural event, and one that cannot be reversed: 'There's no time for a man to recover his hair that grows bald by nature.' Only dumb animals have profuse amounts of hair: 'Because it is a blessing that he bestows on beasts, and what he hath scanted men in hair he hath given them in wit.' And two practical benefits of baldness are mentioned: 'The one, to save the money that he spends in tiring [hair-dressing]. The other, that at dinner they [his hairs] should not drop in his porridge [soup]'. Other Shakespearean quips include: 'A curled pate will grow bald' (*Henry V*, V.ii.168).

Literary Lightbulbs

Poets are almost always bald when they get to be about forty.
— John Masefield

• Gaius Licinius Calvus (a Roman orator and lesser-known poet, but worth mentioning since 'calvus' means 'bald') • Aeschylus • Pierre de Ronsard • Michel de Montaigne •William Shakespeare •Jonathan Swift • Oliver Goldsmith • William Wordsworth • John Clare • Alfred, Lord Tennyson (who in his later years wore a velvet skull-cap to protect his bare scalp from draughts) • Anthony Trollope (whose hair was recorded as 'chestnut' when he applied for a Spanish passport, though he admitted in *The West Indies and the Spanish Main* that 'any but a Spaniard would have declared that as to hair, I am bald') • Edward Lear • Leo Tolstoy • Algernon Charles Swinburne • Thomas Hardy • Paul Verlaine • Henry James • Rudyard Kipling • Edmond Rostand • John Galsworthy • André Gide • André Maurois • Edmund Wilson • Thornton Wilder • Pablo Neruda • Henry Miller • Arthur Miller • Noël Coward • P. G. Wodehouse • Eugène Ionesco (author of *La Cantatrice Chauve*, or *The Bald Prima-Donna*) • Isaac Bashevis Singer • Alan Ayckbourn • Philip Larkin (who once described himself as 'like a balding salmon') • Thomas Keneally • Ken Kesey • Salman Rushdie

Thomas Hardly-any-hair, as portrayed by
Max Beerbohm in 1902

1574 Henry III becomes King of France. He lost all his hair at an early age after dyeing it with harmful chemicals. He took to wearing a kind of turban, or a velvet cap with tufts of hair sewn under the brim.

1587 Mary, Queen of Scots is executed. The executioner bent to pick her head up by her auburn tresses. Yet as he held his arm aloft to the crowd and shouted 'Long live the Queen!', he realised that he was holding only her hair. Her near-bald head still lay at his feet.

1610 Louis XIII becomes King of France. He was bald by the age of 29, apparently as a result of applying injurious 'remedies' to his scalp. He concealed this with huge, curly wigs, setting a trend which swept through Europe.

1643 His son, Louis XIV the Sun(-Reflecting) King, accedes to the French throne. He continued the practice of wearing enormous hairpieces, partly to compensate for his lack of height, but principally because he had begun to lose his hair at 32. His barber was the only person who ever saw him bald. When the King went to bed, he would pass his wig to a page through the drawn curtains of his bed; and in the morning, it would be passed back to him through the still-drawn curtains. (His successor, Louis XV, did not take the whole wig-wearing business quite so seriously. As a teenage monarch, he thought it great fun to go around pulling people's wigs off, knowing that he could do so with impunity.)

1706 Benjamin Franklin is born. As well as being a great scientist, he was an important diplomat, philosopher, writer and printer. Sadly for the bald fraternity though, he wrote in a 1784 letter: 'I wish the bald eagle had not been chosen as the representative of our country; he is a bird of bad moral character; like those among men who live by sharping and robbing, he is generally poor and often very lousy. The turkey is a much more respectable bird, and withal a true original native of America.'

1796 Paul I becomes Emperor of Russia. He was so sensitive about his baldness that he decreed that anyone mentioning it was to be flogged to death.

1797   John Adams becomes US President. He and his son John Quincy Adams, who became President in 1825, were similar in looks and outlook according to Alfred Steinberg in *The First Ten* (1967): 'John Quincy Adams was a short, stout, bald, brilliant and puritanical twig off a short, stout, bald, brilliant and puritanical tree. Little wonder, then, that he took the same view of the office of President as had his father.'

1801   Alexander I becomes Emperor of Russia. He is described as 'the bald-coot bully Alexander' in Byron's *Don Juan* (1819–1824). Possibly in an attempt to divert attention towards the other end of the body, he launched a campaign against the wearing of long trousers; in 1807, his troops were ordered to stop all carriages and, if they found any man wearing trousers, to cut the garment off at the knees.

1804   Napoleon Bonaparte becomes Emperor of France. Despite combing his hair forwards in the manner of Julius Caesar, he could not avoid the nickname 'Le Petit Tondu' (or Short and Shorn, if you prefer). His hair loss seems to have caused some resentment on his part. On the death of his brother-in-law General Leclerc, his sister Pauline cut off her lengthy locks and had them buried in his coffin. 'Of course,' Napoleon commented cynically, 'she knows that her hair will come in all the longer and thicker for being cropped.' It has also been claimed that when he met Emperor Alexander I of Russia in 1807, their conversation was prolonged by an exchange of advice on how to prevent hair loss.

1809   James Madison becomes US President. He was virtually bald, which may have prompted in part the dismissive remark of statesman Daniel Webster: 'I did not like his looks any better than I like his Administration.'

1820   George IV becomes King of England. He was at least a wig-wearer, if he was not bald. When sitting for a sculpture, he whipped off his hairpiece and held it out at arm's length. 'Now, Mr Chantrey,' he asked, 'which way shall it be – with the wig or without it?' Unfortunately for the purpose of this book, the sculptor chose 'with'.

They Blinded with Science (as well as with their Heads)

- **Hippocrates** (c.460–377 BC), generally regarded as the father of medicine. The thin rim of hair left at the back and sides of the head by male pattern baldness is sometimes called the 'Hippocratic wreath'.
- **Paracelsus** (c.1493–1541), German physician who established the role of chemistry in medicine.
- **Isambard Kingdom Brunel** (1806–1859), the most influential civil engineer of the nineteenth century.
- **Charles Darwin** (1809–1882), naturalist who laid the foundation of modern evolutionary theory.
- **Ivan Petrovich Pavlov** (1849–1936), Russian physiologist, Nobel Prize winner and dog handler, best known for his pioneering studies of reflex behaviour.
- **Emil von Behring** (1854–1917), German bacteriologist who won the first Nobel Prize for Physiology or Medicine and is considered to be the father of the science of immunology.
- **Josef Breuer** (1842–1925), Austrian physician and physiologist acknowledged as the principal forerunner of psychoanalysis by none other than. . .
- **Sigmund Freud** (1856–1939), Austrian neurologist generally regarded as the founder of modern psychoanalysis.
- **Wilbur Wright** (1867–1912), who with his brother Orville made the first powered aeroplane flight in 1903.

1837   Martin van Buren becomes US President. He had a couple of nicknames which referred to his bare head of state: 'Old Skinhead' and 'His Royal Balderdash'. (If he was ever called 'Martin van Barren', it wasn't recorded.) He thought about wearing a wig, but eventually decided that it would only have added to the perception of him as an indulgent fop, which he was trying to play down.

1881   James Garfield becomes US President. Like William McKinley, who took up the post in 1897, he experienced some hair loss, though neither man achieved his full bald potential. Both were shot.

1885   The bald Marquess of Salisbury becomes Prime Minister of Great Britain and Ireland.

1901   Edward VII becomes King. His lack of hair was no surprise, since his father Prince Albert sported a combover, and his grandfather on Queen Victoria's side was extremely bald. In the case of the latter, the writer Richard Brinsley Sheridan suggested that this was because grass does not grow on deserts.

1917   Vladimir Ilich Lenin becomes head of government in the Soviet Union. 'The structure of his skull is truly striking,' wrote Anatoly Vasilievich Lunacharsky. One has to study him for a little while and then, instead of the 'first impression of a plain, large, bald head one begins to appreciate its physical power, the contours of the colossal dome of his forehead and to sense something which I can only describe as a physical emanation of light from its surface'. The sculptor Naum Aronson was reportedly captivated by Lenin's head, and begged the revolutionary leader to sit for him, pointing out his striking resemblance to the philosopher Socrates.

How the nobs tried to keep hair on their nobs

1922   Benito Mussolini becomes leader of the government in Italy. Not one of the greatest moments in bald history, admittedly. He used to have his head shaved by one of his police guards.

1940   Winston Churchill becomes Prime Minister of Britain. He led a remarkably full life; in addition to his achievements as a politician and statesman, he found time to win the Nobel Prize for Literature in 1953. It must have helped that he needed to spend little time on his hair; he once snapped at his barber: 'A man of my resources cannot presume to have a hairstyle – get on and cut it.'

1942   General Douglas MacArthur assumes command of the Allied troops in the Pacific during the Second World War. Regrettably, MacArthur attempted to cover up with a combover, prompting Alice Roosevelt Longworth (daughter of President Theodore Roosevelt) to remark: 'Never trust a man who combs his hair straight from his left armpit.' It just goes to show that the greatest achievements can be obscured by a few foolishly positioned strands of hair.

1945   The bald Clement Attlee succeeds Winston Churchill as Prime Minister, heading the first Labour Government to serve a full term and presiding over the creation of the welfare state.

1947   Mohandas K. Gandhi leads India to independence. In 1910, Gandhi came up with the idea of using baldness as a form of contraception at a commune in South Africa. The boys and girls of the commune were in the habit of bathing together in a spring, and he was concerned that the boys might be overcome by lust. After much thought, he suggested to the girls that they should shave their heads as a deterrent. Though they were alarmed at first, he persuaded them to go along with it – and in fact he carried out the cutting himself.

1948   The balding David Ben-Gurion becomes the first Prime Minister of Israel.

1949   The receding Konrad Adenauer becomes Chancellor of West Germany.

1952   The baldest presidential race in US history takes place. Dwight Eisenhower defeated Robert Taft to win the Republican party nomination and went on to beat Democrat Adlai Stevenson. Eisenhower's Secretary of the Treasury was the bald George Humphrey, whose very first encounter with Eisenhower was marked by an exchange about the general recession. 'George,' said Eisenhower as Humphrey entered the room, 'I see you comb your hair the way I do.'

1958 The bald Nikita Khrushchev becomes President of the Soviet Union.

1959 General Charles de Gaulle becomes President of France. He had a shaven head at the tender age of 20, when he attended a military academy. This apparently accentuated his large nose and ears, and he was nicknamed both 'The Great Asparagus' and 'Turkey Cock'.

1962 The receding John Glenn becomes the first American to orbit the earth in space in 1962. He was truly bald by 1998, when he became the oldest ever astronaut at the age of 77.

1968 The bald Pierre Trudeau becomes Prime Minister of Canada.

1969 Edwin 'Buzz' Aldrin walks on the moon during the historic Apollo 11 mission. Though he did so only after the hirsute Neil Armstrong, the baldies in NASA got their own back with the Apollo 12 mission later in the year. Charles Conrad and his similarly bare-beaned colleague Alan Bean got to do some lunar leg-stretching while Richard Gordon, whose follicles were fully operational, was left orbiting the moon and waiting for them to return.

1974 Valéry Giscard d'Estaing becomes President of France and fellow bald politician Gerald Ford becomes US President following the resignation of Richard Nixon. When he was in Congress during the 1960s, Ford annoyed President Lyndon Johnson to such a degree that the latter claimed that Ford 'had played [American] football too long without a helmet'. The barb became much-repeated, possibly because Ford's bare, helmet-like skull lent it an air of plausibility.

1978 Bald heads of state Menachem Begin of Israel and Anwar al-Sadat of Egypt share the Nobel Peace Prize.

1981 The heavily receding François Mitterrand becomes President of France, and Prince Charles marries Lady Diana Spencer. In November 1990, the *National Enquirer* in the US claimed that Charles was trying a pungent combination of camel dung and bear grease in an attempt to keep his hair, much to his mother's displeasure. (Headline: 'ROYAL STINK OVER PRINCE CHARLES'S BALDNESS CURE'.) He clearly inherited his father's follicles; Prince Philip once began an address to a meeting of synthetic fibre manufacturers by stroking his bare head and declaring: 'I'm not very good at producing man-made fibres myself.'

1982   High-foreheaded Yuri Andropov reaches the highest office in the Soviet Union and Helmut Kohl becomes Chancellor of West Germany. The latter is a mere two vowels away from 'Helmet Kahl', a name which would be even more fitting than the author's: 'kahl' is the German word for 'bald'.

1985   Mikhail Gorbachev becomes President of the Soviet Union. His bald head, with its distinctive port-wine birthmark, seemed to reflect the spirit of *glasnost*, or openness, with which he is associated.

1989   The bald F. W. de Klerk becomes President of South Africa and the shaven Tenzin Gyatso (the 14th Dalai Lama of Tibet) wins the Nobel Peace Prize.

1991   Paul Keating becomes Prime Minister of Australia. His balding crown attracted much attention in September 1995, when newspaper photographers were ordered to stop snapping the back of his head in parliament. The order was issued by the Serjeant-at-Arms, who answers to the Speaker, who in turn answers to the Prime Minister – unsurprisingly, it was suggested that Keating was ultimately responsible. Though seemingly sensitive about his hair loss (he often tried to cover his bald patch with his hand,) he strongly denied that the order had originated from him, and set the record straight in the House of Representatives. 'I did not speak to you about this matter at all – ever,' Keating told the Speaker during question time. Somehow, the Speaker resisted the temptation to tell him to keep his hair on.

1995   The bald Jacques Chirac becomes President of France.

2000   The new millennium is marked in London by the opening of a large dome.

CHAPTER ELEVEN

Shining Examples

Of this I am assured, that the things which are next unto God, are the Spheres of the heavens, and they are balde: in like manner are the starres. The Heaven it selfe appeareth balde in our sight: in the praise whereof what so ever we can saie, the same maie well serve to commend baldnesse.
— The Bald Bishop

It is not just the dazzling reflection of the sun which makes the bald stand out in a crowd. They are prominent for many other reasons: their talent, their intelligence, their valour, their sporting ability or their elevated position in society. It seems only fitting that the most outstanding bald icons should be commemorated in a Hairless Hall of Fame.

The Divine and the Abstract

Bald Gods If the ceiling of the Sistine Chapel is anything to go by, God has plenty of hair. But there are three dome-headed deities that we know of. (Disappointingly, the Norse god Balder – son of Odin and Frigg – is not one of them.) The 'Venus Calva', or Bald Venus, was worshipped in a particular Roman temple after the invasion of the Gauls, when women were said to be cutting off their hair for use as bowstrings. And two of the Seven Gods of Luck in Japanese mythology are bald: Hotei, a fat and jolly character sometimes referred to as the 'laughing Buddha'; and Fukurokuju, frequently depicted as a short old man with a conspicuously high-domed head, though you may take the view that such a misshapen head is hardly a sign of luck.

Saints Several are portrayed as bald in the paintings of Raphael. In *The Holy Family with Saints Elizabeth and John*, St Joseph, at the apex of the configuration, is clearly hairless. And in the *Disputa*, St Gregory the Great and St Jerome on the left of the altar, and St Augustine on the right, are similarly scanty on top.

Time The image of Time as bald, with only a lock of hair on his forehead, dates back to ancient Greece. Shakespeare mentions 'the plain bald pate of Father Time himself' in *A Comedy of Errors*, while in Ben Jonson's *The Poetaster*, the character Pantilius Tucca remarks: 'Thou art not to learn the humours and tricks of that old bald cheater, Time.'

Opportunity In Rabelais's *Gargantua*, this abstract concept personified has a remarkably similar appearance to that of Time: 'Opportunity wears all her hair on her forehead; when she is past, you can not bring her back. She has no tuft of hair which you might use to grab her, for she is bald on the back of her head, and never comes back.'

Political Pates

As our Hairless History of the World showed, a battalion of bald men have become world leaders. However, relatively few have been President of the United States. A number of studies and articles have considered whether a man's hair has a significant bearing on his chances of reaching high office there. G. Vance Noble's 378-page book *The Hirsute Tradition in American Politics* (1978) is hardly encouraging to the hairless; his Law of Political Imagery states:

> All other things being equal, a bald man cannot be elected President of the United States.

A corollary to this law states:

> Given a choice between two bald presidential candidates, the American people will vote for the less bald of the two.

Noble's Law seems to hold true – and the politicians know this. It was no accident that Jimmy Carter went for the 'big hair' look in his 1976 campaign posters, or that Ronald Reagan's hair appeared unnaturally black. In 1970, Vice-President Spiro Agnew let his sideburns grow longer to ensure that he couldn't be thought bald, even though he wasn't actually losing his hair: 'It's just an effort on my part to make my photographs make me look as though I'm not bald from halfway up. The grey hair doesn't show in the pictures.'

And he might have gotten away with it too, if it hadn't been for those pesky tax-evasion charges.

In 1972, the balding George McGovern couldn't even beat Richard 'Tricky Dicky' Nixon, despite a sidewinder described by writer Hunter S. Thompson as 'the George McGovern alpine rope throw'. Noble's view is that he would have done much better if he had worn 'a well-styled rug'. In fact, McGovern wore a wig for a couple of weeks when trying for the Democratic nomination, but gave up after bumping into a campaign committee official when taking the piece to be cleaned. Hugely embarrassed, he dropped the bag and left.

Bald men are also underrepresented in other key areas of US politics. In 1990, a paper titled 'Hair Loss and Electability: The Bald Truth' was published in the *Journal of Nonverbal Behavior*. This study found that there was a significantly lower proportion of bald and balding members of Congress than one would expect in a group of men of their ages. (One position in American public life which bald men do attain regularly is the mayorship of New York. Ed Koch, who held the post in the 1970s, once turned down the offer of a free hair transplant by a Long Island doctor, saying that he was quite happy being bald. Even Rudolph Giuliani, whose early failure to be elected mayor was blamed on his combover by the press, made it to the post in the end.)

Precisely why relatively few bald men reach high political office in the US is unclear. The enduring affection for the hirsute John F. Kennedy may have contributed to the phenomenon in recent decades; certainly, Carter and Clinton have sought to recreate his youthful and vigorous image. Yet it surely goes deeper than that. Noble takes the view in his book that 'something in the American psyche rejects the idea that a candidate who has lost his hair is capable of national leadership'. He goes on to define this prejudice more precisely as 'the latent anti-intellectual macho streak that runs through our history, baldness being associated in the popular mind with ivory-tower academics and, for some reason, the absence of aggressive attributes Americans subconsciously seek in a President and commander-in-chief'.

Dwight Eisenhower was elected President in 1952, perhaps because his status as a war hero would have outweighed any fears among the electorate that the bald may lack aggression. More significantly, he was up against the bald Adlai Stevenson, who was just the sort of intellectual disliked (according to Noble) by the American public. Stevenson used long and abstruse words in speeches and made erudite references to French writers; the term 'egghead' was invented to describe him.

The 1990 study of bald politicians took a different view. The authors of the paper conducted an experiment in which people were given a 'campaign brochure' presenting a candidate and his policies. The candidate was shown either in his natural bald state, or wearing a wig, and reactions to the two versions were compared. The interviewees perceived the bewigged candidate as being younger, but did not find him more attractive, dynamic or more deserving of their vote. The authors suggested that the negative self-perceptions of bald men, rather than the views of others, were holding them back.

Of course, the British people would not be influenced by anything as superficial as hair when electing a Prime Minister – or would they? There have been few blatantly bald PMs since 1900; only the Marquess of Salisbury, Winston Churchill and Clement Attlee would fall into this category – and Churchill and Attlee only ever won elections against each other.

The only bald man to have come close to gaining the key to 10 Downing Street since Churchill is Neil Kinnock, who led the Labour party in the 1987 and 1992 general elections. In October 2000, he partly attributed his electoral defeats to his lack of hair, and in passing explained why Attlee had more success: 'Clem Attlee did not exactly have dreadlocks, did he? But he was not such a skating rink as myself and William Hague. And he also wore a hat much of the time, because he was from that blessed era for the likes of us when people still did so.' If Kinnock's hairstyle did put people off, it was probably not the paucity of hair per se; it would more likely have been his persistence with his combover for so many years.

Kinnock was succeeded as Labour leader by the extremely bald John Smith, who died before he was able to contest a general election. As it was, the hirsute Tony Blair took over and led Labour to victory in 1997 – though after just one year in power, he was reporting a decline in resources at the Ministry of Follicles. 'It is certainly getting greyer and less,' he admitted, blaming the loss on pressure of work.

It certainly couldn't have been caused by worrying that his Tory counterpart had more hair. After the 1997 election, William Hague became the Conservative leader. Though he was still in his thirties at the time, Hague had one of the most prominent pates in parliament. In 2001, he resigned after the Conservatives were again heavily defeated at the polls – to be replaced by the equally bald Iain Duncan Smith. A number of commentators questioned the wisdom of choosing another bald man; their misgivings appeared justified when IDS was replaced as leader in 2003 by Michael Howard, though he could hardly have been chosen for his thick head of hair. Howard duly lost the 2005 election.

There have been other notable baldies in British politics, including Roy Jenkins and Norman Tebbit (nicknamed 'The Chingford Skinhead'). Perhaps unwilling to follow in the footsteps of such leading lights, many others have tried to conceal their hair loss. In 1988, a half-used bottle of minoxidil solution was found hidden behind a window ledge in a washroom at the House of Commons; the perpetrator never owned up. As mentioned above, Labour MPs Bryan Gould and Keith Vaz publicly endorsed Andy Bryant's inversion method of treatment. Gould's baldness became common knowledge only after the House of Commons permitted the introduction of TV cameras. Previously, his bouffant sweep at the front had given the impression that he had a fine head of hair; the elevated angle of the cameras in the chamber revealed a gleaming expanse of skin on his crown.

These MPs would have done better to take the bold approach of former Northern Ireland Secretary Mo Mowlam. She lost her hair after treatment for a benign brain tumour, and though she wore a wig in the early stages of recovery, she astonished journalists by suddenly removing it during a press briefing in May 1997. 'I am going to take my hair off,' she declared. 'I don't care about you lot. I have had enough of it today.' Such openness and informality are directly responsible for Dr Mowlam's public popularity.

It is also worth remembering that too much hair can be a disadvantage in politics. Research carried out in the US for the Democrat party in the early 1990s indicated that candidates with unruly locks received 4 per cent fewer votes than those with a short back and sides. And not for nothing did Margaret Thatcher offer Nigel Lawson the following piece of advice when she summoned him to offer him the Chancellorship: 'Nigel, you must get your hair cut this afternoon.'

Brilliant Actors

Arguably (which means that this is the author's view, and anyone who disagrees can step outside now), the two greatest bald icons of the twentieth century were Yul Brynner and Telly Savalas – both actors, and both head-shavers.

Both were initially persuaded by others to shave their heads for acting roles. In Brynner's case, it was the designer Irene Sharaff who came up with the idea during preparations for *The King And I* in 1951. He was almost bald already, with only a black fringe at the sides and back and a few strands on top, but he still wasn't keen on taking it all off. He was worried that a dip on the top of his head would look unsightly, but Sharaff convinced him to go ahead by pointing out that the King of Siam on whom the story was based had spent time in a Buddhist monastery.

Yul's skull became his trademark, and did much to make baldness look sexy. He wore a

KC and the Headshine Banned

Kevin Costner and Sylvester Stallone are not generally thought of as being bald – and it seems they will go to great lengths to keep it that way. Costner pushed his hair forward to create a false hairline in *The Bodyguard*, and was rumoured to have insisted on having his bald patch painted in by computer during the making of *Waterworld*. (If true, this would help to explain why the film was so expensive to make.)

Meanwhile, Stallone was alleged in 1995 to be so sensitive about his hair loss that his aides would tell tall visitors to sit down quickly in his presence to prevent them from spotting his bald patch.

wig for the 1958 film *The Buccaneer*, but he now looked so strange with hair that he quickly went back to baldness. Marlene Dietrich was moved to comment: 'Covering his sensual dome is like putting clothes on Lady Godiva.'

Savalas, best remembered for his 1970s TV role as lollipop-sucking detective Theo Kojak, was persuaded by director George Stevens to shave his head for the role of Pontius Pilate in the 1965 film *The Greatest Story Ever Told*. Like Brynner, Savalas was unsure about the idea at first, as he thought his children might be scared of his new look. Stevens suggested bringing the children along so that they could watch him having his head shaved. He did, and everyone was happy.

There was never anything on Telly again. He went on to work on one film after another, and never had enough time to grow a new head of hair between pictures; by the time he had a couple of free months, he and his audience had become used to his baldness. He refused to wear a hairpiece for any role, remarking that if directors wanted someone with hair, they wouldn't ask him anyway. Yet at the same time, he did not consider himself to be a bald man; he regarded himself as a man who could be hirsute if he wished, but simply preferred to shave. Talk about splitting hairs.

Plenty of other actors have shaved their heads for particular roles. Woody Harrelson was unnaturally bald in *Natural Born Killers*. Laurence Fishburne's head was bare in both *Othello* and *The Matrix*. And Philip Franks shaved his head twice when he played Tom Pinch in a TV adaptation of Dickens' *Martin Chuzzlewit*. (His hair had just about grown back when he was recalled to re-shoot the ending.)

Another Hollywood leading man has seen the light and permanently removed all his hair to become a major bald icon: Bruce Willis. He was not always willing to embrace his baldness, perhaps as a result of all the jokes about his receding hair in the 1980s TV series *Moonlighting*. (The longer the show went on, the more moonlight was reflected.) He was said to be very sensitive about the subject during the shooting of *The Bonfire of the Vanities* (1990); in her book *The Devil's Candy*, which chronicles the making of the film, Julie Salomon reveals that Willis's head was sprayed with black face powder in order to conceal his hair loss. In 1991, *Time* magazine reported that Willis was so distressed by the look of his hair in footage of *Hudson Hawk* that he had every offending frame retouched before the film's release. Although industry experts declared that the expense involved meant the story had to be apocryphal, the idea that Willis might have made such a request seemed to surprise no one.

However, at the request of Quentin Tarantino, Willis shaved his head in 1994 for *Pulp Fiction*. The movie followed some terrible flops for Willis and some terrible flak in the press – and relaunched his career. Soon Willis was a born-again baldy, happy to let chat-show host David Letterman draw on his scalp on TV. He developed a philosophical, humorous attitude to hair loss: 'Baldness is God's way of showing you are only human. He takes the hair from your head and sticks it in your ears.' Others acclaimed his striking new appearance; fellow actor Brad Pitt referred to him as 'O almighty bald one', while Terry Gilliam, who directed him in *Twelve Monkeys* (1995), commented: 'Bruce Willis has got one of the finest bald heads in the world. It is a monument to cranial architecture.'

The one person still pointing at Willis's pate and sniggering is his *Moonlighting* co-star Cybill Shepherd. In 1998 she declared that she intended to dedicate part of her book *Cybill Disobedience* to Bruce's backside. Apparently he had been in the habit of dropping his

The Bald Academy

The bald Carl Reiner has won nine Male Performer Emmys – more than any other actor, though Ed Asner, best known for playing Lou Grant in the TV series of the same name, pushes him close with seven. The bald have also enjoyed great success at Oscar ceremonies. The receding Jack Nicholson has won in three different decades, for *One Flew Over the Cuckoo's Nest*, *Terms of Endearment* and *As Good As It Gets*, and has been nominated on three other occasions.

The golden period for the hairless was the 1980s, when the Oscar for Best Actor went to a bald or balding man five years in a row: 1982 – Henry Fonda, *On Golden Pond*; 1983 – Ben Kingsley, *Gandhi*; 1984 – Robert Duvall, *Tender Mercies*; 1985 – F. Murray Abraham, *Amadeus*; 1986 – William Hurt, *Kiss of the Spider Woman*. In addition, Sir John Gielgud won the Oscar for Best Supporting Actor in 1982 for his role in *Arthur*. Bob Hoskins was nominated for the Best Actor award in 1987 (for *Mona Lisa*), but could not quite secure a sixth successive win for the hair-loss brigade. Still, Sean Connery made amends in 1988 with an Oscar for his wigless work in *The Untouchables*. Hats off to all of them.

Of course, the Oscar statuette itself is bald, as Woody Allen observed when declining to attend the Academy Awards ceremony in 1978: 'I am not interested in an inanimate statue of a little bald man, I like something with long, blonde curls.' As a further incidental note, Sir John Gielgud is not the only bald actor to have been knighted. The royal sword has also passed over the hairless heads of Sir Ralph Richardson and Sir Sean Connery, and Sir Laurence Olivier's hair was very thin in his later years. (He was completely bald-pated for his role as the vicious Nazi dentist in the 1976 film *Marathon Man*, for which he received an Oscar nomination.)

trousers and mooning on the *Moonlighting* set, and Shepherd asked him to give her some warning so that she could prepare herself for the awful sight. 'He could probably use some of that hair now on his head,' she said.

A Dozen Directors Who Rarely Said 'Cut!'

Sergei Eisenstein – *Battleship Potemkin, October*

Cecil B. de Mille – *Cleopatra, The Ten Commandments*

Jean Renoir – *Boudu Sauvé des Eaux, La Règle du Jeu*

Alfred Hitchcock – *Psycho, North by Northwest*

Otto Preminger – *Laura, Anatomy of a Murder*

Michael Powell – *One of Our Aircraft Is Missing, The Life and Death of Colonel Blimp*

Karel Reisz – *Saturday Night and Sunday Morning, The French Lieutenant's Woman*

Richard Lester – *A Hard Day's Night, The Three Musketeers*

John Schlesinger – *Midnight Cowboy, Marathon Man*

Volker Schlöndorff – *The Tin Drum, Swann in Love*

Robert Altman – *M*A*S*H, Short Cuts* (!)

Federico Fellini – *La Dolce Vita, 8$^1/_2$* (Fellini jokingly referred to his own hair loss after spending four days in a Rome clinic in 1986. 'According to the doctors, I'm only suffering from a light form of premature baldness,' he claimed. Premature, indeed. He was 66 at the time.)

Clean Humour

Baldness is a recurrent theme in TV sitcoms. This means that many fine bald actors get plenty of work, though more often than not they are the butt of the jibes. Even in shows where there are few explicit jokes about baldness, there is often an unattractive or uncongenial bald character, such as:

the coarse Louie de Palma (Danny DeVito) in *Taxi*;

the grumpy Victor Meldrew (Richard Wilson) in *One Foot In The Grave*;

the stupid Stupid Dave (Mark Roberts) in *The Naked Truth*;

the bizarre Uncle Fester (Jackie Coogan) in *The Addams Family*;

the bigoted Alf Garnett (Warren Mitchell) in *Till Death Us Do Part*;

the foolish character played by Gregor Fisher in *The Baldy Man* (after the first programmes aired, Fisher claimed to have received threats of violence from irate bald men who did not like him poking fun at them);

George Costanza (Jason Alexander) in *Seinfeld*, who by his own description is totally inadequate, completely insecure, paranoid and neurotic.

Even cartoon series can portray the hairless in an unflattering light. In *King of the Hill*, the two biggest losers in Hank Hill's group of friends are bald; the dim-witted and easily-influenced Bill Dauterive has been alone for years since his wife left, while cap-wearing Dale Gribble is always being cuckolded by John Redcorn, a native American with long, flowing locks.

Similarly in *The Simpsons*, Homer is stupid, thoughtless, and lazy as well as bald – and in the episode 'Simpson and Delilah', his boss Mr Burns blames his general bitterness and unpleasantness on his sudden loss of hair in his senior year at college.

The brighter side of baldness may be found in sitcoms, though you do have to look hard. A revelation of baldness is a sign of sympathy and friendship in *Cheers*. For several series, the barman Sam Malone (Ted Danson) displays great pride in his hair – yet he encourages barmaid Carla to reveal her most embarrassing secret (having slept with barfly Paul) by briefly removing his hairpiece to expose his bald spot.

The discarding of a wig is an act of boldness and self-confidence in 'Golden Gordon', an episode of *Ripping Yarns* (not a sitcom, strictly speaking, but worthy of note here all the same). Gordon Ottershaw (Michael Palin) sets out to save the useless Barnstoneworth United FC by reuniting their finest old players for one final match. He finds the team's star striker Baldy Davitt (Roger Sloman) working in a butcher's shop – and now wearing a very obvious hairpiece, though he claims that he has always been very proud of his fine head of hair. Eventually, Gordon persuades Davitt to play. Just before the referee blows his whistle to start the match, Davitt dramatically removes his toupee to reveal his freshly greased and shining pate. Within seconds, he has blasted the ball into the net, and even the beaten goalkeeper is rushing up to ask for his autograph.

The greatest bald hero of sitcoms, however, is Sergeant Ernie Bilko, the brilliant schemer in *The Phil Silvers Show*. Bilko expresses pride in his pate, claiming that his hair was lost in the service of his country and that the bare skin on top of his head is therefore a badge of honour. On another occasion, he says that his hair loss has been caused by giving away so many locks of his hair to admiring women.

In one episode, a TV comic called Buddy Bickford visits Fort Baxter and makes the mistake of joking about Bilko's baldness. He goes through the usual anti-bald gags, protesting that Bilko's gleaming head is dazzling him, declaring that a midget could use it as a skating rink and comparing it to a ball on a pool table. Bilko exacts full revenge by destroying Bickford's confidence completely.

In another episode titled 'Hair', Bilko launches a strong attack on the hirsute when he discovers that his girlfriend, Sergeant Joan Hogan, has been seen out with an abundantly-haired corporal. Contemptuously calling her a 'hair-lover', he condemns hair for being insanitary, accuses the corporal in question of having dandruff (which Bilko will never have) and suggests that if she likes that sort of thing, Sergeant Hogan should date a sheepdog.

Bilko's one brief lapse from his pro-baldness stance occurs when Sergeant Sowici glues a hairpiece on to his head as he sleeps, making him think when he wakes that a potion tested on him by his barber has had a miraculous effect. Bilko lets all the girls in Sgt Hogan's office run their fingers through his hair, and rushes out to buy shampoo, hair tonic and a hairdryer – items which, he admits, he has wanted to buy for years. When he washes his hair, the hot water causes the wig to slide off - but Bilko is angry with himself rather than upset at the loss of his hair. He realises that he has been the victim of vanity, and that his judgement has been clouded.

Realising that Sowici plans to embarrass him by removing the hairpiece in public, Bilko forestalls him by casually taking it off himself and tossing it aside to a great cheer. He also makes up with Sergeant Hogan, who is not in the least perturbed to learn that he has not really grown new hair; to her, his lack of hair makes no difference at all.

The BAPHTA Awards

Sitcoms aside, the hairless shine in many other areas of television. Indeed, with the number of TV awards now in existence, it is surprising that they have never been acknowledged in their own glittering ceremony. Still, this omission is easily rectified. Ladies and gentlemen, here are the winners of the Bald And Partially Haired Television Awards:

Best Bald Newsreader/Weatherman: Willard Scott

Also nominated: Michael Fish, John Tusa, the late Gordon Honeycombe

Though not well known in Britain, US weatherman Willard Scott wins for his outstanding work in demonstrating that hair is of little importance. He has sometimes worn a wig when presenting the weather forecast or appearing in a commercial; at other times he has appeared bald. He is so casual about the matter that in November 1984 he wore a different hairpiece every half-hour on NBC's *Today* programme, and once took it off in the middle of an appearance on *The David Letterman Show*. When he is not on the air, however, the hair is never on him.

Best Bald Talk Show Host: Montel Williams

Also nominated: Clive Anderson, Jack Docherty

Another success for America. Clive Anderson has a forehead which is still in the process of becoming a fore-and-aft-head. Jack Docherty was excessively sensitive about his bald spot on his Channel 5 show, covering it with his hand when bowing to the audience. The head of Montel Williams, however, is absolutely hairless and gleams like a beacon.

Best Bald Quiz/Game Show Host: Richard O'Brien

Also nominated: Paul Daniels, Jim Bowen, Robert Robinson

Richard O'Brien, who presented the early series of *The Crystal Maze*, shaves his head completely because otherwise, he has said, he would look like a chartered accountant – which would hardly be appropriate for the creator of *The Rocky Horror Show*.

Best Bald Quiz/Game Show Participant: Lee Hurst

Also nominated: Alan Coren, Ian Hislop, Wolf

Lee Hurst just wins this category, despite telling the questionnaire in the *Guardian* in May 1998 that his favourite word is 'hair'. He stoutly fought his corner in *They Think It's All Over* against the hairy Rory McGrath and anyone else who mocked his baldness. When comedienne Jo Brand asked if she could run her fingers through his hair, he responded by offering to take his trousers off. Wolf from *Gladiators* is nominated simply to annoy him. He confessed to the *Radio Times* in October 1998: 'I wish I could have my hair back. It's heredity and I can't stand it. I'm not narcissistic, but I would like a bit more. You see an alcoholic lying in a corner asleep in a bin bag with a full head of liced hair and you think, why me? I'm healthy, I'm fit, I'm strong, I take vitamins and here's this guy . . .'

Best Bald Sports Commentator: Brian Moore
Also nominated: David Coleman, Barry Davies, Murray Walker

Four equally legendary commentators, you may think. The late Brian Moore, however, was lifted head and shoulders above the rest when his dome-like skull was immortalised in the title of a Gillingham FC fanzine: *Brian Moore's Head Looks Uncannily Like London Planetarium*. Also worthy of note is the US sports presenter Terry Bradshaw; though he goes bald now, he was paid for wearing a toupee when he played quarterback for the Pittsburgh Steelers.

Best Bald Presenter: Clive James
Also nominated: Desmond Morris, Ainsley Harriott, Ian Wright, Frank Bough

Clive James walks away with this award on the strength of his article 'Baldies of the world come out!', which appeared in the *Observer* in October 1977. The piece took a critical look at men who use ridiculous and unconvincing methods to disguise their loss, and proclaimed the author's own nonchalance on the subject: 'Touchy to the point of paranoia in every other department of symbolic virility, your reporter is for some reason relatively carefree about the fact that the top of his head glows in the dark.'

Best Bald Comedian/Entertainer: Alexei Sayle
Also nominated: Jasper Carrott, Russ Abbot, Harry Hill, Matt Lucas, Jim Tavaré, Mick Miller

Jasper Carrott has performed plenty of material on baldness, lamenting the lot of bald men who cannot travel on buses because of cheeky kids, and mocking those who try to compensate for a bare pate with a ponytail ('It looks like the cat's disappeared up the backside of a turkey'). Russ Abbot saw the error of his transplants in 1994, and had the reseeded receded areas cleared by electrolysis. Matt Lucas, who lost his hair at the age of six, reportedly tried pills, seaweed, homeopathic remedies and eventually a scratchy wig in his early years, but now goes bare whenever he is not performing. However, Alexei Sayle wins for a single observation in his TV comedy-drama *Sorry about Last Night* (1995). Siobhan Redmond's character says of his: 'He's balding. I've told him it doesn't matter, but he won't listen. Why do men never believe it doesn't matter, but think we're telling the truth about the knob-size thing?'

Best Bald Soap Opera:
Coronation Street

Also nominated: *EastEnders, Brookside*

Brookside had the shaven Mick Johnson and the receding Jimmy Corkhill, plus Barry Grant who ended up bald. In the Mitchell brothers, *EastEnders* boasted the two most striking bald heads in the soap world, as well as Roy Evans, Frank Butcher, Dr Anthony Trueman, Jim Branning and even the Millennium Dome in the opening credits. But neither can match *Coronation Street*. This soap has featured such bald and balding characters as Alec Gilroy, Fred Gee, Fred Elliott, Percy Sugden, Derek Wilton, Jack Duckworth, Eric Firman, Mick Hopwood, Patrick the taxi driver and Reg Holdsworth. When Reg (Ken Morley) decided to wear a wig in order to appear more dynamic at work, the hairpiece fell down from behind a sun visor in their car and caused his wife Maureen to swerve off the road. Reg was constantly subjected to the jibes of others, such as this one from Maud Grimes: 'His hair's not his own and his mind's not his own either.' And finally, a soap villain: the male heads in *Emmerdale* are so hairy that one might suspect that sheep dung is an effective baldness remedy after all.

The Pate Gallery

William Hogarth (1697–1764)

William Blake (1757–1827)

Paul Cézanne (1839–1906)

Pierre-Auguste Renoir (1841–1919)

Henri Matisse (1869–1954)

Piet Mondrian (1872–1944)

Pablo Picasso (1881–1973)

Gino Severini (1883–1966)

Marcel Duchamp (1887–1968)

Jackson Pollock (1912–1956)

To this gleaming array of talent, we may also add Théodore Géricault, who deliberately had his head shaved as part of his preparations for painting *The Raft of the Medusa* (1818–1819). He wished to cut himself off from his old life, his friends and his family so that he could devote himself completely to the task, and believed that he would be less likely to leave his house if he no longer sported the curled, reddish-blond hair of which he had always been proud. The idea worked; over the following months, he rarely went outside, ate in his studio and slept in an adjoining bedroom.

Paul Cézanne: self-portrait

Polished Pop Acts

Pop music boasts many bald artists, partly because of the longevity of certain performers, partly because of the increasing popularity of head-shaving. Every act in this Topless 20 has reached the top ten in the UK album or singles chart (an asterisk denotes a UK No.1):

Michael Stipe* – vocalist, R.E.M. Note: 'Shiny Happy People' is not a reference to jolly bald folk, and 'The Sidewinder Sleeps Tonite' has nothing to do with combovers.

Erroll Brown* – vocalist, Hot Chocolate.

Phil Collins* I can feel it combing in the hair tonight . . . or maybe not.

Elton John* So far, his hairpiece has not been seen to dangle in the wind.

Richard and Fred Fairbrass* – vocalist and bass guitarist, Right Said Fred. Fred Fairbrass claimed in 1993 that their baldness contributed greatly to their appeal, since their heads were the most obvious phallic symbols in Britain – an image apparently emphasised by Richard's frequent skull-rubbing. He described himself and his brother as being 'two big willies on stage'. But if the Fairbrasses were big, bald willies, what did that make bubble-permed lead guitarist Rob Manzoli?

Louis Armstrong* (Several other jazz greats have been bald, notably Count Basie, Euble Blake, Stephane Grappelli and Ben Webster.)

Seal*

Mick Fleetwood* – drummer, Fleetwood Mac. They had a 1977 hit with 'Go Your Own Way'. His hair did.

Moby* Charmingly described as a '36-year-old bald-headed fag' by Eminem in the latter's 'Without Me'.

Billy Corgan – vocalist, Smashing Pumpkins/Zwan

Outhere Brothers* Should perhaps have been called the Hairout Brothers.

Isaac Hayes*

Garry Christian – vocalist, The Christians. One hopes that their song 'When the Fingers Point' was not inspired by any attention his head may have received in the street.

Paul and Phil Hartnoll – or collectively, Orbital. They released a single in 1999 titled 'Nothing Left'.

Adamski* In 1992, he remarked that walking along Brighton beach first thing in the morning and feeling the wind on his bald head was the ultimate hangover cure.

Shovell – percussionist, M People.

Carl Douglas* Had a huge hit with 'Kung Fu Fighting'. In fact his head was a little bit frightening.

Sice* – vocalist, Boo Radleys

Ashley Slater – vocalist, Freakpower

Buster Bloodvessel – vocalist, Bad Manners. He deserves the final word in this list after his strong pro-baldness comments to the *Sun* in November 1998. Dismissing hair potions as utterly worthless (but using a shorter word), he remarked that those who try to make money out of the bald are merely trying to exploit foolish feelings of insecurity. He advocated simply shaving the head and getting on with life. For a man who had a hit with 'Ne-Ne Na-Na Na-Na Nu-Nu', he talks a lot of sense.

Many of the references to baldness in pop and rock songs use hair loss to signify the onset of age, most famously in the opening line of The Beatles' 'When I'm Sixty-Four' (1967): 'When I get older, losing my hair'. A slightly negative view of baldness may be detected in this song, inasmuch as there is a fear that a bald man might no longer be the recipient of such tokens of affection as a valentine, birthday greetings or a bottle of wine. Thirty years later, young and shamelessly hairy group Hanson expressed this even more bluntly in 'MmmBop': 'When you get old, start losing hair/ Can you tell me who will still care?'

The Kings of Leon song 'Bucket', from their 2004 album *Aha Shake Heartbreak*, talks of going bald at the age of 18 - but this is scarcely more uplifting. (Another song from the same album, titled 'Milk', refers to having a combover.)

Hair loss sounds a particularly sad state of affairs in the Crash Test Dummies song 'Afternoons & Coffeespoons' (1994): 'Someday I'll have a disappearing hairline/ Someday I'll wear pyjamas in the daytime'. The title and lyrics of this song, incidentally, allude to 'The Love Song of J. Alfred Prufrock' by T. S. Eliot - a poem which contains the lines:

> Time to turn back and descend the stair,
> With a bald spot in the middle of my hair –
> (They will say: 'How his hair is growing thin!')

The view of baldness as something regrettable and depressing is echoed in David Bowie's 'Ashes to Ashes' (1980), in which having no hair is mentioned in the same breath as having no money. Similarly in 'One Last Love Song' (1994) by The Beautiful South: 'Save me from baldness and saving the earth'. And not forgetting 'I Think I'm Going Bald' by Rush, featured on the 1975 album *Caress Of Steel*:

> I looked in the mirror today;
> My eyes just didn't seem so bright.
> I've lost a few more hairs.
> I think I'm going bald,
> I think I'm going bald.

The condition brings some joy in Joni Mitchell's 'Just Like This Train', from her 1974 album *Court and Spark* – but only because she is relishing the thought of it happening to someone else: 'Dreaming of the pleasure I'm going to have/ Watching your hairline recede/ (My vain darling)'. It is generally believed that the hairline in question belonged to James Taylor. There can be no doubt, however, that the subject of the following verse from 'Snooker Loopy' by the Matchroom Mob with Chas and Dave is snooker star Willie Thorne. For one thing, he is mentioned by name. And for another, he sings the final line himself:

> But old Willie Thorne, his hair's all gone,
> And his mates all take the rise.
> His opponent said, 'Cover up his head,

'Cos it's shining in my eyes.'
When the light shines down on his bare crown,
It's a cert he's gonna walk it,
But it's just not fair giving off that glare.
(Thorne:) Perhaps I ought to chalk it.

Two songs view female baldness with some disapproval. The Who were insistent on a 1965 B-side that they didn't want no bald-headed woman, on the grounds that 'it'll make me mean, yeah Lord, it'll make me mean'. Why this should be is never made clear – though fittingly the A-side was 'I Can't Explain'. Even the King has sung of a woman losing her crown: Elvis Presley collapses in giggles in a live recording of 'Are You Lonesome Tonight' after changing one line of the lyrics to: 'Do you gaze at your bald head and wish you had hair?' (Legend has it that Elvis lost it because a man in the audience took off his toupee at the mention of the bald head.)

There are many more invocations of baldness in reggae songs, but this is because of the cultural significance of hair in Rastafarian society. The dreadlocked Rastas have traditionally viewed the close-cropped police and soldiers as instruments of 'Babylon', or decadent western culture. In 'Crazy Baldheads' (1976), Bob Marley advocates fighting back against the hairless oppressors: 'Them crazy, them crazy/ We gonna chase those crazy baldheads out of town'. Those who do not follow Rastafarianism cannot be God's chosen people, Marley claims in 'Time Will Tell' (1978): 'Jah would never give the power to a baldhead'.

Other reggae records from the 1970s include: 'Get Out Bald Head' by Big Joe, 'Run Baldhead' by Time Unlimited, and 'Mr Baldwin' by The Gladiators – a song which invites and encourages general laughter at the expense of the said Mr Baldwin. (Not one of the author's favourites.) Special loathing is reserved for barbers who cut off Rastas' dreadlocks in Jamaican prisons, the inspiration behind songs such as 'I Killed The Barber' by Dr Alimentado. The homophony of 'barber-man' and 'Baba-man' (i.e. 'Babylonian man') was seen as a significant coincidence.

Happily, there are a number of songs offering a more positive view of bare pates. In his ska classic 'Skinhead' (1995), Laurel Aitken claims: 'When a skinhead walks down the street/ Every chick's heart skips a beat'. Buster Bloodvessel, lead singer of Bad Manners, growls defiantly in 'Samson and Delilah' (1982): 'You can't cut my hair 'cause I haven't any there!' In 'The Joy of Living' (1995), the lead singer of Oui 3 nonchalantly declares that a lack of hair leaves 'all the more room for another slammin' hat'. And in 1997, Howie B released a single titled 'Angels Go

Bald: Too' – but since this is an instrumental piece, there are no lyrics to elucidate further.

The greatest hymn to the hairless, however, comes from New York group Four Bitchin' Babes. They may be largely unknown in Britain, but their 1993 song 'Bald-Headed Men' deserves the widest possible recognition:

> Everybody knows it's testosterone
> That turns a bushy-haired man into a chrome dome,
> But testosterone is what makes a man a man;
> The more that he's got, the more that he can
> Do the things that make the women go OY!
> I'll take a bald-headed man over a big-haired boy.
> Big-haired boys make very good friends,
> But they cannot compare to bald-headed men.
> (She said it before, she'll say it again)
> I like bald-headed men. . .
>
> Try looking in your mirror from a whole different place,
> You're not losing hair, you're gaining face.
> Be confident, be cool, it won't be long when
> You find you are proud to be one of the bald-headed men.

Well said, sisters.

The Glabrous World of Sport

Football in particular boasts many outstanding bald players, despite being the sport in which the hairless receive the most taunts. The crowd will always pick on a bare pate, with songs such as:

> Baldy, Baldy, over there,
> What's it like to have no hair?
> Is it hot or is it cold?
> What's it like to – be bald?

Even when fans sing in support of a bald player, baldness is seen as a handicap to which a blind eye is turned:

Steve Bould, Steve Bould,
Stevie, Stevie Bould.
He's got no hair but we don't care,
Stevie, Stevie Bould.

Team-mates are scarcely more sympathetic. Here, for example, is then Sunderland captain Kevin Ball looking forward to the year ahead in a match programme from January 1996: 'The crystal ball wasn't too clear at first, then we realised we were staring at Steve Agnew's head.' It is rarer for players to mock bald spectators – but it has been known. In 1995, Dennis Wise scored for Chelsea at Aston Villa and ran straight over to a bald Villa fan, slapping his own head. Wise explained later that the fan had been shouting abuse at him during the pre-match warm-up.

There is some evidence that referees pick on players with no hair. During the 2000–2001 season, disciplinary figures for the English Premiership showed that seven of the ten players cautioned and sent off most often had little or nothing on top. It was also revealed that former referee Kevin Lynch (bald himself) had helped to solve one club's disciplinary problems by advising the players to shun the hairless look. 'Those haircuts do look aggressive,' he commented. 'Human nature is such that refs may look at players and say, "He looks like a hard man."'

But to demonstrate the quality and quantity of footballers with 'nothing on me 'ead, son', here is a bald squad composed of players who have graced the English and Scottish Premier Leagues in recent seasons. Habitual head-shavers have been recognised as well as the naturally bald, since they receive as much abuse for their lack of hair. However, those such as David Beckham and Paul Gascoigne who have merely flirted with the style have been omitted – even though the latter's brief hairless spell was predicted in the Bible ('Baldness is come upon Gaza' —Jeremiah 47:5).

1   Brad Friedel (Blackburn)
2   Danny Mills (Man City)
3   Steve Stone (Portsmouth)
4   Lee Carsley (Everton)
5   Sol Campbell (Arsenal)
6   Bobo Balde (Celtic)
7   Thomas Gravesen (Everton)

8	Claus Jensen (Fulham)
9	Dion Dublin (Aston Villa)
10	John Hartson (Celtic)
11	Gianluca Vialli (Chelsea)

Substitutes:

12	Fabien Barthez (Man Utd)
13	Chris Marsden (Southampton)
14	Matt Elliott (Leicester)
15	Temuri Ketsbaia (Dundee)
16	Nicolas Anelka (Man City)

The most appropriate team manager would be Jim 'Bald Eagle' Smith. Gary McAllister's claim is scotched by a remark he made in 1994, when as a player with hair, he missed a penalty for Leeds and claimed afterwards that the floodlights reflecting on the bald head of Norwich keeper Bryan Gunn had dazzled him. (Former Holland and Rangers manager Dick Advocaat is ruled out completely by the hair transplant he had carried out in the late 1990s.)

If you think that team looks strong, consider how a Rest of the World XI from the last ten years might line up.

1	Borislav Mihailov (Bulgaria)
2	Roberto Carlos (Brazil)
3	Lilian Thuram (France)
4	Juan Sebastian Veron (Argentina)
5	Franck Leboeuf (France)
6	Zinedine Zidane (France)
7	Klas Ingesson (Sweden)
8	Iordan Letchkov (Bulgaria)
9	Ronaldo (Brazil)
10	Hasan Sas (Turkey)
11	Attilio Lombardo (Italy)

Mihailov gets the goalkeeper's shirt ahead of his compatriot Zdravko Zdravkov and Bogdan Stelea of Romania to ensure that his astonishing hairpiece features in the highlights. When Bulgaria qualified for the 1994 World Cup finals, Mihailov was so bald that his shirt might have read 'Mihairov'. Yet by the time the finals began, he had acquired a full head of hair. However, the hot and humid weather in the US made his newly laid carpet so uncomfortable that his hairdresser had to fly over to attend to it. Meanwhile, fellow Bulgarian international Iordan Letchkov made a huge impact on the tournament with an unashamedly hairless dome – caused, he has claimed, by radiation from the Chernobyl nuclear reactor.

One player is dishonourably ruled out from our World XI: Borja Aguirretxu of Spain. In 1997 he tested positive for the steroid nandrolene. Facing a two-year ban from football, the Celta Vigo defender offered the shaky defence that the drug was contained in tablets he had been taking to combat baldness. The standard defender's tactic – shouting angrily at his fallen hair for taking a dive – would have been a better course of action.

Bald footballers are by no means a modern phenomenon, as an Oldies XI demonstrates.

1	John Shaw
2	Terry Hennessey
3	Terry Mancini
4	Ricardo Pavoni
5	Ray Wilkins
6	Uwe Seeler
7	Ralph Coates
8	Alfredo Di Stefano
9	Bobby Charlton
10	Alan Gilzean
11	David Armstrong

The legendary Pelé (yes, he has hair; but his name means 'bald' in French) loses out to the lesser-known South American Ricardo Pavoni, whose hair-weave scored a late equaliser for Uruguay against Bulgaria in the 1974 World Cup finals. His practised finish may lend a little credibility to Bobby Charlton's suggestion in the *Ryan Giggs Soccer Skills* TV series that poor heading technique had contributed to his own baldness.

If it were possible for our bald teams to play each other, the quality of football would be outstanding – and would deserve an outstanding referee. One candidate outshines all others: Pierluigi Collina of Italy. In 2002, he was presented with an award on a sports show on Italian TV – but when the presenters made jokes about a 'Collina hair lotion', he stormed off, smashed his trophy and threw the pieces in a bin backstage.

Most other sports can point to their own hairless heroes – or would, if pointing weren't rude. **American football** has the legendary San Francisco 49ers quarterback Y. A. Tittle, voted the NFL's most valuable player in both 1961 and 1963. Still in the States, **baseball**'s most famous bald player is Joe Garagiola, who went on to become a leading TV broadcaster and was elected to the Baseball Hall of Fame in 1991. Many top **basketball** players have had nothing on top, notably Kareem Abdul-Jabbar (winner of six NBA championships, six MVP awards and the highest points scorer in NBA league history), Charles Barkley and Michael Jordan, the highest-earning sportsman in history.

Athletics has featured a number of bald heads in recent years, since many sprinters have deliberately opted for the aerodynamic look. However, naturally balding stars include Miruts Yifter of Ethiopia (gold medallist over 5,000 and 10,000 metres at the 1980 Olympics) and Ed Moses from the US (400 metres hurdles champion at the 1976 and 1984 Olympics, and undefeated for a record 122 consecutive races during his career). Another leading hurdler, Britain's Kriss Akabusi, deserves a special mention after laughing off the jibe from decathlete Daley Thompson on TV in 1996: 'That's not a forehead, it's a seven!'

Swimmers often remove all their body hair as well as the hair on their head so that they will slip through the water more easily. Duncan Goodhew had a natural advantage in this respect, though one can't help wondering whether there is something about the breaststroke which affects the follicles; fellow British swimmers David Wilkie and Adrian Moorhouse have both lost most of their hair since winning Olympic gold at this event.

In **cycling**, Bjarne Riis and the late Marco Pantani won the Tour de France in 1996 and 1998 – which may suggest that our old friend Professor Wheeler had a point after all. Cueballs in **snooker** have been skilfully struck by Willie Thorne and by Peter Ebdon, World Champion in 2002. Andre Agassi has demonstrated his overhead smash in **tennis** for some years.

Though naturally balding **boxers** are uncommon (one notable example being Sir Henry Cooper, who won three Lonsdale Belts during his career), head-shaving is popular in the sport. George Foreman enjoyed far greater popularity when he returned from retirement with a gleaming pate than he did in his dour, hirsute heyday in the 1970s. Fellow world heavyweight champion Evander Holyfield took the look a stage further by emerging almost earless from a contest with Mike Tyson. One of the first, and still most famous, head-shavers in boxing was world middleweight champion Marvelous Marvin Hagler, who once claimed that he cut off his hair because 'with four sisters about the house, I could never get my hands on a comb'. Yet his opponent Roberto Duran suggested that he may have had another intention in mind: 'Hagler uses his bald head as a third hand. I'm a far cleaner fighter.'

One would expect to see several bald heads in the worlds of **cricket** and **golf**, where participants play at a high level into their forties and beyond. Yet curiously, there are relatively few pates on parade. In the case of cricket, this may be partially explained by certain players acquiring and advertising hairpieces. Whereas old-timers like Brian Close were proud to display their helmet-hard heads, Graham Gooch and Greg Matthews were determined to field extra cover. Gooch offered the following poor explanation for his decision: 'If you get your front teeth knocked out, you don't leave a gap in your teeth, do you?' Still, at least he displayed a sense of humour about his new appearance; when he retired after scoring a century for Essex against the West Indies, the reason he gave was: 'My hair was hurting.'

In January 2002, Gooch went in to bat for his hair clinic after the ASA investigated a complaint that its advertising was misleading. To prove that his hairpiece could withstand all sorts of exertions, Gooch dived into a swimming pool, took a shower and even had two bikini-clad models stroking his scalp. (The bikinis were worn for strict scientific reasons, of course.) The hairpiece survived intact – but the ASA still ordered the clinic to amend its ads.

Virtually all professional golfers are hirsute – even Jerry Pate. One exception is John Daly, who shortly after winning the Open Championship in 1995 lived up to his 'Wild Thing' nickname by shaving his head. He said that some people had told him his hair was too short, others that it was too long – 'so I thought to hell with it, take the lot off'. Interestingly, Daly saw that head-shaving could be both an act of defiance and a punishment: 'My wife laughed when I told her I was a skinhead. If she gives me any flak about it, I'll shave her head as well.'

In any sphere of human activity you care to name, many of the people we look up to have little or no hair to look up to. If you were previously of the opinion that getting ahead with a bald head is impossible, you may stand corrected. More importantly, our line-up of luminaries should give heart to anyone anxious about losing their hair. Remember: receding is no bar to succeeding.

INTERLUDE VI
Bald Eagles and Hairless Mexicans

In fact he roared so loud that it loosened all the roots of his hair and tinkle tinkle all his lovely mane fell off, and landed on the ground 'PLIP-PLAP-PLOP' 200,000 times, one for every hair. Suddenly Mr Gronk the lion saw himself in the Daily Mirror and, oh! he saw that he was now bald! A Bald Lion? 'Oh dearie me, I'll be the laughing stock of the hyenas,' he said.

— Spike Milligan, *The Bald Twit Lion*

According to Pliny the Elder in his *Natural History*, 'Man alone of all creatures, groweth to be bald.' In fact, this is not the case. The very word 'alopecia' derives from a Greek word meaning 'fox-mange'. (Foxes are prone to losing their fur in patches, though it is also possible that the term refers to the way grass withers and dies in areas where they have urinated.) Curiously, a number of animals which one would expect from their names to be bald are not, while others universally thought of as hairy, furry or woolly are liable to lose their outer layer.

Birds

The bald eagle is a prime example of the former category; since its body is dark brown and its head is white, it appears bald from a distance, yet it is entirely covered with feathers. Similarly, the baldpate (a type of duck) and the proverbially bald coot only appear so because of white feathers on their heads.

There are some birds which do become bald. The male wattled starling of East Africa loses the feathers on its head as the breeding season approaches. Vultures also go bald, though feeding rather than breeding is responsible in their case; they lose the feathers on their heads through sticking them into dead carcasses. In addition, a previously unknown species of bald parrot was discovered in the Mato Grosso region of Brazil in 2002.

Sheep

In 1994, scientists discovered that almost half of the mature sheep in Western Australia were experiencing bald patches and a general thinning of their wool fibres. The condition was estimated to cost the national wool industry around 50 million Australian dollars a year. The explanation offered was somewhat surprising: 'It's stress-related. The same mechanism seems to affect women during pregnancy.' It seems that the ewes experienced stress while pregnant, and all of the sheep were affected at the end of the summer when food was scarce. Their bodies reacted by shutting down certain functions, such as the growing of wool, in order to conserve energy.

Sheep have also caused baldness in another species. In the early 1990s, researchers at Adelaide University transplanted a sheep gene into mice to see if they would become woolly. In the event, precisely the opposite happened. The hair became fragile, and the mice were left entirely bare.

Apes

The orang-utan and chimpanzee both experience some degree of baldness on reaching maturity, as does the stump-tailed macaque. The balding process in macaques works in exactly the same way as in humans; for this reason, macaques were used in early experiments using minoxidil. The treatment made their hair grow back – in fact, it worked far better on the macaques than on the men who later spent a fortune on it. (Which begs the question: who are the real monkeys here?)

Cats and Dogs

Among the animals acknowledged by Pliny to be born without hair are certain breeds of cat and dog. Hairless cats were kept by ancient civilisations such as the Aztecs, and they were being bred in New Mexico in the early twentieth century. Although these 'Mexican Hairless' cats later became extinct, another breed of hairless cat was developed in Ontario, Canada, during the 1960s. Called the Sphynx, it was bred from a hairless mutant of the American Shorthair. This type is now most popular with Dutch breeders, particularly those who are allergic to cat fur.

There are two recognised breeds of hairless dog: the Mexican Hairless and the Chinese Crested. (The Mexican Hairless is in fact not native to Mexico, and probably originated in the Orient.) Neither breed is entirely without hair; the Mexican Hairless has a tuft of coarse hair on its skull and a small amount on the lower half of its tail, while the Chinese Crested has some hair on its head, feet and tail. However, this is not enough to prevent other dogs from laughing at them in the manner of Muttley from *Wacky Races*.

Other breeds of dog may lose their hair, though this is rare and generally caused by illness. One case which became national news in Britain in 1993 involved a King Charles spaniel owned by a couple in Bristol. At the age of seven, the dog suddenly lost all its hair and looked like a plucked chicken. Local vets were baffled; vitamin supplements, a high-protein diet and a variety of skin creams all failed to have any effect. For some time, the only thing which helped was a coat made out of a fluffy car-seat cover by a friend of the owners, which at least made the poor pooch look as though it had fur. People from all over the country wrote to offer advice. Two years later – which indicates just how many suggestions were tried out – some success was finally reported. After a cream called Grass's Skin Cure had been applied for eight months, the spaniel grew new fur on its ears and lower back, and started to sprout light hairs over the rest of its body.

Incidentally, this dog was not the first to wear a hairpiece. Lassie wore one during film-making, though this was not to conceal baldness. Rather, it was to disguise the fact that Lassie was actually a Laddie.

CHAPTER TWELVE

Bald? Join the Club

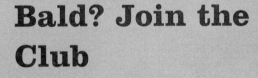

Eggheads of the world unite; you have nothing to lose but your yolks.
— Adlai Stevenson

It's not just birds of a feather that flock together. A number of clubs have been formed by the bald over the years, each one an attempt to assert their own worth in a world which often pokes fun at them.

Possibly the earliest club for those with little hair was the one mentioned in *The Times* in the spring of 1795: 'A club has been formed called the Crop Club, every member of which is obliged to have his head cropped for the purpose of evading the tax on powdered heads . . . the new crop is called the Bedford level.' The tax mentioned was a guinea a year – a considerable sum in those days. Why the severe haircut was known as the 'Bedford level' is unclear; it might have been more appropriate to look a few miles down the road from Bedford and call it the 'Baldock level'.

A century later, a Bald Head Club was formed in the New York Stock Exchange. It had 28 members initially, and 16 of these took part in a demonstration on the trading floor the day after the club was founded. At the head of the procession was a Mr William French, who usually wore a brown wig, but removed it on this occasion to reveal (in the words of the *New York Times*) 'a glossy surface of scalp, embossed at the neck and over each ear with patches of hair, about the size of half-dollar pieces'. As the procession moved around the floor, with the banner and Mr French's wig held high, the participants met with 'the accompaniment of cheers from the brokers and handclapping and other manifestations of approval from the spectators' gallery'.

A baldness club on a much more ambitious scale was founded in the US in around 1910. The Bald Head Club of America was set up in Litchfield City, Connecticut, by journalist John Rodemeyer. The stated aim of the club was 'to promote and foster a sentiment of

fraternity among those whose domes of thought protrude through and tower above the foliage that affords shade and adornment'. Not that a big shiny dome was an essential requirement for membership; a bald spot the size of a half-dollar was considered sufficient.

The club grew steadily, and its annual convention in 1921 was packed – indeed, an overflow room had to be opened at the venue – and a good deal of coverage in the press followed, including this from the *New York Times*:

> Although some Connecticut people thought they detected a
> display of Aurora Borealis, it was only the expansive
> refulgence diffused from the glistening domes of 350
> Connecticut lights, all members of the Bald Head Club of
> America . . . The group picture was taken with the setting sun
> gleaming on the hundreds of nude knobs.

The club continued to flourish, and hit the headlines again in 1926. The government announced a proposal to set up a hair research college which would study the causes of baldness and look for a cure. Rodemeyer strongly objected on the grounds that there is nothing wrong with baldness and that setting up the college would therefore be a waste of money. He publicly called on the Governor of Connecticut and the State Attorney to oppose the move; although the two were on opposite sides of the political divide, both were members of the Bald Head Club.

Many other clubs for the hairless sprouted up around the world in the second half of the twentieth century. In 1956, Italy's thousand-strong Bald-Headed Association gained international recognition when it bestowed honorary membership upon Dwight Eisenhower and Nikita Khrushchev. The association's motto was 'Bald-headed men of the world unite'; the aim of their gesture towards the two world leaders was evidently to put this slogan to the ultimate test.

The first 'world rally' of bald men (though only 50 participants were present) took place in the French seaside town of La Baule in May 1960. The assembled multitude discussed whether baldness hinders a professional career, and whether it is an obstacle to married bliss, before a panel of women chose a 'Mr Bald Head'. Despite the unpromising start, there is still an International Association of Bald-Headed Men based in France; their 1997 conference was held in Fontainebleau, where club president Henri Braye set the tone by asserting: 'It is a sign of intelligence and sex appeal. We are proud of our smooth pates.' (As distinct from their smooth pâtés.)

In Japan, there is an annual 'Bright Head Contest' – a beauty pageant for bald men.

In Poland in January 1995, the Bald People's Party embarked on a hunger strike to publicise their demands for greater representation in the highest levels of government. (They must have forgotten just how unpopular the bald Polish leader General Wojciech Jaruzelski had been.) Spokesman Witold Slusarski outlined the aims of the new party: 'The protesters want the new constitution to guarantee bald people top state posts. This includes naming people who once had hair to head the key foreign, defence and interior ministries.' A noble cause – but the effect of their hunger strike was somewhat diminished by their insistence on having a lunch break.

Britain has been home to at least three baldness clubs. The Wrockwardine Wood Bald-Headed Men's Club was formed in Shropshire in around 1960. Members proudly sported ties bearing the image of a gleaming, hairless pate, and the association was as quick to reject the idea of a cure as the Bald Head Club of America had been in 1926. When offered the chance in 1968 to try out a herbal remedy, the club secretary declared: 'It would destroy the spirit and atmosphere of our club, which we formed to help people lose their shyness about being bald.' A rival association started up in Staffordshire in the early 1970s, principally to provide the Shropshire club with some friendly competition.

In 1995, another club for the bald-headed was formed in Steyning, Sussex. Based at the Star Inn, the Bald-Headed Club of Great Britain has three categories of membership: baldies, wispies and wiggies. To qualify as a baldy – the most senior level – a broad, bare expanse of scalp skin is required. Wispies are those still at the thinning and receding stage, while wiggies are members with hair who cover their heads with bald wigs in order to join. (At one club dinner, a shortage of bald wigs prompted one member to improvise by pulling a condom over his head.) Women are allowed to join, though after a year there was only one female member; she claimed to be bald but refused to say where.

The BHC has its own distinctive handshake; members shake with one hand, and slap each other on the heads with the other. And

In an episode of *The Golden Girls* Blanche has a nightmare that she is stuck in a confined space with a crowd of bald men, and fears that this portends disaster. Then her nightmare comes true; she finds herself on a plane full of hairless men, and is convinced that they are going to crash. She is only calmed by her room-mate Dorothy, who points outs to her that the captain has switched off the 'No Bald Men' sign. As it turns out, the men are simply off to a reunion of baldies in the Bahamas.

as one might expect of an association based at a pub, there are special club drinks. As well as Bald-Headed Beaujolais, there is Bald-Headed Bitter – which comes without a frothy head. The only drink off-imits to members is the hair of the dog. The club has also raised considerable amounts of money for charity by such means as allowing youngsters to come and break eggs on their bald pates.

The United States remains, however, the home of the largest and most active bald organisations; it is still the land of the free from hair. Two major groups emerged during the final quarter of the twentieth century. By far the more militant of the two was the New York-based Bald Urban Liberation Brigade (or BULB), formed in 1991. Having informed the press of their intention to embark on 'a radical media campaign to wrest the toupees from the chrome domes of America's leading celebrities', BULB proceeded to stick up posters around the city, featuring alleged wig-wearers with the caption 'Absolutely Bald'. (These were inspired by the 'Absolutely Queer' posters pasted up by gay activists as part of an 'outing' campaign.) Among the group's victims were Ted Danson, Larry Hagman, John Wayne, William Shatner, Burt Reynolds, Charlton Heston, Paul Simon and Charles Bronson. Bronson was furious and threatened to sue if the allegation was not retracted.

Though BULB enjoyed a lot of media coverage at the time, the group soon receded into the background. They did not come close to rivalling the size, longevity or lasting impact of the Bald-Headed Men of America.

The BHMA was started in North Carolina in 1972 by John T. Capps III. He began to lose his hair at the age of 15, and had a fine head of skin by the time he applied for a sales job with a printing company. Though young and dynamic, he was turned down – and was told specifically that this was because he had no hair. Shocked by this, Capps set up the organisation to cultivate a sense of pride and dignity among the bald, to offer support to anyone feeling depressed or discriminated against on account of their hair loss, and to demonstrate that the bald can be just as lively and humorous – if not more so – than the hirsute.

From humble beginnings, the club has grown and grown – 'through lack of growth', as Capps himself has pointed out – and by the 1990s had more than 30,000 members in around 40 countries (including Mikhail Gorbachev, the only honorary member, who was sent his certificate during the 1987 summit talks with Ronald Reagan). Remarkably, this has been achieved without active recruitment; word of mouth and responses to press and TV features on the club have been responsible for the rise in numbers.

The BHMA is based in Morehead City, North Carolina – or as it is commonly dubbed,

'More Head, Less Hair City'. The city has done much to recognise the organisation; the street on which the club has its HQ was renamed Bald Drive, and the local chamber of commerce puts up 'Welcome Baldies' road signs when the club's annual convention is being held. In 1988, a company marketing a 'hair-restoring' lotion tried to muscle in on the convention by picketing outside the venue, but the counties controlling the land in question were quick to stop it.

Proof that the author has been certified

As soon as they join, new members are actively encouraged to be proud of their pates. Everyone receives a membership card, badge and certificate. A newsletter (*Chrome Dome*) is published from time to time, but by far the biggest event in the club's calendar is the annual convention.

This takes place on the second weekend of September in the 'Baldroom' of Morehead City's Holiday Inn. Although there are sessions during which members can discuss their experiences of being bald, and recount how they came to terms with having no hair, the emphasis here is firmly on fun. All manner of contests are arranged; there is a Bald-As-A-Golf-Ball golf tournament, and awards are presented to the smoothest, sexiest, tallest, shiniest, most kissable, most distinguished and best all-round bald heads. There are also prizes for the best bald look-alike and the most tanned bald head (the 'Solar Dome' award).

The merchandise on sale includes the usual mugs, T-shirts and sweatshirts, but there are also more unusual items such as brushes which come with cloth pads instead of bristles and combs designed in a large U-shape so that they touch only the fringes of hair at the sides of the head. There are a number of bumper stickers bearing club slogans, such as:

The BHMA is very big on pro-baldness slogans, you understand. Others include: 'Slick is sexy'; 'Skin is in'; 'If you haven't got it, flaunt it'; 'It's hard to be humble when you shine'; and 'The Lord is just, the Lord is fair. He gave some brains, the others hair.'

By making jokes at their own expanse, the members of the BHMA and the other baldness clubs display an immunity to the barbs of any would-be detractors and reveal a healthy, accepting attitude to life. They have encouraged self-respect irrespective of hair; they have proved that the unfurry need never feel inferior.

Or, to coin a new slogan which any of these organisations is welcome to adopt: 'The bald, as one, will never be outdone.'

INTERLUDE VII
Places to
Baldly Go . . .

Upon my life Sir Nevis I am piqu'd
That I have so far panted tugg'd and reek'd
To do an honour to your old bald pate
— John Keats

1	Baldock, Herts	8	Baldrine, Isle of Man
2	Baldersby, N. Yorks	9	Baldovie, Dundee
3	Balderton, Notts	10	Baldinnie, Fife
4	Balderston, Lancs	11	Baldernock,
5	Baldslow, E. Sussex		E. Dunbartonshire
6	Toot/Marsh Baldon, Oxon	12	River Balder, N. Yorks
7	Baldhu, Cornwall		

Rest of the World

Bald Head

13 Headland, Maine

14 Cape, W. Australia

15 Bald Head Island, N. Carolina
(*This would have been an ideal location for the Bald-Headed Men of America convention, but the developers of this upmarket resort turned their noses up at the idea. Snobs.*)

16 Bald Hills, suburb, Brisbane, Australia

17 Bald Hill Dam, Sheyenne River, North Dakota

Bald Mountain
18 Colorado
19 Idaho
20 Maine
21 New Brunswick, Canada

22 Bald Mountains, Appalachian range, Tennessee (*Includes peaks called Big Bald and Big Butt.*)

Baldy Mountain
23 Montana
24 Manitoba, Canada

25 Mount Baldy, Indiana

26 Baldo, Italy

27 Baldy Peak, Arizona

28 Bald Butte, Oregon

Bald Knob
29 Town, Arkansas
30 Village, Virginia
31 Hill, Missouri

32 Baldface Mountain, New York State

33 El Balde Village, San Luis province, Argentina

34 Baldur Village, Manitoba, Canada

35 Baldeo Town, Uttar Pradesh, India

36 Baldegg Village, Switzerland

37 Baldoon Locality, Ontario, Canada

38 Baldone Village, Latvia

39 Balder Oilfield, North Sea

And what locations can the hirsute claim as their own? Hairy Hill in Alberta, Canada.

CHAPTER THIRTEEN

The Last Strands

I knew t'would be a bald conclusion.
— William Shakespeare, *The Comedy of Errors*, II.ii.110

And now the end is near, and so we face the final parting. But before we go our separate ways, we should consider how the future looks to the bald. And more importantly, how the bald should look to the future.

Pharmaceuticals companies are currently investing millions of pounds, if not billions, in the search for a truly effective and safe cure for baldness. Though the companies are careful not to let slip any important information to their rivals (which, paradoxically, may be delaying the ultimate breakthrough), it appears that three broad paths are being explored.

1) Altering Chrome Dome Chromosomes

Genetic engineering is one possible route to roots which do not wither and die. Since one's inherited genetic make-up determines whether or not hair follicles are turned off by dihydrotestosterone, it follows that if susceptible follicles could be genetically altered in some way, they could be made immune to the hormone's effects.

Considerable progress has been made in this direction. In 1995, Doctors Robert Hoffman and Lingna Li of AntiCancer Inc. in San Diego, California reported in *Nature Medicine* that they had found a method to deliver genetic material to hair follicles. Microscopic particles of fat called liposomes are used to envelop the genetic material. When the liposomes are applied to the hair follicles, the fat is absorbed and the genes are deposited inside.

To prove that this works, Hoffman and Li loaded liposomes with melanin (the dark pigment found in skin and hair) and applied the cream to white mice. The hair of the mice was turned dark from the roots up, and there were no side-effects or spillovers into the bloodstream. The skin did not change colour; only the follicles were affected. This success was followed up by experiments to see whether an easily detectable marker gene could be carried to the follicles of the mice – again, the liposomes duly delivered.

While the discovery of this delivery method (the DHL of DNA, if you like) was a great breakthrough, the small matter of finding the right genetic cargo remains outstanding. But there have been some significant developments in the search:

In 1995, a team of researchers at Bradford University managed to isolate regulatory cells from 'balding' hair follicles and grow a culture of them in a test tube. This had previously been achieved only with cells from 'non-balding' follicles. By comparing the two types of cell, the scientists hoped to pinpoint the crucial genetic difference between them – and consequently, to find the gene which ensures resistance to the effects of dihydrotestosterone.

In the June 1995 issue of *Nature Genetics*, Dr Pragna Patel from the Baylor College of

On the Fringes

In November 1999, another possible road to re-covering one's head came to light. The magazine *Nature* reported on the work of Dr Colin Jahoda of Durham University, who had demonstrated that hair follicles from one person could be transplanted successfully on to another person.

Dr Jahoda used his wife as a guinea pig in his experiment, though without giving her the hairy appearance of a guinea pig; he settled for removing a small piece of his scalp and placing it on a wound on her arm. After just a few weeks, new hair of a different colour, length and thickness to that of his wife was sprouting where the transplant had taken place.

Usually, the body's immune system rejects foreign tissue, but hair follicles seem to enjoy a special 'immuno-privileged' status which makes them resistant to rejection. And their special powers do not end there; Dr Jahoda's donor cells interacted with the surrounding skin tissue on his wife's arm, converting those cells into new hair follicles.

Yet while the principle of the procedure has been established, the day when it will be possible to regain a full head of hair by this method is still a long way off. Apart from any other considerations, finding willing hair donors is likely to prove near-impossible – unless the desperately cash-strapped could be persuaded to flog off their follicles instead of their kidneys in future.

Medicine in Houston, Texas, reported on a gene which has caused members of a large Mexican family to grow thick, dark hair everywhere over their faces except on their lips and eyes. (The condition, which causes those affected to be called werewolves, is known as congenital generalised hypertrichosis.) Again, it was hoped that by pinpointing and studying the gene responsible, important clues leading to a treatment for baldness might be uncovered.

In January 1998, the journal *Science* reported on the discovery of a specific gene responsible for hair loss. Scientists studying a village in Pakistan where alopecia universalis (the loss of all facial and body hair) is common managed to identify the gene by comparing the chromosomes of affected individuals with those of specially bred hairless laboratory mice. A mutation in a particular section of DNA was found to be present in both groups.

Most promisingly, researchers at the Max Planck Institute for Immune Biology in Freiburg, Germany, claimed in December 2000 that they had managed both to identify and manipulate the gene which determines hair growth. They created a cream which made mice go bald where it was applied, and it was predicted that a DNA shampoo could soon be developed to enable users to keep their hair. Not that the prospect of such a product pleased everyone. A spokesperson for Greenpeace Germany expressed concern about the shampoo finding its way into drinking water: 'Will we end up with hairy fish or will people get hairy tongues?'

2) A Way to Stymie the Enzymes

The second possibility is that a more effective method will be found to block the enzymes in the body which convert testosterone to dihydrotestosterone. (If DHT is not produced, it follows that the genetically susceptible hair follicles cannot be switched off.) It is thought that finasteride may work in this way. However, in view of the potential side-effects of finasteride (impotence and reduced sex drive, as if you'd forgotten), the public will need a good deal of reassurance that any new super enzyme-blocker is completely safe before using it.

3) The Grow-Between

Creating new follicles on the scalp to grow new hair is an idea which has only recently been considered, but this is now the third major branch of research into potential baldness remedies. In November 1998, the journal *Cell* announced that biologists at the University of Chicago had succeeded in inducing the formation of new follicles in adult skin cells – something which usually only happens when the body is an embryo in the womb.

The researchers discovered that a molecule called beta-catenin acts as a signal which instructs cells to become hair follicles. In an experiment using mice that had been genetically engineered to produce large amounts of beta-catenin in the skin throughout their adult life, the team was able to stimulate the formation of new follicles in the spaces between existing follicles to create a breed of unusually hairy rodents. Some mice even grew three strands of hair from a follicle instead of one.

Sun, November 1998

Although the researchers stressed that they had not yet found a cure for baldness, they were sure that their discovery represented a great step forward. It is conceivable that a chemical could one day be rubbed into human skin to stimulate the production of beta-catenin and, in turn, the formation of new hair follicles. Other applications are possible too; for example, sheep could be made to grow thicker wool.

There is much more research to be carried out first, however – not least because certain unfortunate side-effects of beta-catenin are already evident. For one thing, the feet of the mega-hairy mice grew considerably larger than usual. Rather more worrying is that the mice developed skin tumours, probably because the supply of beta-catenin was never-ending. The Chicago scientists acknowledged the problem, but suggested that it may be possible to find a way to produce the molecule in the body until new follicles are established and then halt production.

The enormous sums of money being ploughed into the various fields of research may seem ludicrous, even obscene, given that the intended result is purely cosmetic. One might understandably take the view that these billions would be much better spent on seeking a cure for cancer or Aids. Yet the companies involved are not entirely to blame for this state of affairs. They would not be investing so heavily in the race for an effective baldness remedy were there not millions of people prepared to spend a fortune to buy one. The vanity and insecurity of these individuals may therefore be held ultimately responsible for this (mis)use of money, time and expertise.

If, even after all of this book's celebrations of baldness, you are still concerned about losing your hair, one of the slogans of the Bald-Headed Men of America may prove instructive at this point: 'What's in your head is more important than what's on top.' This slogan was intended by the BHMA simply to mean that brains matter more than hair – but if we interpret 'what's in your head' as 'your mental attitude towards baldness', the message is just as valid. By resolving to be less anxious or fearful, you render all remedies redundant. To borrow another BHMA saying, coming to terms with baldness is a case of mind over matter; if you don't mind, it doesn't matter.

Admittedly, being carefree about being hair-free is not easy for everyone. A lack of confidence and a poor self-image can take a lot of effort to correct. But the effort is always worthwhile. It is not just that you will save money on chemicals or carpet for your head; once you can accept your baldness, you will be a stronger person all round. You could start by asking yourself why you are upset about becoming bald. Is it because you think that other people are looking at your shining head in a negative light? If so, does this fear have any foundation in reality, or is it purely imaginary? Despite the odd joke and jibe, most people do not actually care about whether others have hair or not. And if it is genuinely the case that others look down on your thinning hair, doesn't that simply show how shallow they are?

Or look at it this way: are there not much more important things in life to wrinkle your expanding forehead about? Just as it seems ludicrous for pharmaceuticals companies to spend billions on finding a way to retain strings of dead cells on the scalp when so many life-threatening conditions require cures, it is folly to fret about your follicles when you could be concerning yourself with matters of far greater consequence. If the state of the world seems too daunting to tackle, your career and your relationships with those around you are

The Bald Bishop

Bishop Synesius concluded his treatise by declaring:

that baldnesse is excellent, that it is
heavenlie, that it is the end of Nature, that
it is the thing whereby we attaine
heavenlie wisedome, and that it purchaseth
to them which have it, the possession of
innumerable benefits, as well of the bodie
as of the minde.

Those with an abundance of hair should do the decent thing:

Let them notwithstanding, that are mossie
headed learne this lesson: that if they
meane to be sober, honest and prudent, the
next way for them so to be, is often to be
shorne and shaven. And let them
furthermore esteeme such happie and
fortunate, as neede not the edge of the
scissors or rasour.

It is an appropriate entreaty from a bishop; after all,
what person in charge of a flock does not want to see it
shorn regularly?

certainly more deserving of your attention than the loss of your locks. (Should you be
convinced that your career and your relationships are being adversely affected by the loss
of your hair, you should realise that it is your anxiety about the condition rather than the
condition itself which is causing the problems.) Bear in mind too that losing hair does not

compare with losing, say, an eye or a limb. It is not a contagious condition. And it is not as if your hair aches before falling out, like teeth usually do.

You should also consider the alternatives if you are not prepared to cultivate a more positive outlook. There are really only two other options open to you. You could try to cure or cover your loss by using one of the existing methods described earlier – but all of these come with drawbacks which you can mix and match from the following list: expensive; inconvenient; of limited effectiveness; painful; potentially harmful; liable to cause embarrassment by actively drawing attention to your insecurity and desperation. Otherwise, you could wait for the ultimate baldness cure to be discovered as a result of all the research currently being undertaken. But how long do you think that is likely to take? Even if the remedy were discovered tomorrow, it would take years of testing before it became readily available to the public. Are you prepared to be dissatisfied and anxious for that period of time? Moreover, if and when such a treatment does become available, you can be sure your new hair will cost an arm and a leg as the companies will need to earn back all they have invested.

The best way to adopt a more positive attitude is to take control of how your hair looks by having it cut very short. (If you are feeling really bold, you could shave your head completely; most people are likely to find a close crop a big enough step for starters.) By doing this, you are saying: 'I have chosen the way my hair looks; my lack of hair has not been imposed on me by nature, nor am I trying to cling to what I no longer have.' You demonstrate to others – and more importantly, to yourself – that you are strong and decisive. Besides, the close crop and the shaven head are now established 'looks'; cutting the hair off is the easiest way to create a fashionable style.

Eventually you may learn, like Sergeant Bilko, to wear that skin like a badge. You can use it to create an image of toughness – or as an erogenous zone, if you choose. Either way, by being open and honest about your baldness, you seize the initiative and assert your authority. You are in control.

You can further improve your self-image and the way you are perceived by working on your fitness and taking up a healthy diet. Isn't it better to spend money on your whole body at a gym than merely on the topmost tufts at the chemist's, wigmaker's or transplant clinic? Dressing well will also boost your confidence. And smile, for goodness' sake. Being cheerful will make you far more attractive and popular than having hair.

Don't worry, be slappy.

ACKNOWLEDGEMENTS

The author wishes to express his thanks to the following for their help in researching this book: the British Library; the British Library Newspaper Library in Colindale; the libraries of the London Boroughs of Barnet, Camden, Kensington and Chelsea and Westminster; Advertising Archives; John Mason of the Institute of Trichologists (Incorporated); Ian McCann for his help with the subject of baldness in reggae; John Capps III and Carl Bivens of the Bald-Headed Men of America.

Every effort has been made to contact the copyright holders of all material included in this book before publication. Any such individual or organisation who has not been traced or who has not responded is invited to contact the publisher in order to be fully credited in any subsequent edition.

Introduction

p. 4: 'For, such is the nature of wisdom . . .'
Abraham Fleming, Introduction to *A Paradoxe, proving by Reason and Example, that Baldnesse is much better than Bushie Haire, &c* (1579), a translation of *De Calvitii Encomium* by Bishop Synesius of Cyrene.

Chapter One: The Causes of Calvities

p. 5: '. . . radiation from ceiling panels may be a cause of baldness . . .'
Sir Leonard Hill, *Warming for Health and Comfort* (1938).

p. 6: '. . . many cases of baldness were caused by the absorption of lead, and of arsenic . . .'
New York Times, 12 September 1930.

p. 6: 'China's Disaster Reduction Press claimed that beards cause baldness . . .'
The Times, 18 May 1994.

p. 6: 'butcher-boys, valets and the lower classes of the Irish . . .'
Newsweek, 28 February 1983.

p. 7: 'The most liable of all seem to be those who indulge in excessive brain-work . . .'
G. R. Brandle, *A Treatise on Premature Baldness* (1897).

p. 7: '. . . although the skull and scalp stop growing after about 20 years . . .'
San Francisco Chronicle, 23 April 1978.

p. 8: 'The wasting of the brain which leads to baldness'
Hippocrates, *Epidemics*, Book VI, iii, 1.

p. 11: 'various over-seasoned foods and condiments . . .'
G. H. Wheeler, *An Abridged Lecture. . . on the Prevalent Disorders of the Hair, Causing Greyness and Baldness* (1899).

p. 12: 'Eye fatigue was put forward as a cause of baldness . . .'
New York Times, 22 November 1934.

p. 12: 'Robert Holton removed several dark hairs from his comb . . .'
Gore Vidal, *In a Yellow Wood* (E. P. Dutton and Co. Inc., 1947). Reproduced by kind permission of Time Warner Book Group UK. For the US, its dependencies, the Philippines and Canada: Reproduced with permission of Curtis Brown Group Ltd, London on behalf of Gore Vidal. Copyright © Gore Vidal 1947.

p. 14: 'the fashion for shingled hair . . . would have dire consequences'
New York Times, 25 March 1927.

p. 14: '. . . shingling would cause women to grow moustaches and beards'
New York Times, 27 March 1927.

p. 14: 'Sikh boys twisting their uncut hair tightly on the top of the head . . .'
Disorders of Hair Growth: Diagnosis and Treatment (McGraw-Hill, 1994), ed. Elise A. Olsen.

p. 14: 'Afro-Caribbean styles featuring tight braiding . . .'
ibid.

p. 14: 'The Afro itself may damage the hair . . .'
Los Angeles Times, 22 June 1972.

p. 15: '. . . poor blood supply can hardly be the principal factor behind baldness . . .'
W. Montagna and K. S. Carlisle, Considerations on Hair Research and Hair Growth (Springer-Verlag, 1981).

p. 16: 'In my own experience, psychological trauma . . .'
Ian Martin-Scott, Baldness and the Care of the Hair (W. & G. Foyle Ltd, 1966).

p. 17: 'Joseph Smietana was a one-man baldness plague . . .'
Chicago Tribune, 4 March 1981.

p. 18: '. . . baldness resulted from the muscular contractions caused by having a chuckle . . .'
Gilles Lambert, The Conquest of Baldness (Souvenir Press, 1961).

p. 20: 'This matter of baldness . . .'
Winfield Townley Scott, 'Baldness and the Swan', To Marry Strangers (Thomas Y. Crowell Co., 1945).

p. 20: 'Solti was once labelled "the screaming skull" . . .'
Independent, 25 November 1985.

p. 20: 'Anyone who hasn't read Cortázar is doomed . . .'
Pablo Neruda, quoted in Guardian, 18 July 1998.

p. 22: '. . . believed to be caused by the chemical element thallium . . .'
Chicago Tribune, 17 November 1988.

p. 22: 'This Serpent is extreamly cold . . .'
Jonathan Swift, 'The Description of a Salamander' (1705).

p. 23: 'the shock of an explosion at a nearby chemical plant . . .'
San Francisco Chronicle, 23 May 1980.

p. 24: '. . . lost every hair on his body following a 200-foot bungee jump . . .'
Sun, 9 August 1994.

p. 24: 'The cause of this condition is a lack of hot fluid . . .'
Aristotle, The Generation of Animals, V.iii.

p. 25: 'Those who are bald become this way because they have a phlegmatic constitution . . .'
Author unknown, The Nature of the Child (Hippocratic Corpus).

p. 25: '. . . prolonged exposure to the sun's rays was a prominent factor in hair loss . . .'
New York Times, 25 December 1910.

p. 26: 'It takes the hair right off your bean'
Graham Lee Hemminger, 'Tobacco', Penn State Froth (1915).

p. 26: 'Trichotillomania . . . Estimates of the number of female sufferers in the United States have been as high as eight million'
Sunday Times, 8 October 1989.

p. 27: 'By's beard the Goat, by his bush-tail the Fox . . .'
John Davies of Hereford, 'On Kate's Baldness', ed. Geoffrey Grigson, The Faber Book of Epigrams and Epitaphs (Faber and Faber, 1977).

p. 28: 'Oh, if some Nymph of Drury's artful Race . . .'
Ellis Pratt, 'The Art of Dressing the Hair' in J. Stevens Cox, Illustrated Dictionary of Hairdressing and Wigmaking, (Batsford Academic and Educational, 1984).

p. 28: 'The Falklands thing was a fight between two bald men over a comb'
Jorge Luis Borges, Time, 14 February 1983.

p. 29: 'Hair loss was also commoner after the war . . .'
Martin-Scott, Baldness and the Care of the Hair.

p. 30: '. . . an experiment carried out at the Winfield State Mental Hospital'
San Francisco Chronicle, 4 October 1992.

p. 30: '5-alpha-reductase converts the testosterone to dihydrotestosterone'
Montagna and Carlisle, Considerations on Hair Research and Hair Growth.

Chapter Two: Cures for Coots

p. 31: 'the ashes of an ass pizzle . . .'
Pliny the Elder, Natural History, Book 28.

p. 32: 'Ebers papyrus . . .'
Luigi Giacometti Ph.D., Archives of Dermatology Vol. 95 (1967); William P. Taylor, Bald Is Beautiful (Macmillan, 1983).

p. 33: 'berries of myrrh . . . cactus sap'
Lambert, The Conquest of Baldness.

p. 33: 'boxwood was a traditional English country remedy . . .'
Mary Chamberlain, Old Wives' Tales (Virago, 1981).

p. 33: 'Jean Adrien Helvetius listed the parts of the human body . . .'

p. 34: 'I have discovered an essential oil that will make the hair grow . . .'
Honoré de Balzac, César Birotteau (1838).

C. J. S. Thompson, *Magic and Healing* (Rider and Co., 1947). Used by permission of The Random House Group Limited.

p. 34: 'The virtues of southernwood . . .'
G. L. Gomme, *Popular Superstitions* (1884).

p. 35: 'Willow twigs were often used during the Middle Ages'
The Times, 18 November 1974.

p. 35: 'Grapefruit juice and alum were suggested by John Capps III'
Washington Post, 21 July 1983.

p. 35: 'Bear's grease was still common in the late nineteenth century . . .'
Cox, *Illustrated Dictionary of Hairdressing and Wigmaking*.

p. 36: 'To wash with dog's piss . . .'
John Moncrief of Tippermalluch, *The Poor Man's Physician* (1731).

p. 36: 'It was reported in 1989 that a Swiss farmer called Gerhardt Flit . . .'
San Francisco Chronicle, 26 February 1989; Richard Sandomir, *Bald Like Me: The Adventures of Baldman* (Collier Books, 1990).

p. 36: 'Cow licks were touted as a cure for baldness'
The Times, 15 December 1986.

p. 36: 'Beef marrow was often melted and applied to the scalp in the Victorian era . . .'
Daily Telegraph, 19 August 1983; Karen Thesen, *Country Remedies from Pantry, Field and Garden* (Pierrot Publishing Ltd, 1979).

p. 37: 'Donkey's teeth, ground down and boiled in oil . . .'
Sandomir, *Bald Like Me*.

p. 37: 'The Rawlinson manuscript in the Bodleian Library . . .'
Notes and Queries, Series II, Volume II (1915).

p. 37: 'I have prescribed Humagsolan in a good many cases . . .'
Franz Nagelschmidt, *The Loss of Hair and Its Treatment by Light* (Sollux Publishing Co., 1926).

p. 37: 'the boiled flesh of a mole was commonly rubbed on the scalp'
Wayland D. Hand, *American Folk Medicine* (University of California Press, 1976).

p. 37: 'mole's blood was seen as a cure . . .'
ibid.

p. 37: 'translated from the *Lilium Medicinae* . . .'
Thompson, *Magic and Healing*.

p. 37: 'The person making it up must fill a jar . . .'
Patrick Logan, *Irish Country Cures* (Appletree Press, 1981). Reproduced by permission of Appletree Press.

p. 37: 'Pigeon poo was used by the Egyptians and by Hippocrates . . .'
Cox, *Illustrated Dictionary of Hairdressing and Wigmaking*.

p. 38: 'a pomade of goose droppings'
Lambert, *The Conquest of Baldness*.

p. 38: 'poultices made of chicken manure'
Chamberlain, *Old Wives' Ta....*

p. 38: 'Python fat has been applied to the head'
San Francisco Chronicle, 26 February 1989.

p. 38: 'Have you ever seen a bald sheep?'
Taylor, *Bald Is Beautiful*.

p. 38: 'Dr B. Norman Bengtson of Chicago claimed to have grown new hair'
New York Times, 4 November 1931.

p. 38: 'Spider's webs have been tried'
Sandomir, *Bald Like Me*.

p. 38: 'Friedrich-Christian Lesser suggested in his *Théologie des Insectes* of 1742 . . .'
Philip Ward, *Dictionary of Common Fallacies*, (Oleander Press, 1978).

p. 38: 'Magnified one thousand times, the insect . . .'
Robert Graves, 'The Blue-Fly', *Complete Poems* (Carcanet Press, 2000). Reproduced by permission of Carcanet Press Limited. Poem first published in *Poems 1953* (Cassell and Co.).

p. 38: 'Mr Pil Chun of Tewksbury, Massachusetts, patented a method of acupuncture . . .'
New York Times, 31 July 1995.

p. 39: '"Capsuloids", a treatment common in the early 1900s . . .'
British Medical Association, *Secret Remedies* (1909).

p. 39: 'Earwax'
San Francisco Chronicle, 26 February 1989.

p. 39: 'Placenta extracts formed part of a preparation . . .'
Montreal Gazette, 29 March 1988.

p. 39: 'Human urine is poured into the bladder of a goat . . .'
Logan, *Irish Country Cures*.

p. 40: 'To promote the growth of a boy's hair . . .'
Sir James George Frazer, 'The Magic Art and the Evolution of Kings', *The Golden Bough* (Macmillan, 1911). Reproduced by permission of the Master and Fellows of Trinity College, Cambridge.

p. 40: 'A technique called "popping" was practised by German-born Rita Hartinger . . .'
New York Times, 24 February 1968.

p. 40: 'lightning was said to have restored the hair of a 62-year-old man in Falmouth . . .'
Los Angeles Times, 5 July 1980.

p. 41: 'The mild electrical treatment that we use is pleasant . . .'
G. H. Wheeler, *An Abridged Inaugural Address on Modern Remedies for Baldness and Greyness* (1897).

p. 42: 'Lead-based remedies were common . . .'
Cox, *Illustrated Dictionary of Hairdressing and Wigmaking*.

p. 43: 'mustard gas promoted hair growth . . .'
Muriel MacFarlane, *A Complete Guide to Growing New Hair* (Cornell, 1993).

p. 43: 'Ammonia was an important constituent . . .'
Cox, *Illustrated Dictionary of Hairdressing and Wigmaking*.

p. 43: 'Turpentine formed part of a remedy . . .'
New York Times, 3 November 1901.

p. 43: 'Radioactive paint was mentioned as a treatment . . .'
Martin-Scott, *Baldness and the Care of the Hair*.

p. 43: 'Tying arteries in the temples . . .'
Le Devoir, 21 August 1984; *Montreal Gazette*, 18 April 1987.

p. 43: 'Massaging the scalp . . .'
Wheeler, *Abridged Inaugural Address*.

p. 43: 'Hair Today, for example, was a herbal shampoo . . .'
San Francisco Chronicle, 14 July 1983.

p. 43: '. . . products which "have quite taken the place of the old-fashioned shampoo" . . .'
Wheeler, *Abridged Inaugural Address*.

p. 44: 'mix five drops of essential oil of sage . . .'
Reader's Digest Family Guide to Alternative Medicine (1991).

p. 44: 'Magnetic insoles have also been proposed . . .'
D. J. Drabble, *Baldness and Hair Care* (Roberts Publications, 1980).

p. 45: 'the Frenchman Emile Coué visited New York . . .'
New York Times, 15 January 1924.

p. 46: 'a hair-growing competition in 1995 . . .'
Independent, 13 April 1996.

p. 46: 'Vodka-based treatments . . .'
New Orleans Times-Picayune, 11 May 1982.

p. 46: 'George De Leon, a researcher in New York . . .'
Sunday Times, 2 October 1977.

p. 47: 'Professor Nathan Zuntz asserted in 1920 . . .'
New York Times, 11 February 1920.

p. 47: '. . . trend in the north of England for smearing Marmite on the head'
Mirror, 29 March 1995; *Take a Break*, May 1995.

p. 47: '. . . experienced some regrowth on his bald spot after rubbing curry into his scalp'
Independent, 10 April 1996.

p. 47: 'rub the scalp with a clean cloth, raw onions or fig leaves until it grows flushed'
Lambert, *The Conquest of Baldness*.

p. 47: 'cold Indian tea and fresh lemon juice were applied . . .'
San Francisco Chronicle, 4 October 1992.

p. 48: 'Andras Banfi announced in 1979 that he had invented a miracle hair restorer . . .'
New York Times, 27 April 1980.

p.48: 'Around ten years later, Beijing was going mad . . .'
New York Times, 26 January 1988; *Guardian* 20 October 1988

p. 49: '. . . this had to be done by a doctor who was dressed in black'
Frazer, 'The Magic Art', *The Golden Bough*. Reproduced by permission of the Master and Fellows of Trinity College, Cambridge.

p. 50: 'A combination of arsenic and prayer was declared to be effective . . .'
National Observer, 19 October 1974.

p. 50: 'Frequent shaving . . . was recommended frequently'
New Statesman, 3 October 1969.

p. 50: 'Lichtmann's Improved Cap for Promoting the Growth of Hair'
Rodney Dale and Joan Gray, *Edwardian Inventions* (W. H. Allen, 1979).

p. 51: 'Eel fat was tried during the eighteenth century'
Cox, *Illustrated Dictionary of Hairdressing and Wigmaking*.

p. 51: 'One marketed in Japan came with the instruction . . .'
Sandomir, *Bald Like Me*.

p. 52: 'John Hartson signed up for a course of "advanced laser therapy"'
Independent, 7 October 1998.

p. 52: 'the female hormone oestrogen has been employed . . .'
San Francisco Chronicle, 14 July 1983.

Interlude I: 'I'm not bald . . .'

p. 55: '. . . I'm alive.'
Spongebob Squarepants. Reproduced by permission of MTV Networks International.

Chapter Three: Drugs, Plugs . . .

p. 55: 'Developed from a chemical extracted from rat's urine'
Independent, 2 March 1988.

p. 55: 'Jan R. AufderHeide offered the following explanation'
New York Times, 17 March 1987.

p. 56: 'After four months, 8 per cent of patients show good results . . .'
Times, 25 July 1991.

p. 56: 'as successful as a farmer pouring fertiliser on to a concrete yard'
The Times, 25 July 1991.

p. 58: 'The treatment involves considerable expense . . .'
Consumer's Digest, July/August 1993.

p. 58: '. . . it must be applied twice a day'
Los Angeles Times, 29 January 1988.

p. 58: 'It has to be used for four months'
Chicago Tribune, 30 January 1997.

p. 58: 'The chances . . . are very slim'
New Statesman, 3 February 1989, reporting the Lancet.

p. 58: 'Minoxidil seems to be effective . . .'
San Francisco Chronicle, 19 August 1988.

p. 58: 'a client of a hair clinic in New York was so furious . . .'
Sandomir, Bald Like Me.

p. 58: '. . . it tends to do so on the crown . . .'
Chicago Tribune, 30 January 1997.

p. 58: '. . . there is a possibility of side-effects'
Consumer's Digest, July/August 1993.

p. 59: '. . . it does not come cheap'
Guardian, 23 December 1997.

p. 59: '. . . you have to keep taking it for life'
Daily Mail, 13 January 1998.

p. 59: 'It takes around three months . . .'
ibid.

p. 59: 'Finasteride must not be used by women'
Guardian, 23 December 1997.

p. 59: 'It can lead to . . .'
ibid; Independent, 5 November 1997.

p. 59: 'One of the first methods of implanting hair in the scalp . . .'
Clive Anderson and Ian Brown, Patent Nonsense (Michael Joseph, 1994).

p. 61: '. . . took action against a California company called Medi-hair . . .'
Washington Post, 16 January 1971.

p. 61: 'the New York dermatologist Dr Norman Orentreich . . .'
Toronto Globe and Mail, 26 March 1988.

p. 61: 'policemen, construction workers and salesmen are keenest . . .'
Chicago Tribune, 24 May 1991.

p. 61: 'Elton John's transplants were carried out in Paris . . .'
San Francisco Chronicle, 27 October 1978.

p. 62: 'Francis Rossi of Status Quo . . .'
Independent, 15 March 2000.

p. 62: '. . . as is Gary Numan'
Guardian, 1 November 1997.

p. 62: 'Bobby Hull . . . spent $900 on transplants'
New York Times, 14 December 1971.

p. 62: 'this did not deter one man in France . . .'
Spectator, 3 November 1990.

p. 62: 'Senator William Proxmire of Wisconsin tried to cover up his new hair transplant . . .'
Chicago Tribune, 16 May 1972.

p. 63: 'a doctor fashioned a hairline in the shape of an inverted triangle . . .'
New Orleans Times-Picayune, 1 April 1973.

p. 63: 'The "flap operation", sometimes known as the "Juri flap" . . .'
Daily Telegraph, 2 July 1976.

p. 63: 'The Lamont method . . .'
Taylor, Bald Is Beautiful.

p. 63: 'the surgical removal of the bald spot . . .'
New York Times, 7 June 1984; 25 November 1992.

p. 64: 'Tom Jones admitted in 2003 that he had undergone a scalp reduction'
Mail on Sunday, 9 February 2003.

Chapter Four: . . . and Rugs

p. 65: 'This is on me . . .'
Alan Bennett, Prick up Your Ears: The Screenplay (Faber and Faber, 1987). Reproduced by permission of Faber and Faber Ltd.

p. 66: 'In ancient Egypt, wigs were status symbols . . .'
Desmond Morris, Bodywatching (Jonathan Cape, 1985).

p. 66: 'Since you cover your temples and the crown of your bald head with kidskin . . .'
Martial, Epigrams, Book XII.

p. 66: 'Caligula is said to have worn a wig to disguise himself'
John Woodforde, The Strange Story of False Hair (Routledge and Kegan Paul, 1971).

p. 66: '. . . sometimes sewing bunches of hair to the brim of their hats'
ibid.

p. 66: 'a group of wigmakers marched through the centre of London'
ibid.

p. 67: 'There was an old person of Brigg'
Edward Lear, *More Nonsense* (1872)

p. 67: 'the secret of then-young singer Tony Bennett . . .'
Sandomir, *Bald Like Me*.

p. 67: 'those selling 'Crown Toppers' in the 1960s . . .'
Sunday Times Magazine, 19 November 1967.

p. 67: 'Woolworth's started selling wigs from just £2 each'
Woodforde, *The Strange Story of False Hair*.

p. 67: 'two armed robbers held up a wig shop in Manhattan'
New York Times, 22 April 1974.

p. 67: 'There was an old person of Dutton'
Edward Lear, *A Book of Nonsense* (1846)

p. 68: '. . . to owe more than $100,000 to a Los Angeles wigmaker'
People, 15 December 1996.

p. 68: '. . . so desperate for a part in the film *Striptease* . . .'
Independent, 16 January 1998.

p. 68: 'Can't act. Slightly bald. Can dance a little.'
ed. Colin Jarman, *Guinness Dictionary of Poisonous Quotes* (Guinness Publishing, 1991).

p. 68: 'Frank Sinatra was once said to have employed a man . . .'
New York Times, 19 June 1967.

p. 68: 'Lorne Greene . . . took five or six silvery pieces'
ibid.

p. 69: 'Now I wear a wig, but I introduced it gradually . . .'
John Nettles, *Nudity in a Public Place* (Robson Books, 1991). Reproduced by permission of Robson Books, an imprint of Chrysalis Books Group Plc.

p. 69: 'Marlon Brando on Frank Sinatra'
Daily Mail, 30 March 1977.

p. 69: 'Sean Connery differs from most wig-wearing actors . . .'
Michael Freedland, *Sean Connery: A Biography* (Weidenfeld and Nicolson, 1994).

p. 70: 'The jazz drummer Lenny Hastings used to wear one . . .'
The Times, 26 September 1983.

p. 70: 'the true appearance of later-disgraced pop singer Gary Glitter . . .'
News of the World, October 1993.

p. 70: 'Charles Alfieri spoke publicly about famous wearers . . .'
Daily Telegraph, 10 July 1998.

p. 70: 'William Shatner, who as Captain Kirk in *Star Trek* refused to baldly go anywhere . . .'
ITV Teletext, 24 March 1995.

p. 71: 'George Burns was highly displeased when a newspaper columnist . . .'
ed. Clifton Fadiman, *Faber Book of Anecdotes* (Faber and Faber, 1985).

p. 71: 'Members of a Bruce Forsyth appreciation society . . .'
Sunday Mirror, 21 July 1996.

p. 71: 'By and by comes Chapman the periwig-maker . . .'
The Diary of Samuel Pepys, 3 November 1663.

p. 72: 'I have to tell you that I, too, have taken steps . . .'
Dad's Army, 'Keep Young and Beautiful'. Reproduced by kind permission of Jimmy Perry and David Croft.

p. 72: 'After dinner came my Perriwigg-maker . . .'
ibid., 13 November 1663.

p. 72: 'a man from Elgin, Morayshire, hit the headlines . . .'
Sun, March 1994.

p. 73: 'a New York realtor on holiday in Florida . . .'
Chicago Tribune, 24 May 1991.

p. 73: 'the Brooklyn supermarket owner whose wig was speared . . .'
New York Times, 19 June 1967.

p. 73: 'a judge attending an assizes service in Oxford . . .'
James Derriman, *The Pageantry of the Law* (Eyre and Spottiswoode, 1955).

p. 74: 'Frederick the Great's wig fell off . . .'
Woodforde, *The Strange Story of False Hair*.

p. 74: 'A syrup-sporting non-league footballer . . .'
Radio Five Live, 11 January 1997.

p. 74: 'railway authorities in Kent put up posters in stations . . .'
Daily Star, 2 December 1997.

p. 74: 'the management at Blackpool Pleasure Beach had issued a similar warning . . .'
Sun, 1 June 1994.

p. 75: 'By this time in his career Frankie Howerd's hair . . .'
Barry Took, *Star Turns: The Life and Times of Benny Hill and Frankie Howerd* (Weidenfeld and Nicolson, 1992). Reproduced by permission of Weidenfeld and Nicolson, a division of The Orion Publishing Group.

p. 75: '. . . pioneered in 1992 by cosmetic surgeon Anthony Pignataro . . .'
Washington Post, 1 September 1995.

p. 76: 'two of Sean Connery's wigs – each costing around £800 . . .'
Sun, 18 August 1992.

p. 76: 'the chairman of a leading football club . . .'
www.bbc.co.uk/scotland/sportscotland/offtheball

p. 76: 'a "rug war" broke out between DJs . . .'
Chicago Tribune, 26 June 1990.

p. 77: 'a hawk at a falconry display in Devon . . .'
Sun, 27 August 1992.

p. 77: 'a barn owl at the Gentleshaw Wildlife Sanctuary . . .'
Sun, 14 March 1994.

p. 77: 'it was reported that a snowy owl had performed the same trick . . .'
news.bbc.co.uk, 4 February 2003.

p. 77: 'The victim of the most famous wig theft . . .'
Fred Laurence Guiles, *Loner at the Ball*, (Bantam Press, 1989).

p. 77: 'The legendary newsreader Reginald Bosanquet once lost his rug . . .'
Nigel Rees, *Guinness Book of Humorous Anecdotes* (Guinness, 1994).

p. 77: 'A burglar in Basingstoke lost his hairpiece . . .'
Woodforde, *The Strange Story of False Hair*.

p. 77: 'In the case of a Chicago salesman, it caused the misdemeanour . . .'
Chicago Tribune, 27 December 1968.

p. 78: 'a man from Abbeville in France bought a new wig . . .'
Daily Record, 2 January 1992.

p. 78: 'Clement of Alexandria declared in the first century . . .'
Woodforde, *The Strange Story of False Hair*.

p. 78: 'the writer Tertullian was vehement in his condemnation . . .'
ibid.

p. 78: 'the Council of Constantinople excommunicated a number of Christians . . .'
ibid.

p. 78: 'the Bishop of Toul in France was warning that the fashion was unchristian . . .'
ibid.

p. 78: 'Look, once I've done the midday bulletin . . .'
Extract from *Drop The Dead Donkey* written by Andy Hamilton and Guy Jenkin, a Hat Trick Production for Channel 4 Television. Permission courtesy of Channel 4, Hat Trick Productions, Andy Hamilton and Guy Jenkin.

p. 79: 'Ray Milland came out as a proud pilgarlic . . .'
Sunday Times, 5 January 1975.

p. 79: 'The magician Paul Daniels used to sport . . .'
Daily Mirror, 6 September 1983.

Interlude II: Proverbs for Pilgarics

p. 80: 'A hair on the head is worth two in the brush'
Oliver Herford, quoted in *The Successful Toastmaster*, ed. H.V. Prochnow and H.V. Prochnow Jr (Harper and Row 1966).

p. 80: Proverbs from Czech Republic, China, Congo, Tamil people, Estonia, Hindustan and Wales.
ed. S.G. Champion, *Racial Proverbs* (Routledge and Kegan Paul 1938).

p. 80: Proverbs from Latvia, Punjab, Suffolk, Khrushchev and Spain.
Cox, *Illustrated Dictionary of Hairdressing and Wigmaking*.

p. 80: Proverb from Scotland.
John Ray, *Proverbs: Scottish* (1678)

Chapter Five: Combovers and Other Covers

p. 82: '. . . Hair thin and thoughtfully distributed . . .'
J. M. Barrie, *The Little White Bird* (Hodder & Stoughton, 1902). Reproduced by permission of Great Ormond Street Hospital Children's Charity.

p. 83: 'I am firstly confident that I am being of practical service . . .'
Eric Oakley; *A Method of Disguising Your Male Baldness Using Your Own Hair from the Sides* (Sales Doctors Ltd, 1975).

p. 83: 'From both sides you gather up your scanty hair . . .'
Martial, *Epigrams*, Book X.

p. 86: 'I will not grow the hair above my ear . . .'
Bill Zavatsky, 'Bald', published in *American Poetry since 1970: Update*, ed. Andrei Codrescu (Four Walls, Eight Windows, 1989). Copyright © 2005 by Bill Zavatsky. Used by permission of the author.

p. 88: 'I could observe in detail the Byzantine complexity of the coiffure . . .'
Nettles, *Nudity in a Public Place*.

p. 88: 'You use ointment to pretend you have hair . . .'
Martial, *Epigrams*, Book VI.

p. 89: 'This is paint, Frank . . .'
The Fabulous Baker Boys (1989). Courtesy of Granada International Media Limited for material from *The Fabulous Baker Boys* supplied for inclusion in this publication.

p. 89: 'What it signifies . . .'
Frank Johnson, *The Times*, 6/7 September 1983. © NI Syndication, London 1983.

p. 90: 'a 58-year-old Blackpool man had hair tattooed . . .'
Sun, 22 August 1992.

p. 92: 'a 55-year-old man was awarded compensation of £950 . . .'
Daily Mail, 6 May 1998.

Chapter Six: Getting Scalped

p. 93: 'Finot used the wonderful joke at the expense of Macassar Oil . . .'
Balzac, *César Birotteau*.

p. 94: 'an individual called Bartlett who operated in the late nineteenth century . . .'
Lambert, *The Conquest of Baldness*.

p. 94: 'Andrew Taylor Still, who declared in 1874 . . .'
Ward, *Dictionary of Common Fallacies*.

p. 94: 'it was left to assiduous investigators such as Arthur J. Cramp . . .'
James Harvey Young, *The Medical Messiahs* (Princeton University Press, 1967).

p. 95: 'the British Medical Association investigated the claims . . .'
Secret Remedies (BMA, 1909).

p. 97: 'a US congressional committee analysed preparations such as Hair-A-Gain . . .'
San Francisco Chronicle, 8 March 1992.

p. 97: 'the US Food and Drug Administration seized over 750,000 vitamin capsules . . .'
New York Times, 27 March 1962.

p. 97: 'Curtis Howe Springer of Ontario, California, was convicted on ten counts . . .'
New York Times, 19 July 1970.

p. 98: 'Virgil Ganyard and Maryland Nance Jr. of the National Hair and Scalp Clinic . . .'
Washington Post, 2 July 1975.

p. 98: ' . . . a herbal potion being promoted by 74-year-old Ma Evans from Australia . . .'
San Francisco Chronicle, 19 July 1979.

p. 98: 'Bob Murphy of Reno, Nevada, was accused by the US Postal Service . . .'
San Francisco Chronicle, 8 March 1992.

p. 99: ' . . . an elusive multimillionaire called Glenn Braswell . . .'
San Francisco Chronicle, 14 July 1983.

p. 99: 'a Chicago clinic was charged by the local State Attorney's Office . . .'
Chicago Tribune, 28 July 1992.

p. 99: 'a man was found guilty at Middlesex Guildhall Crown Court . . .'
Independent, 2 February 1994.

p. 100: ' . . . complaints about hair-loss treatments were on the increase'
Independent, 10 April 1996.

p. 100: 'the High Court forbade Quest Hair Research from publishing advertisements . . .'
Times, 17 January 1996.

p. 100: 'the ASA asked newspapers and magazines not to accept an ad . . .'
Minutes of Evidence to Select Committee on Health, House of Commons, 22 April 1999.

Interlude III: 'Oi, Spamhead!'

p. 101: 'I prepare myself to receive the litanies . . .'
Zavatsky, 'Bald'.

Chapter Seven: The Significance of Slapheadedness

p. 104: 'Perhaps you'd like to explain to me . . .'
Red Dwarf, Episode 34 ('Emohawk'). Reproduced by kind permission of Rob Grant and Doug Naylor.

p. 106: 'a Fijian chieftain used to take the precaution . . .'
New York Times, 4 January 1959.

p. 106: 'Alexander the Great ordered his whole army to have their hair cropped . . .'
Charles Mackay, *Extraordinary Popular Delusions and the Madness of Crowds* (1852).

p. 106: 'Native American warriors used to leave . . .'
ibid.

p. 106: 'If I were fierce and bald and short of breath . . .'
Siegfried Sassoon, 'Base Details', *Counter-Attack and Other Poems* (William Heinemann, 1918). Copyright Siegfried Sassoon by kind permission of George Sassoon. United States: 'Base Details' from *Collected Poems of Siegfried Sassoon* by Siegfried Sassoon, copyright 1918, 1920 by E. P. Dutton. Copyright 1936, 1946, 1947, 1948 by Siegfried Sassoon. Used by permission of Viking Penguin, a division of Penguin Group (USA) Inc.

p. 106: 'Dr E. William Rosenborg of the University of Tennessee . . .'
New Orleans Times-Picayune, 29 March 1981.

p. 107: ' . . . to show symbolically that they are no longer free to be courted'
Lambert, *The Conquest of Baldness*.

p. 107: 'a return to the newness and bare innocence of a baby . . .'
J.C. Cooper, *An Illustrated Encyclopedia of Traditional Symbols* (Thames and Hudson, 1978).

p. 107: ' . . . reflection of the sun'
ibid.

p. 107: 'the crown of thorns worn by Jesus . . .'
ibid.

p. 107: '. . . Krishna will use to pluck them up . . .'
ibid.

p. 107: 'Buddhists in Thailand similarly leave a tuft of hair . . .'
Michael Caine, *Not Many People Know That!* (Robson Books 1984).

p. 108: '. . . women as well as men shaved their heads at the front'
Taylor, *Bald is Beautiful.*

p. 108: 'Major Witton B. Persons and Captain Lawrence J. Carr . . .'
New York Times, 22 September 1938.

p. 108: 'Bald heads forgetful of their sins . . .'
W. B. Yeats, 'The Scholars', *The Wild Swans at Coole* (Macmillan, 1919). By permission of A. P. Watt Ltd on behalf of Michael B. Yeats.

p. 108: 'Learned we found him . . .'
Robert Browning, 'A Grammarian's Funeral', *Shortly After the Revival of Learning* (1855).

p. 109: 'A bald-headed man at the altar . . .'
ed. C.L. Daniels and Professor C.M. Stevans, *An Encyclopedia of Superstitions* (1903).

p. 110: 'In the seventeenth century, the Cavaliers considered the Roundheads . . .'
Mackay, *Extraordinary Popular Delusions and the Madness of Crowds.*

p. 111: 'It is foolish to tear out one's hair in grief . . .'
Cicero, *Tusculanum Disputationem*, Book III.

p. 111: 'every player in the Brazilian football team . . .'
Guardian, 13 December 1997.

p. 111: 'the entire US volleyball team wielded their razors . . .'
San Francisco Chronicle, 29 July 1992.

p. 111: 'the players of Polish football club LKS Lodz . . .'
Guardian, 12 August 1998.

p. 112: '. . . it was common for a jealous husband to shave his wife's head . . .'
MacFarlane, *A Complete Guide to Growing New Hair.*

p. 112: 'French women believed to have collaborated . . .'
Morris, *Bodywatching.*

p. 112: 'Julius Caesar ordered that prisoners from Gaul should be shorn'
Sandomir, *Bald Like Me.*

p. 113: 'football clubs in Bulgaria took to punishing poorly performing players . . .'
Guardian, 22 March 2003.

p. 113: 'a New York man sought similar redress from his hairdresser . . .'
Guardian, 23 October 1997.

p. 113: 'In some African tribes, such as the Masai and the Dinka . . .'
Morris, *Bodywatching.*

p. 113: 'In his 1991 biography . . .'
Dermott Hayes, *Sinead O'Connor: So Different* (Omnibus Press, 1991).

p. 113: 'I went on holiday to Greece . . .'
Hot Press, 4 December 1986. Reproduced by permission of www.hotpress.com

p. 114: 'A while back when these people from a record company . . .'
Melody Maker, November 1987. Reproduced courtesy of Melody Maker.

p. 114: 'People always ask me if I shaved my head to look aggressive . . .'
Q Magazine, March 1990 (Issue 42).

p. 114: 'Ms Weaver turned the storyline to her own advantage . . .'
Sun, 21 August 1992.

p. 115: 'the experience of 19-year-old Shannon Faulkner of Charleston . . .'
Washington Post, 2/11 August 1994.

p. 115: 'If Ligeia has as many years . . .'
Martial, *Epigrams*, Book XII.

p. 116: 'He was introduced to all the people . . .'
Ursula K. LeGuin, *The Dispossessed* (Victor Gollancz, 1974). Reproduced by permission of Victor Gollancz, a division of The Orion Publishing Group. For the US, its dependencies, the Philippines and Canada: Copyright © 1974 by Ursula K. LeGuin. Reproduced by permission of HarperCollins Publishers Inc.

p. 116: 'The operation of the mechanism of displacement upwards . . .'
Charles Berg, *The Unconscious Significance of Hair* (George Allen and Unwin, 1951).

p. 118: 'Hair itself has several sexual meanings . . .'
Ernest Jones, *On the Nightmare* (Hogarth Press, 1931). Reproduced by kind permission of Jackie Jones.

Chapter Eight: 10 Disadvantages of Depilation

p. 119: 'A ram had been trained by its owner to butt a discus . . .'
Fable from *Codex Bernensis.*

p. 120: 'a balding man was usually reckoned to be five years older . . .'
Thomas Cash, 'The Psychosocial Effects of Male Pattern Balding: Does Losing it mean "Losing it"?', *Hair Loss Journal*, 4 (2), 3-4 (1988).

p. 120: 'He looks about forty, as he is beginning to be bald . . .'
Lord Birkenhead, *Rudyard Kipling* (Weidenfeld and Nicolson, 1978).

p. 120: 'Dr David Przybyla of Denison University in Ohio announced the results . . .'
Atlanta Journal and Constitution, 12 September 1996.

p. 121: 'Julian Dicks claimed in February 1997 . . .'
Under the Moon, Channel 4 Television, 26 February 1997.

p. 122: 'a New York lawyer found that 70 per cent of his business fell off . . .'
New York Times, 27 May 1994.

p. 122: 'Our Maker designed the head . . .'
Plato, *Timaeus*, Section LXXVI.

p. 123: 'the Greek tragedian Aeschylus was killed by an eagle . . .'
ed. Fadiman, *Faber Book of Anecdotes*.

p. 123: 'the speed of hair loss on the crown, rather than the degree . . .'
American Journal of Epidemiology, November 1995.

p. 123: 'I don't advise a haircut, man . . .'
Withnail and I (1987). Extract from Bruce Robinson, *Withnail and I; and How to Get Ahead in Advertising* (Bloomsbury 1989). Reproduced by permission of Bloomsbury Publishing Plc.

p. 124: 'men with male pattern baldness are likely to develop higher cholesterol levels . . .'
New York Times, 31 May 1990.

p. 124: 'a nightclub in Newcastle-upon-Tyne turned away . . .'
Daily Mirror, 1995.

p. 124: 'a man was refused entry to the US . . .'
New York Times, 5 June 1921.

p. 125: 'Tis not that both my eyes are black . . .'
Sir Owen Seaman, 'The Penalties of Baldness', *In Cap and Bells* (1899).

p. 127: 'J. R. Planché was the butt of a joke made by journalist Theodore Hook'
S.A. Bent, *Familiar Short Sayings of Great Men* (1887).

p. 127: 'Groucho Marx was once refused entry . . .'
ed. Fadiman, *Faber Book of Anecdotes*.

p. 127: 'Mrs Patrick Campbell could be equally tactless . . .'
ibid.

p. 127: '. . . the Athenian philosopher Diogenes had a disagreement with a bald man . . .'
tr. Olivia and Robert Temple, *Aesop* (Penguin 1998).

p. 127: 'he invariably found hair in the soap at service stations . . .'
Los Angeles Times, 4 April 1983.

p. 128: 'a ticket seller at a theatre in Gdansk . . .'
New York Times, 1 February 1924

p. 128: 'I'd rather have fingers than toes . . .'
Gelett Burgess, 'On Digital Extremities', *Poems of Gelett Burgess* (1903).

p. 128: 'In August 1995, the *British Journal of Psychology* . . .'
Wells, P.A., Willmoth, T., & Russell, R.J.H (1995). 'Does fortune favour the bald? Psychological correlates of hair loss in males.' *British Journal of Psychology*, 86(3), 337-344.

p. 129: 'a 43-year-old civil servant from Hitchin in Hertfordshire . . .'
Times, 2 July 1993.

p. 129: 'a 17-year-old student at Leeds University poisoned himself with coal-gas . . .'
Times, 21 October 1958.

p. 129: 'A man in Cheshire committed burglary and assault . . .'
Nova, October 1975.

p. 129: 'a 31-year-old Yorkshireman accused of theft . . .'
ibid.

p. 130: 'a 25-year-old Londoner hijacked a lorry . . .'
Independent on Sunday, 18 September 1994.

p. 130: 'a West Midlands man was jailed for five and a half years . . .'
Sunday Mirror, 5 April 1998.

p. 130: 'the driver of a goods train . . .'
Nova, October 1975.

p. 130: 'And the pilot of a helicopter . . .'
Los Angeles Times, 14 September 1989.

Interlude IV: 'Slapping Back'

p. 132: 'American entertainer Steve Allen offered one suggestion . . .'
New York Times, 9 April 1967.

p. 133: 'In a *Roseanne* episode . . .'
Roseanne, Episode 702 ('The Homecoming')

p. 133: '. . . delivered by American playwright Marc Connelly . . .'
ed. Fadiman, *Faber Book of Anecdotes*.

Chapter Nine: 40 Advantages of Alopecia

p. 134: 'There's one thing about baldness: it's neat'
Don Herold, quoted in *Medical Quotes*, ed. John Daintith and Amanda Isaacs (Facts on File, 1989)

p. 135: 'I might never have made anything of my life . . .'
Duncan Goodhew, quoted in *Coping with Sudden Hair Loss*,

Elizabeth Steel (Thorsons, 1988). Reproduced by kind permission of Wendy Jones.

p. 136: 'There is more felicity on the far side of baldness . . .'
Logan Pearsall Smith, *Afterthoughts* (Constable and Co., 1931). Reproduced by kind permission of Constable & Robinson Ltd.

p. 136: 'Forty times over let Michaelmas pass . . .'
William Makepeace Thackeray, 'The Age of Wisdom', *Ballads* (c.1860).

p. 137: 'He had, in fact, an ancient, mildewed air . . .'
Oliver Wendell Holmes, 'Rip Van Winkle MD', *Medical Poems* (1893).

p. 138: 'I don't think a man that's a little bald looks bad . . .'
Giuseppe Cassieri, *La Cocuzza* (1960); tr. Raymond Rosenthal, *The Bald Man* (Martin Secker and Warburg, 1963).

p. 138: 'I can't answer for women . . . but I find him very attractive as a man's man'
Sean Connery, quoted on ITV Teletext, 4 May 1999.

p. 138: 'There are times when I think I'm absolutely beautiful . . .'
Marsha Daly, *Telly Savalas* (Sphere, 1975).

p. 139: 'George Foreman, who chose to remove all his hair in 1977 . . .'
New York Times, 5 May 1993.

p. 139: 'On the other hand, Tommy Lee . . .'
ibid.

p. 140: 'When Brendan Bracken became Minister of Information . . .'
Rees, *Guinness Book of Humorous Anecdotes*.

p. 140: 'Dr Arthur C. Curtis argued that hair was becoming less important . . .'
Guardian, 10 December 1966.

p. 140: 'a higher incidence of baldness indicates an evolutionary shift . . .'
Newsweek, 6 October 1997.

p. 141: 'It was a witty retort, for example, that King Archelaus . . .'
Plutarch, *De Garrulitate*, XIII.

p. 141: 'Now see here! I cut my own hair . . .'
Robert Frost, quoted in *The Successful Toastmaster*, ed. Prochnow and Prochnow.

p. 141: 'Bill Clinton was strongly criticised after he had a haircut . . .'
Atlanta Journal and Constitution, 26 May 1993.

p. 141: 'Former Conservative leader William Hague once remarked . . .'
BBC Ceefax, 13 July 1997.

p. 141: 'the poet Philip Larkin, in a letter . . .'
ed. Anthony Thwaite, *Selected Letters of Philip Larkin, 1940-85* (Faber and Faber, 1993). Reproduced by permission of Faber and Faber Ltd. US Rights: Excerpt from 24 March 1949 from *Selected Letters 1940-1985* by Philip Larkin. Copyright © 1992 The Estate of Philip Larkin. Reprinted by permission of Farrar, Straus and Giroux, LLC.

p. 143: 'after crashing his car near the harbour, a man in Shoreham, Sussex . . .'
Sun, 8 February 1995.

p. 142: 'A man from Allentown, Pennsylvania, had the honour of having a sandwich named after him . . .'
The Morning Call (Allentown, PA), 29 September 1984.

p. 143: 'A friend of Valsalva, Morgagni says . . .'
H. P. Truefitt, *New Views on Baldness* (1863).

p. 144: 'bald men are much less prone to cancer of the bronchus'
MacFarlane, *A Complete Guide to Growing New Hair*.

p. 144: 'In ancient Egypt, it was widely believed that shorn hair could be used . . .'
Giacometti, *Archives of Dermatology Vol. 95*.

p. 144: 'A man nicknamed "Jack the Snipper" . . .'
New York Times, 22 December 1911.

p. 145: 'American Senator William Proxmire . . . was once held up at gunpoint'
Chicago Tribune, 16 May 1972.

p. 145: 'In a letter of 1767, the Countess of Suffolk mentions a remark . . .'
Woodforde, *The Strange Story of False Hair*.

p. 146: 'William Hague again: "It makes life very simple . . ." '
ITV Teletext, 26 March 2001.

p. 146: 'Heineken refreshes the pates other beers cannot reach'
Campaign Poster Advertising Awards 1988.

p. 146: 'a man from Welling in Kent used his head to publicise his local snooker club . . .'
Sun, 12 April 1996.

p. 146: 'Republican Senator Jake Garn of Utah campaigned for election . . .'
Time, 13 January 1975.

p. 147: 'the hairless owner of a tyre-retreading business in Tega Cay . . .'
Los Angeles Times, 14 September 1989.

p. 147: 'The proprietor of a Miami lighting business . . .'
New Orleans Times-Picayune, 17 November 1985.

p. 147: 'The bald manufacturer of a hot barbecue sauce in Tallahassee . . .'
The Morning Call (Allentown, PA), 29 September 1984.

p. 147: 'The bare-pated owner of a commercial cleaning company . . .'
Sandomir, *Bald Like Me*.

p. 147: 'the owner of the Old Mill Inn in Basking Ridge, New Jersey . . .'
New York Times, 21 October 1987.

p. 147: 'a Houston sandwich shop called Neptune Subs . . .'
Ananova.com, 13 November 2000.

p. 147: 'the Houston Rockets basketball club offered free admission . . .'
USA Today, 8 March 1993.

p. 148: '. . . a pension in October 1891 for "loss of hair" . . .'
New York Times, 25 June 1893.

p. 148: 'an eleventh-century Pope decreed that all those with luxuriant locks . . .'
Mackay, *Extraordinary Popular Delusions and the Madness of Crowds*.

p. 148: 'St Anselm, Archbishop of Canterbury at around the same time . . .'
Woodforde, *The Strange Story of False Hair*.

p. 148: 'St Wulstan, Bishop of Worcester from 1062 to 1095, always carried a small knife . . .'
Mackay, *Extraordinary Popular Delusions and the Madness of Crowds*.

p. 149: 'Harvard College condemned long hair . . .'
New York Times, 9 April 1967.

p. 149: 'the military regime in Greece banned long hair . . .'
New York Times, 10 May 1967.

p. 149: 'police in Saigon seized long-haired youths . . .'
New York Times, 13 October 1970.

p. 149: 'Singapore began to refuse entry to men . . .'
New York Times, 14 September 1972.

p. 149: 'Kenya barred visitors with long hair . . .'
New York Times, 12 March 1972.

p. 149: 'Chile forbade its students from following the fashion'
New York Times, 4 March 1972.

p. 149: 'South Korean President Park Chung Hee banned it . . .'
New York Times, 20 May 1973.

p. 149: 'the state of California cut jobless benefits . . .'
Los Angeles Times, 9 March 1973.

p. 149: 'the Bavarian State Interior Ministry banned public appearances . . .'
New York Times, 18 February 1974.

p. 149: 'Albania prohibited the hirsute from entering the country . . .'
Guardian, 20 April 1979

p. 149: '. . . caused the mulleted footballer Chris Waddle some concern . . .'
ed. Peter Ball and Phil Shaw, *The Book of Football Quotations* (Stanley Paul, 1989).

p. 149: 'the Real Madrid midfielder Fernando Redondo was dropped . . .'
Guardian, 9 September 1995.

p. 150: 'Leonardo Ricatti was told by Italian Serie B club Avellino . . .'
ITV Teletext, 12 August 1996.

Interlude V: 'As bald as . . .'

p. 151: 'His hat and wig were hanged upon a knob behind him . . .'
Robert Louis Stevenson, *St Ives* (1897).

p. 151: . . . cueball, grapefruit, lunar sea of senility.
Robert Baldwin and Ruth Paris, *The Book of Similes* (Routledge and Kegan Paul 1982).

p. 151: . . . billiard ball, cucumber, lizard, Heaven, baby's bottom.
Cox, *Illustrated Dictionary of Hairdressing and Wigmaking*.

p. 151: . . . cannon ball, winter tree.
F.J. Wilstack, *A Dictionary of Similes* (Harrap, 1917).

p. 151: . . . electric lightbulb.
David Lodge, *Therapy* (Secker and Warburg, 1995).

p. 152: . . . egg.
Alfred, Lord Tennyson, *Harold* (1876).

p. 152: . . . balloon.
Percival Wilde, *Tinsley's Bones* (Victor Gollancz, 1943).

p. 152: . . . badger's bum.
Nigel Rees, *Why Do We Say*. . . (Blandford, 1987).

p. 152: . . . palm of your hand.
R.H. Barham, 'The Jackdaw of Rheims' (1870).

Chapter Ten: A Hairless History of the World

p. 153: 'Many a crown . . .'
Elizabeth Barrett Browning, *Aurora Leigh*, Book I (1857).

p. 154: 'the word "caesaries", which denotes a thick head of hair'
Cox, *Illustrated Dictionary of Hairdressing and Wigmaking*.

p. 154: 'His baldness was a disfigurement which displeased him greatly . . .'
Suetonius, *De Vita Caesarum*.

p. 154: 'His hair was thin and he had none on the top of his head . . .'
ibid.

p. 154: 'he was murdered beside the Lake of Curtius . . .'
ibid.

p. 154: 'His body had been depilated . . .'
ibid.

p. 154: 'He was so sensitive about his baldness . . .'
ibid.

p. 155: 'The Goths mistrusted anyone who did not have long hair . . .'
J. M. Wallace-Hadrill, *The Long-Haired Kings* (Methuen 1962).

p. 155: 'At dawn I sighed to see my hairs fall . . .'
Po Chü-I, 'On His Baldness' (AD 832); tr. Arthur Waley, *Chinese Poems* (George Allen and Unwin, 1946). © Copyright by permission of The Arthur Waley Estate.

p. 156: 'chaplain preached a sermon on the torments which awaited him . . .'
Mackay, *Extraordinary Popular Delusions and the Madness of Crowds*.

p. 156: 'his queen, Eleanor of Guienne, was less than impressed . . .'
ibid.

p. 156: 'King Edward II of England loses most of his hair . . .'
ed. Elizabeth Longford, *The Oxford Book of Royal Anecdotes* (OUP, 1989).

p. 156: '. . . according to the contemporary chronicler Adam of Usk'
ibid.

p. 157: 'Elizabeth I . . . became almost totally bald'
Caine, *Not Many People Know That!*

p. 157: 'The German tutor Paul Hentzner describes her thus . . .'
A. and V. Palmer, *Quotations in History* (Harvester Press, 1976).

p. 158: 'Poets are almost always bald . . .'
John Masefield, quoted in *A Dictionary of Literary Quotations*, ed. Meic Stephens (Routledge, 1990).

p. 158: '. . . whose hair was recorded as "chestnut" . . .'
Anthony Trollope, *The West Indies and the Spanish Main* (1859).

p. 159: '. . . lost all his hair at an early age after dyeing it with harmful chemicals . . .'
Woodforde, *The Strange Story of False Hair*.

p. 159: '. . .executioner bent to pick her head up by her auburn tresses . . .'
ed. Fadiman, *Faber Book of Anecdotes*.

p. 159: '. . . bald by the age of 29, apparently as a result of applying injurious "remedies" . . .'
Lambert, *The Conquest of Baldness*.

p. 159: '. . . principally because he had begun to lose his hair at 32 . . .'
Woodforde, *The Strange Story of False Hair*.

p. 159: 'I wish the bald eagle had not been chosen . . .'
Benjamin Franklin, Letter to Sarah Bache, 26 January 1684.

p. 159: 'He was so sensitive about his baldness . . .'
Caine, *Not Many People Know That!*

p. 160: 'John Quincy Adams was a short, stout, bald, brilliant . . .'
Alfred Steinberg, *The First Ten: The Founding Presidents and their Administrations* (Doubleday, 1967).

p. 160: '. . . launched a campaign against the wearing of long trousers . . .'
ed. Mary Packard, *Ripley's Believe It or Not!: Special Edition 2004* (Scholastic Inc., 2003)

p. 160: 'On the death of his brother-in-law General Leclerc . . .'
ed. E. Fuller, *A Thesaurus of Anecdotes* (Crown Publishers, c.1942).

p. 160: 'when he met Emperor Alexander I of Russia in 1807 . . .'
Lambert, *The Conquest of Baldness*.

p. 160: 'When sitting for a sculpture, he whipped off his hairpiece . . .'
ed. Longford, *The Oxford Book of Royal Anecdotes*.

p. 162: ' "Old Skinhead" and "His Royal Balderdash" . . .'
San Francisco Chronicle, 23 April 1978.

p. 162: '. . . this was because grass does not grow on deserts'
ed. Longford, *The Oxford Book of Royal Anecdotes*.

p. 162: 'The structure of his skull is truly striking . . .'
Anatoly Vasilievich Lunacharsky, *Revolutionary Silhouettes*, tr. Michael Glenny (Allen Lane, 1967).

p. 162: 'Naum Aronson was reportedly captivated by Lenin's head . . .'
Dmitri Volkogonov, *Lenin: Life and Legacy* (HarperCollins, 1994).

p. 163: 'A man of my resources cannot presume to have a hairstyle . . .'
Taylor, *Bald is Beautiful*.

p. 163: 'Never trust a man who combs his hair straight from his left armpit'
ed. Ned Sherrin, *The Oxford Book of Humorous Quotations* (OUP, 1995).

p. 163: 'Gandhi came up with the idea of using baldness as a form of contraception . . .'
Louis Fircher, *The Life of Mahatma Gandhi* (Jonathan Cape, 1951).

p. 163: '. . . whose very first encounter with Eisenhower was marked by an exchange . . .'
Paul Boller, *Presidential Anecdotes* (OUP, 1981).

p. 164: 'he was nicknamed both "The Great Asparagus" and "Turkey Cock"'
Charles Williams, *The Last Great Frenchman* (Little, Brown and Co., 1993).

p. 164: 'Charles Conrad and his similarly bare-beaned colleague . . .'
Sandomir, *Bald Like Me.*

p. 164: 'Ford annoyed President Lyndon Johnson to such a degree . . .'
Boller, *Presidential Anecdotes.*

p. 165: 'Prince Philip once began an address to a meeting . . .'
ed. Fadiman, *Faber Book of Anecdotes.*

p. 165: '. . . newspaper photographers were ordered to stop snapping the back of his head . . .'
Times, 21 September 1995.

Chapter Eleven: Shining Examples

p. 167: 'The "Venus Calva", or Bald Venus . . .'
ed. P.G.W. Glare, *Oxford Latin Dictionary* (Clarendon, 1982).

p. 168: 'Opportunity wears all her hair on her forehead . . .'
François Rabelais, *La Vie très Horrificque du Grand Gargantua* (1534).

p. 168: 'This is his Law of Political Imagery . . .'
G.V. Noble, *The Hirsute Tradition in American Politics* (Bedford University Press, 1978).

p. 168: 'Vice-President Spiro Agnew let his sideburns grow longer . . .'
New York Times, 31 August 1970.

p. 169: '. . . the balding George McGovern . . .'
San Francisco Chronicle, 8 June 1987.

p. 169: 'Ed Koch, who held the post in the 1970s . . .'
New York Times, 8 November 1979.

p. 171: 'a half-used bottle of minoxidil solution was found hidden behind a window ledge . . .'
Times, 22 June 1988.

p. 171: 'candidates with unruly locks received 4 per cent fewer votes . . .'
Times, 23 March 1994.

p. 171: 'In Brynner's case, it was the designer Irene Sharaff . . .'
Peter Hay, *Broadway Anecdotes* (OUP, 1989).

p. 172: 'Covering his sensual dome is like putting clothes on Lady Godiva'
Sandomir, *Bald Like Me.*

p. 172: 'Costner pushed his hair forward . . .'
Guardian, 26 August 1995.

p. 172: 'Meanwhile, Stallone was alleged . . .'
Guardian, 30 September 1995.

p. 172: '. . . was persuaded by director George Stevens to shave his head . . .'
Daly, *Telly Savalas.*

p. 173: 'He was said to be very sensitive about the subject . . .'
Julie Salomon, *The Devil's Candy* (Cape, 1992).

p. 173: 'Baldness is God's way of showing you are only human . . .'
Sunday Mirror, 29 September 1996.

p. 173: 'Brad Pitt referred to him as . . .'
Guardian, 27 May 1995.

p. 173: 'Bruce Willis has got one of the finest bald heads in the world . . .'
GQ Magazine, 1995.

p. 173: 'she declared that she intended to dedicate part of her book . . .'
Independent, 18 September 1998.

p. 175: 'According to the doctors . . .'
Federico Fellini, quoted in *Variety*, 1966.

p. 176: 'Fisher claimed to have received threats of violence . . .'
Virgin Radio, 28 November 1995.

p. 178: 'he wore a different hairpiece every half-hour on NBC's *Today* programme . . .'
San Francisco Chronicle, 14 July 1983; *USA Today*, 20 December 1984.

p. 178: 'he would look like a chartered accountant . . .'
Big Breakfast, Channel 4 Television, 4 August 1995.

p. 179: 'I wish I could have my hair back . . .'
Radio Times, 10-16 October 1998.

p. 179: '. . . paid for wearing a toupee when he played quarterback for the Pittsburgh Steelers'
TV Guide, 20 August 1994.

p. 179: 'He's balding. I've told him it doesn't matter . . .'
Alexei Sayle, *Sorry About Last Night*, BBC Television (1995). Reproduced by kind permission of Alexei Sayle.

p. 180: 'His hair's not his own . . .'
Coronation Street. Courtesy of © Granada Manchester 2004 for material supplied for inclusion in this publication.

p. 180: 'Théodore Géricault, who deliberately had his head shaved . . .'
Lorenz Eitner, *Géricault: His Life and Work* (Orbis Publishing, 1983).

p. 181: 'Fred Fairbrass claimed in 1993 . . .'
Sunday Times Magazine, 24 October 1993.

p. 182: 'Walking along Brighton beach in the morning . . .'
Sunday Times Magazine, 26 April 1992.

p. 182: 'Dismissing hair potions as utterly worthless . . .'
Sun, 26 November 1998.

p. 183: 'Time to turn back and descend the stair . . .'
T. S. Eliot, 'The Love Song of J. Alfred Prufrock', *Prufrock, and*

other Observations (The Egoist, 1917). Reproduced by permission of Faber and Faber Ltd.

p. 186: 'Wise explained later that the fan had been shouting abuse . . .'
Comment after Aston Villa v Chelsea, 14 October 1995.

p. 186: 'Those haircuts do look aggressive . . .'
Daily Mirror, April 2001.

p. 188: 'the hot and humid weather in the US made his newly laid carpet so uncomfortable . . .'
Times, 9 July 1994.

p. 188: '. . . caused, he has claimed, by radiation from the Chernobyl nuclear reactor'
Guardian, 13 July 1994.

p. 188: 'Borja Aguirretxu . . . tested positive for the steroid nandrolene'
Guardian, 15 February 1997.

p. 188: 'The lesser-known South American Ricardo Pavoni . . .'
Telegraph Magazine, 18 July 1975.

p. 189: 'when the presenters made jokes about a "Collina hair lotion" . . .'
GQ-magazine.co.uk, 11 October 2002.

p. 190: 'Gooch went in to bat for his hair clinic . . .'
Guardian, 9 January 2002.

p. 190: '. . . so I thought to hell with it, take the lot off'
Los Angeles Times, 7 August 1995.

Interlude VI: Bald Eagles and Hairless Mexicans

p. 191: 'In fact he roared so loud . . .'
Spike Milligan, *The Bald Twit Lion* (Dobson Books, 1968). Re-produced by kind permission of Spike Milligan Productions Limited.

p. 191: 'Man alone . . . groweth to be bald'
Pliny the Elder, *Natural History*, Book XI.

p. 192: 'The male wattled starling of East Africa loses the feathers . . .'
New Orleans Times-Picayune, 29 March 1981.

p. 192: 'Vultures also go bald . . .'
Michael Caine, *And Not Many People Know This, Either!* (Robson Books, 1985).

p. 192: 'a previously unknown species of bald parrot was discovered . . .'
Guardian, 20 May 2002.

p. 192: 'scientists discovered that almost half of the mature sheep in Western Australia . . .'
Guardian, 9 May 1994.

p. 192: 'researchers at Adelaide University transplanted a sheep gene into mice . . .'
Times, 7 August 1990.

p. 192: 'The orang-utan and chimpanzee both experience some degree of baldness . . .'
ed. Arthur Rook and Rodney Dawber, *Diseases of the Hair and Scalp* (Blackwell Scientific Publications, 1982).

p. 192: 'macaques were used in early experiments using minoxidil . . .'
Sandomir, *Bald Like Me*.

p. 192: 'Hairless cats were kept by ancient civilisations . . .'
Albert Pintera, *Cats* (Hamlyn Colour Guides, 1979).

p. 193: 'another breed of hairless cat was developed in Ontario . . .'
ibid.

p. 193: '. . . two recognised breeds of hairless dog . . .'
Ernest H. Hart, *An Encyclopedia of Dog Breeds* (TFH Publications, 1975).

p. 193: '. . . a King Charles spaniel owned by a couple in Bristol . . .'
Daily Mail, 7 June 1993; 12 June 1995.

p. 193: 'Lassie wore one during film-making . . .'
Daily Mirror, 4 April 1996.

Chapter Twelve: Join the Club

p. 196: 'a Bald Head Club was formed in the New York Stock Exchange . . .'
New York Times, 8 February 1896.

p. 196: 'The Bald Head Club of America was set up in Litchfield City . . .'
New York Times, 21 August 1920.

p. 197: 'The government announced a proposal to set up a hair research college . . .'
New York Times, 26 January 1926.

p. 197: 'Italy's thousand-strong Bald-Headed Association gained international recognition . . .'
New York Times, 5 June 1956.

p. 197: 'The first "world rally" of bald men . . .'
Times, 24 May 1960.

p 197: 'club president Henri Braye set the tone by asserting . . .'
Sunday Mirror, 1997

p. 197: 'In Japan, there is an annual "Bright Head Contest" . . .'
Taylor, *Bald is Beautiful.*

p. 197: 'In Poland in January 1995, the Bald People's Party . . .'
Eastern Evening News (Norwich), January 1995.

p. 198: 'The Wrockwardine Wood Bald-Headed Men's Club was formed in Shropshire . . .'
Shropshire Star, 7 August 1968.

p. 198: 'A rival association started up in Staffordshire . . .'
Shropshire Star, 12 August 1970; 11 September 1970.

p. 198: 'another club for the bald-headed was formed in Steyning . . .'
Sunday Mirror, 21 April 1996.

p. 199: 'the more militant of the two was the New York-based Bald Urban Liberation Brigade . . .'
Atlanta Journal and Constitution, 12 September 1991.

p. 199: 'The BHMA was started in North Carolina in 1972 . . .'
Observer, 25 November 1990.

p. 199: 'including Mikhail Gorbachev, the only honorary member . . .'
New York Times, 9 November 1988.

Interlude VII: Places to Baldly Go . . .

p. 202: 'Upon my life Sir Nevis I am piqu'd . . .'
John Keats, 'Upon my life Sir Nevis I am piqu'd' (1818).

p. 202: 'the developers of this upmarket resort . . .'
Sandomir, *Bald Like Me*.

Chapter Thirteen: The Last Strands

p. 206: 'a team of researchers at Bradford University managed to isolate regulatory cells . . .'
Daily Mail, 11 July 1995.

p. 208: 'Most promisingly, researchers at the Max Planck Institute . . .'
Metro, 21 December 2000.

MUSIC CREDITS

Chapter Seven

Hair (from the musical play 'Hair')
Music by Galt MacDermot
Words by James Rado and Gerome Ragni
© 1968 EMI Catalogue Partnership, EMI Unart Catalog Inc and EMI United Partnership Ltd, USA
Worldwide print rights controlled by Warner Bros. Publications Inc/ IMP Ltd.
Reproduced by permission of International Music Publications Ltd.
All Rights Reserved.

Chapter Eleven

When I'm Sixty-Four
Words & Music by John Lennon & Paul McCartney

MmmBop
Words & Music by Isaac Hanson, Taylor Hanson & Zachary Hanson
© Copyright 1997 Jam 'N' Bread Music/Heavy Harmony Music, USA.
© 1997 Warner/Chappell Music Ltd, London W6 8BS
Reproduced by permission of International Music Publications Ltd.
All Rights Reserved. International Copyright Secured.

Afternoons & Coffeespoons
Words & Music by Brad Roberts
© Copyright 1993 705 7052 Canada Limited.
Universal/Island Music Limited.
Used by permission of Music Sales Limited.
All Rights Reserved. International Copyright Secured.

One Last Love Song
Words & Music by Paul Heaton & David Rotheray
© Copyright 1994 Island Music Limited.
Universal/Island Music Limited.
Used by permission of Music Sales Limited.
All Rights Reserved. International Copyright Secured.

I Think I'm Going Bald
Words & Music by Neil Peart, Geddy Lee & Alex Lifeson
© Copyright 1975 Core Music Publishing Corporation.
Carlin Music Corporation.
Used by permission of Music Sales Limited.
All Rights Reserved. International Copyright Secured.

Just Like This Train
Words & Music by Joni Mitchell
© Copyright 1974 Crazy Crow Music.
Sony/ATV Music Publishing (UK).
Used by permission of Music Sales Limited.
All Rights Reserved. International Copyright Secured.

Snooker Loopy
Words & Music by Chas & Dave
Reproduced courtesy of Chas & Dave, Snout Music Ltd.

Crazy Baldheads
Words & Music by Vincent Ford & Rita Marley
© Copyright 1976 Odnil Music Limited/ Fifty Six Hope Road Music Limited.
Blue Mountain Music Limited.
Used by permission of Music Sales Limited.
All Rights Reserved. International Copyright Secured.

Time Will Tell
Words & Music by Bob Marley
© Copyright 1978 Odnil Music Limited/ Fifty Six Hope Road Music Limited.
Blue Mountain Music Limited.
Used by permission of Music Sales Limited.
All Rights Reserved. International Copyright Secured.

Skinhead
Words & Music by Laurel Aitken

PICTURE CREDITS

A NOTE ON THE AUTHOR

Kevin Baldwin has worked in advertising and as a television researcher. He is the author of three books on football including Norfolk 'n' Good: A Supporter's View of Norwich City's Best-ever Season. He lives in Barnet. Honestly he does.